From Across the Spanish Empire:

SPANISH SOLDIERS WHO HELPED
WIN THE AMERICAN REVOLUTIONARY WAR, 1776-1783

ARIZONA, CALIFORNIA, LOUISIANA, NEW MEXICO,
AND TEXAS MILITARY ROSTERS

BY LEROY MARTINEZ, J.D.

CLEARFIELD

Reprinted for Clearfield Company by
Genealogical Publishing Company
Baltimore, Maryland
2015

ISBN 978-0-8063-5784-3

Table of Contents

Acknowledgments

Julianne Carvajal-Burton, PhD

Alan Kemp, PhD

Charles R. Lampman, Commander USN (Retired)

Julia Lopez

Henrietta Martinez Christmas

Mildred Murry, PhD

Jesse Villareal

Cathy Romero

Elizabeth Macey

Claudia Verano Da Metz

Ed Tinoco

v

Forward

by

Judge Edward F. Butler, Sr.

President General 2009-2010 National Society Sons of the American Revolution

I have had the pleasure of knowing Leroy Martinez for over 10 years. During that time we have frequently conferred, including several face to face meetings in California and Arizona. Our time together has been spent analyzing the archival records that clearly prove that Spain was a principal ally in the American Revolutionary War.

Leroy has been an indefatigable researcher. His research has allowed him to piece together an interesting story. Unfortunately, for 100 years or more, France has been given credit for much of the financial support provided by Spain. This book clearly dispels that myth. He shows that King Carlos III was clearly the leader of the Borbon Compact, being senior in age and experience to King Louis of France.

His book shows the consistent assistance received through Joseph Gardoqui and sons in Bilbao, Spain. He shows how General Bernardo de Galvez quarterbacked the Spanish army and Spanish Militia under his command into repeated victories by eliminating the English from both the Mississippi River Valley and the Gulf Coast.

This book should be on the required reading list of all American History teachers. Every young Hispanic student should be taught that their ancestors played an important role in the battle for American independence.

Ed

Illustrations

Spanish colonial military flag in Spanish North, Central, and South America.
The red and white color design represents the Bourbon family of Spain.

Chapter I:

Introduction

Although the declaration of Independence was signed on July 4, 1776, Spain contributed to the American effort as early as May of that year. The American Revolution should be considered a world event as many countries were involved to some degree. Research from the Library of Congress showed this author record of Spain's involvement before the Declaration of Independence.

For this reason, I have included a chronology of events for illustrative purposes.

Members of the sons of the American Revolution (SAR) began accepting membership of descendants of Spanish soldiers after Spain declared war with the British during 1779. Today, memberships of Spanish soldiers are included as of 1776.

As an aid to Dr. Granville Hough, I began helping applicants with SAR applications in 2004. Several of these applicants were New Mexico Spanish descendants. Since then, I have helped others throughout the United States. Primary sources helped the applicants more so than secondary sources, which motivated me to transcribe as many archival Spanish records as possible. This book is the result of my collection of records.

I hope it will help anyone interested in their family history. Most importantly, I hope that genealogists and historians will appreciate the fact that Spain participated in the American Revolution, just like other countries, and should also be acknowledged. Almost all the neutral trading nations of Europe joined as part of the armed Neutrality. These nations were eager to see the British less powerful over the seas.

This book is intended to aid persons interested in the Spanish Military and Presidios (forts) that had been part of America during the American revolutionary War, 1776 to 1783.

This book includes all Spanish military documents I was able to find, which I translated from Spanish to English.

The Sons of the American Revolution Society can use the Spanish records to process applicantions for membership. Copies of the Spanish archival records are in my private collection. Copies were also accepted and are placed in the National Library of the Sons of the American Revolution Society, located in Kentucky.

The Daughters of the American Revolution has different membership uidelines from the SAR. These guidelines include soldiers who served under Governor Bernardo Galvez and other Spanish soldiers in the southwest who contributed to the Revolutionary War effort.

Other researchers may use this information to learn more about their military ancestors.

.Historians can use the translated archival records for historical knowledge and to understand that Spain, as well as other countries, was part of the American Revolution.

The primary sources of this work are from manuscripts found at various archives.however, I have referred to some secondary sources to enhance readers' ability to study the subject matter pertaining to Spain's involvement in this conflict. This is not a book written from compiled information of other authors. Any information for these primary archive copies can be accessed through this author or the National Library of the Sons of the American Revolution Society.

Countries involved with the American Revolution throughout the world: Almost all the neutral trading nations of Europe joined as part of the Armed Neutrality. These nations were eager to see the British less powerful over the seas.

Britain's allies were Loyalist colonists (one-third of colonists) and some Native Americans.

In contrast, enemies of Britain included:

Belligerent Powers: One-third of United States colonists, 1775-1783, France, 1778-1783, Spain, 1779-1783, Holland, 1780-1783, Restive or unhelpful: Ireland, Unfriendly Powers (Armed Neutrality): Russia, 1780 Denmark-Norway, 1780 Sweden, 1780 Holy Roman Empire, 1781 (The Roman Empire generally included parts of Germany, Austria, Bohemia and Moravia, parts of Italy, Belgium, Netherlands, Switzerland, Hungary, Flanders, Pomerania, Schlewig, and Holstein) Prussia, 1782 Portugal, 1782, and Two Sicilies', 1783.
Source: *Dr. Mildred Murry private papers*

Foreign Aid Prior to the American Declaration of Independence: The idea of foreign assistance was introduced to Congress by Benjamin Franklin. France was not the only foreign power to express willingness to do so. Under the Bourbon Compact Rule, France and Spain acted in concert in world affairs. Spain's King Carlos III was the uncle of the King of France. Benjamin Franklin was a well-traveled person with previous contacts in Europe, particularly in France.

On November 29, 1775, Benjamin Franklin introduced the idea of seeking foreign aid in order to prepare for the separation of Colonials from Britain. A secret Foreign Committee was formed with five persons chosen: Benjamin Harrison, Benjamin Franklin, Thomas Johnson, John Dickinson, and John Jay. Spanish intelligence learned that Britain had obtained all vital information coveyed at the Continental Congress. The five Secret Committee members were to covertly acquire foreign assistance without sharing its origin with other Congressional members.

Benjamin Franklin received a letter from the Prince Gabriel Antonio de Bourbon of Spain through the Spanish Ambassador on December 12, 1775, that included writing from a secret "Sallust". Benjamin Franklin's response was to send the Prince a copy of the first Colonial Congressional Minutes. The Prince noted in his letter that Spain and the American Colonials had much in common as neighbors and that there should be a friendship between the rebels and Spain.

On this same date, Joseph Hewes wrote that his orders from Richard Smith were to try to get wine, proceed to the Island of Saltitudas for salt, then continue to another Spanish location to pick up gun powder and muskets for the rebel colonists.

About February 1776, a letter likely written by Samuel Adams indicated "Measures to Be Pursued in Congress," via foreign aid from France, Spain, Holland, and Denmark. These measures included the Alliance of France and Spain, the Ambassadors sent to each court, the lead and salt needed, treaties of Commerce, the preparation for the Declaration for Independence, the prevention of exportation of silver and gold, and other strategems.

Richard Smith's diary, dated February 29, 1776, included the foreign commercial alliances chiefly with France and Spain. Richard Adams' entry dated February 29, 1776 included the intent for commercial alliances in particular with France and Spain. In the interest of foreign commercial trade and assistance, a letter signed on March 2, 1776, by Benjamin Franklin and John Dickinson, indicated that Silas Deane was to travel covertly as a merchant to France to meet certain persons and obtain clothing, ammunition, arms, etc. for the Continental defense. Remittances would be paid to both France and Spain.

France and Spain used Spanish Bilboa and a fictitious French Hortalez merchant companies to give covert aid to American Colonials. (It should be noted that Spain covertly, through the merchant Diego de Gardoqui in Bilbao, sent money, muskets, munitions, medicine, and military supplies in great amounts to aid the Americans. Diego de Gardoqui was rewarded as the first Spanish ambassador to the new United States.)

Time was of essence and the American Colonials were eagerly awaiting Foreign Commissioner Silas Deane's mission response. Colonials were unaware that France and Spain had already prepared for assistance through the merchants mentioned. Charles Carroll, Sr. on August 1, 1776, wrote that a French ship had landed at Chester with arms and ammunition and a letter indicating that France's intent was to help protect the Colonials from the British. As Stephen Ceronio wrote on October 23, 1776, agents for the Hortalez Company had delivered arms, ammunition, and clothing for the Continental defense.

No sooner had the American Rebels begun their plans for independence, than were plans of foreign assistance sought. Foreign assistance was requested before July 4, 1776. The letters of the Delegates to Congress and other documents reveal that France, Spain, Holland, Denmark, Berlin, and Tuscany were among the first to provide foreign assistance. Former merchants continued the transatlantic trade, but now it was conducted in a covert fashion. One merchant from Spain was the Biboa Family Company and the French and Spanish fictitious Hortalez Company. The Caribbean Dutch Island of St. Eustatius became successful for international commerce. It is interesting to note that commerce from this Island was founded by Sephardic Jewish families. In addition, all Spanish ports were open to American ships and for commerce. Supplies, arms, ammunition, money and more were sent to Island ports in order to avoid direct British contact. In conclusion, France and Spain acted together time wise, even if in a different and covert manner. The American Revolution foreign assistance began before the actual Declaration of Independence and until the 1783 Treaty of Paris, which included the American colonies, France and Spain. The final ratification for the Treaty of Paris for all countries involved was during 1784.

Spanish Coins

4

Sources:

December 12, 1775, Philadelphia, Gabriel Antonio de Bourbon, Letters of Delegates to Congress, Volume 2, p. 479.

February 9-23, 1776, Philadelphia, Measures to Be Pursued in Congress, Letters of Delegates to Congress, Volume 3, p. 219.

February 29, 1776, RichardSmith's Diary, Volume 3, p.312.

March 2, 1776, Philadelphia, Minutes of Proceedings, Letters of Delegates to Congress, Volume 3, p.321.

July 1, 1776, Philadelphia, Colonies in their Limits, Letters of Delegates to Congress, Volume 4, p.356

October 23, 1776, Philadelphia, Committee of Secret Correspondence, Volume 5, p.367

August 1, 1776, Philadelphia, Charles Carroll, Sr., Letters of Delegates to Congress, Volume 4, p.596

Chapter II

Events from 1565-1784

1565 St. Augustine, Florida settled by Pedro Menendez de Aviles followed by earlier explorations.

1598 Onate Expedition to settle New Mexico Province followed by earlier explorations. This included Texas, Southern Colorado, Southwest Kansas, Oklahoma panhandle, part of Utah, and part of Arizona.

1610 New Mexico capital moved to Santa Fe from the San Juan Pueblo area.

1762 Spain enters war with Britain and is allied with France in Seven Years' War.

1762, August 23 Havana, British capture Cuba from Spain.

1763, February Treaty of Paris ends the Seven Years' War in America: Spain loses Florida as part of the treaty, but the King of France cedes Louisiana west of the Mississippi River to Spain to compensate Spain for its loss of Florida.

1769, July-August Spain takes formal possession of Louisiana with regiments from Havana, detachments of Aragon and Guadalajara, America New Spain dragoons, and Havana militia.

1775, November 29 Continental Congress establishes a committee to seek foreign aid mostly from France and Spain.

1776, May 1 Spain and France secretly agreed to send money and future aid to the Continental Army.

1776, May American George Gibson and William Linn sent to Spanish New Orleans for arms and supplies.

1776, August General Charles Henry Lee, second in command, sent Capt. George Gibson and 16 colonists from Fort Pitt to Spanish New Orleans for additional aid.

1776, September Spain sent 9000 pounds of gunpowder up the Mississippi River to Fort Pitt, and 1000 pounds of gunpowder by ship to Philadelphia. This plan was intended before July 4, 1776.

1776, November 25 King Carlos III orders Gov. Bernardo Galvez to secretly provide intelligence about the British.

1776, November 26 Spanish Governor Bernardo Galvez received orders to send gunpowder to the colonist via the Mississippi River. The gunpowder total cost was about $70,000. Secret commissioners were sent to English colonies as spies.

1776, December 24 Spanish royal order to aid American colonists in secret because both France and Spain wanted to remain neutral for the time being.

1777, Spain sent 2000 barrels of gunpowder, lead, and clothing up to the Mississippi River to the colonists. Also, Spain sent 1 million "Livres" and additional provisions for reaching Fort Pitt (Pennsylvania).

1777 Secret Committee Chairman Benjamin Franklin requested and was granted 215 cannons, 4000 tents, gunpowder, 13,000 grenades, 30,000 muskets, bayonets, uniforms, 50,000 balls, and gunpowder.

1777 October Patrick Henry wrote two letters to Galvez thanking Spain for its help and requesting more aid. He suggested that the Floridas should be returned to Spain after the war.

1778-1779 George Rogers Clark obtained supplies from Galvez in New Orleans. These supplies were used in attacking the British at Kaskaskia, Cahokia, and Vincennes.

1778, January Patrick Henry wrote another letter to Bernardo Galvez requesting more supplies.

1778, February The treaty of alliance between France and the United States obligated Spain to assist France against the English. Galvez began to recruit an army and militia in Louisiana.

1778, March James Willing left Fort Pitt with 30 men to New Orleans and received more supplies for the war. They were welcomed by Galvez in New Orleans, and Willing left to return to Fort Pitt. James Willing was protected from the British by Galvez in New Orleans.

1779, May 8 Spain formally declares war against the British and becomes allies with all of the British enemies e.g. France and the Continental Army.

1779 Spain seizes Baton Rouge and Natchez from the British. Soldiers included detachments from regiments Louisiana, Louisiana militia (men 18- 60 years), and the New Orleans Carabineers.

1779-1782 Spanish ranchers in Texas area provided up to 15,000 cattle to support Galvez' soldiers, along with several hundred horses, mules, bulls. Some of these cattle were sent to the Continental troops at Valley Forge.

1779 Males over 18, including Indians, in New Spain were required to become members of the militia in Louisiana in the Southwest.

1779, June 21 Spain declared war on England.. Spani's King Carlos III ordered all Spanish subjects around the world to fight the English wherever they could be found.

1779, August 27-September 7 Galvez Spanish Army in New Orleans travels 90 miles up the Mississippi River to attack Fort Bute, in Manchac, Louisiana.

1779, August 29 King Carlos III proclaimed that the Spanish troops in America was to drive the British out of the Gulf of Mexico and the Mississippi River.

1779, September 20 Galvez' Army captures the British Baton Rouge and Fort Natchez.

1779, November 8 Jefferson wrote to Galvez thanking him for Spain's assistance.

1779, November Fort Omoa, Honduras, is recaptured by Spain against the British. Combattants include the Guatemala Dragoons and militias. Spain originally crossed over land to reach the Pacific Ocean.

1780 Carlos III issued a royal order requesting a one-time voluntary donation in New Spain, called "Donativo," amounting to two Pesos per Spaniard and one peso per Native American throughout Spain's New World Empire. Almost 1 million pesos was received in New Spain and half that amount was later forwarded to the Continental Army for aid in the American Revolution.

1780, January 28 - March 14 Galvez led the attack on the British Fort at Mobile, today's Alabama.

1780, May 26 Spanish military at Fort San Carlos, St. Louis, aided Clark in the conquest of the territories northwest of the Ohio River, and against the British Indian attack on St. Louis in 1780.

1780, May Spanish Fort in Upper Louisiana, (today St. Louis, Missouri), repulses the British and Indian attack from losing the Mississippi River location. Spanish soldiers were the regiments of Louisiana and the St. Louis militia.

1780, October 16 Galvez led the Spanish fleet of 15 warships and 59 transport ships from Havana to attack Pensacola.

1780, November 22 Fort Carlos Spanish Commander Balthazar de Villiers went across the Mississippi River with a detachment of Spanish soldiers to capture the English Fort Concordia.

1781, January 2 Spanish soldiers travel up the Mississippi River to British Fort St. Joseph, Illinois, to capture the fort and destroy the British stockade.

1781, January The British failed in attacking Las Adeas Fort, near Mobile. Spanish defenderss were regiments from Havana, Principe, Espana, Navarro, and Louisiana militia.

1781, March 9 Spanish siege of Pensacola, West Florida. Soldiers were regiments of Soria, Corona, Aragon, Rey, Guadalajara, Hibernia, Flandes, Napoles, 2nd Catalonian Volunteers, Espania, Navarra, Zamora, Extremadura, Leon, and Principe. Detachments were from Toledo, Mallorca, Louisiana, and Havana: Louisiana dragoons, America dragoons, detachment of Louisiana militia, Havana Grenadiers of Mulatto and Moreno militia.

1781, June 28 Natchez recaptured from the British, after it was taken in May 1781. Soldiers were from the detachments of Regiment Louisiana and Louisiana militia.

1781, August Washington and others drank a toast thanking the Spanish King and French King at the home of Robert Morris, Philadelphia.

9

1781, October 19 General Charles Cornwallis surrendered at Yorktown. Funds to pay the French soldiers and money came from private citizens of Cuba.

1782, May 8 Bernardo Galvez' army, aided by American Navy Commander Alexander Gillon of the *South Carolina* frigate, captured Nassau, Bahamas. Soldiers were from Guadalajara, Espana, the New Spain's Corona regiment, Havana Pardo and Moreno regiments.

1783, April 18 British retake Nassau, Bahamas, the British naval fleet location used during the American Revolution against the colonists and Spain.

1783, April Spanish capture the Arkansas post. Spanish soldiers and militia defeated the British

1783, September 3the signing of the Treaty of Paris 1783 ended the war between England, the United States, Spain, and France. Ratifications were not finished until 1784.

1784 U.S. Congress formally cited Galvez and Spain for their aid.

1784 Congressional records indicated that a portrait of Galvez be placed in the Congressional assembly room.

2014 Congress votes to admit Bernardo Galvez as a Citizen of the United States.

2014 Efforts have been addressed to replace the portrait of Galvez and have it placed back in the halls of Congress.

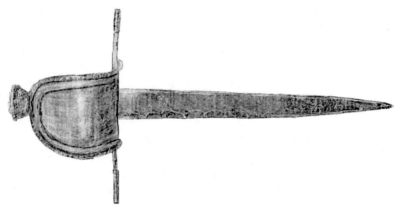

Short Sword

10

Sources:

Edward E. Butler, Sr., Judge, *Sons of the American Revolution* magazine, pages 20-22.

René Chartrend, *the Spanish Army in North America 1700-1793.*

Alejandro Quesada, *Spanish colonial fortifications in North America 1565-1822*

Eric Beerman, *The Americas, Vol.45s, No. 1, July 1988, pp.79-95*

*Conclusion:*This book is intended to add some history of Spain's contribution to the American Revolution along with the names of Spanish Soldiers within the American borderland and adjacent regions.

Spanish and British Ships at Battle

Chapter III

Reference to Spanish Words

Aide-de-camp:	a junior officer to the general
Alferez:	1st or 2nd Lieutenant
Apalachicola:	Appalachian
Arkanzas:	Arkansa
Armero:	armorer
Artillery:	heavy, towed weapons, cannons
Ayundante Mayor:	Major Leader
Bachiller:	Bachelor education
Battalion:	a unit of two or more companies
Bayonet:	a spear or long knife attached to a musket
Breeches:	tight just below the knee length pants
Cadete:	cadet
Campana:	on campaign
Cape:	cover the soldier's body for warmth or rain
Capellan:	chaplain
Carbinero:	soldier carrying a light musket firearm
Cartouche:	a pouch for pistol or long arm musket weapon. Sometimes on the front waist
Cartridge:	musket ball and powder wrapped in paper to reload musket
Cavallada:	horse-herd or land used for raising horses
Cavo:	corporal
Cockade:	A bow or rosette representing the color used by a country. Red for Spain
Colonel:	an officer just below a general
Compania volante:	flying company. Quick response military soldiers
Company:	a unit in infantry, cavalry, and artillery
Coronel:	Colonel
Criollo:	Descended from Spanish Families
Cuera:	Leather jacket worn by special soldiers as armor

Destacado:	on detached service
Donativo:	King Carlos III 1780 request for donation for the war effort against Britain
Dragon:	Dragoon soldier
Dragoon:	a heavily armed mounted infantry soldier who is ready to fight on the ground
Ejercito:	army
El Viejo:	the older
Engineer:	knows how to build defenses, bridges, buildings for protection
Ensign:	junior officer
Filacion:	military enlistment papers with soldiers physical description
Fusil:	a light musket with rain protection on locking mechanism
Gaiters:	lower leg covering and protection
Gorget:	a metal collar plate worn by officers. Once used for neck protection
Grenadero:	grenade soldier
Grenadier:	soldiers who can also carry and throw grenade
Habana:	Havana, Cuba
Legajos:	government papers
Light infantry:	trained to fight in various situations
Livres tournois:	money in French
Maravelis:	money in Spanish
Marines:	soldiers assigned to a naval ship
Militia:	citizens acting as soldiers at needed times. Age 18 and older
Moreno:	darker complexion person
Mulatto:	part African and European descent
Musket:	made of wood stock, metal barrel, and a miguelet locking mechanism of Spanish style
Pardos:	black or darker complexion soldier
Pesos:	Spanish coin equaling one dollar
Pistols:	two musket handmuskets per soldier
Plaza de armas:	location in center square where troops drill, parade, or muster
Presidio:	military fort

Puesto	post or small garrison
Real Reglamento:	Royal Regulations as during 1772
Relaciones:	papers relating to a category used by Spain
Soldado de Cuera:	leather Jacket soldier
Sombrero:	hat
Standard:	small flags representing their companies or squadrons
Tambor:	drummer
Teniente:	lieutenant
Tiradores:	marksman
Tricorne hat:	three sides turned up
Trinite:	trinity
Tropa Liquera:	flying troops, cavalry
Vaquieros:	cattleman or cowboy
Ymbalidos:	retired or injured soldier

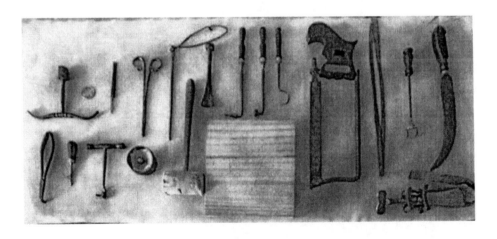

Medical Tools

15

Chapter IV

Spanish Governors

Arizona (Governor of Soñora up to Tucson)

California

Fernando Rivera y Moncada, Military Commander (1774-1777)

>   Died in battle while attempting to cross the Yuma River, Arizona

Felipe de Neve, first Civil Governor (1777-1782)

Pedro Fages (1782-1791)

>   Transpacific sea travel to the Philippines stopped because of British blocade from 1776-1783. Pacific coast settlers went without the usual supply ships. Only the Spanish coast guard traveled the Pacific coast to protect settlers from British or her British privateers.

Louisiana (Upper) above today's Louisiana and into the Illinois Region

Pedro Piernas (1770-1775)

>   First to work with American Colonials

Francisco Cruzat (1775-1778)

Fernando de Leyba (1778-June 28, 1780)

>   Governor with small force who defeated a large group of British soldiers and Native American allies from Canada in the Battle of St. Louis (Fort San Carlos)1780.

Francisco Cruzat (September 24, 1780-1787)

>   French Napoleon eventually sold the Spain's portion of the Louisiana Purchase to Americans during 1803. This is called the "Three Flags Ceremony" each year.

Louisiana (Lower), part of Texas, and Alabama

Luis de Unzaga (1770-1777)

>   Unzaga was appointed by O'Reilly who left in 1770. Unzaga continued to strengthen the French colonists and the Spanish administrators. He was the first to aid the American colonist from New Orleans and up the Mississippi River.

Bernardo de Galvez (1777-1785)

Galvez is known for aiding the American colonists from 1777 to 1783. Galvez provided protection for revolutionary colonists against the British before 1779. Built a military force to gain land and forts against the British up the Mississippi River and in the Gulf Coast in connection with General George Washington as part of Spain's strategy.

New Mexico

Pedro Fermin de Mendinueta (1767-1777)
Francisco Trevre (acting, 1777)
Juan Bautista de Anza (1778-1788)

Texas

Baron de Ripperdda (1770-1778)
Domingo Cabello (1778-1786)

West Florida

Colonel Arturo O'Neill y Tyrone (May 9, 1781-1792) Capital at Pensacola

Spanish Governor's Palace

Spanish Presidios' or Posts

Chapter V

Spanish Presidios and Posts in America Prior to 1821

Spanish Missions and/or settlements were preceded by forts or garrisons. In the Spanish Colonial Americas the term *Presidio's* means forts in Spanish. At times Jesuit priests were left in Southeast Frontier when the local Native Americans were friendlier. Though Spanish Exploration was vast the areas settled took more time. French from Canada and Northeastern America also created posts and had French Jesuits set up missions. In this writing I am focusing on New Spain's North American military Presidios or garrisons. This is a work in progress and hope for any assistance with names, years, state, specific locations, and above all, the source or citation.

Spanish settlements were sometimes fortified. For example, about every twenty-five miles there were fortified settlements from Santa Fe, New Mexico, to Mexico City, then called New Spain. Buenaventura Cerro was a fortified village, in Chimayo, about twenty-five miles north of Santa Fe. Some ruins and some continuously used dwellings are still in existence. The Living History Museum "Golondrinas" was the first such fortified settlement twenty-five miles south of Santa Fe, New Mexico. There the soldiers could rest, eat, and change horses.

Spanish Missions were sometimes fortified. An example was the San Miguel Mission, located in Downtown Santa Fe, New Mexico. It is also the Oldest continuously used church in America. Santa Fe, New Mexico is the Oldest Capital in America. California has four Presidios, and twenty-one Missions. The California Spanish Missions are comprised of both religious and military posts. Thus, it is not easy to provide all Spanish fortified locations.

Known Past Presidios and Garrisons (puesto or post) in Northern New Spain are as follows:
Alabama
Presidio San Estevan 1795
Garrison Apalachicola, 1689-1692, Trinity
Presidio Mobile, 1712, also called Presidio Santa Maria de Galve, 1781

Alaska
There was military and mission presence. However, it is unknown if there was a garrison. Some locals were baptized and crosses left on hill slopes.

Arizona
Presidio de Santa Cruz de Quiburi, 1775-1780, Fairbank
Presidio Tubac, 1752-1776
Presidio San Augustin Del Tucson, 1776-1856

Arkansas

Presidio San Carlos, 1765, near Gillett, new presidio built and named San Estevan de Arkanzas, 1791
Presidio Esperanza, 1797-1803, near Memphis

California Baja

Presidio Loreto, Co. 1, 1697

California Alta

Presidio San Diego, Co. 2, 1769-1831
Presidio Monterey, Co. 3, 1770
Presidio San Francisco, Co. 4, 1776
Presidio Santa Barbara, Co. 5, 1782

Florida

Presidio San Augustin El Viejo, 1565-1763 1881, St. John's County, north of Anastasia Island
Presidio Santa Maria, 1675?-1702, near Fernandina Beach
Presidio San Fernando, 1686-1702, near Old Fernandina
Presidio San Carlos, 1740s, Old Fernandina, Dad County, facing the harbor
Presidio Santa Lucia de Canaveral, 1565-1566, in lower East Florida, Jenson Beach
Presidio San Anton, 1566-1569, east peninsula, Dry Tortugas
Presidio Tequesta, 1567-1568, lower tip, Monroe County, at Lake Sable
Presidio San Mateo, 1665-1668, northeast, 9 miles from Port George or foot of St. John's bluff
    Also called, Caroline, St. Mathias, and San Juan
Presidio Salamototo, 1665-1706, northeast
Presidio Santa Fe, 1680s-1703, north center of Peninsula, Tolosa, Bradford County, near Brooker
Presidio San Francisco, 1702-1705, north center of Peninsula
Presidio San Luis, 1656-1704, near border of Georgia
Presidio San Joseph, 1719-1723, west
Presidio Caroline, 1564-1568 1569-1669 Jacksonville
Presidio Elena, 1670s-1702, Talbot Island, near Jacksonville
Presidio George, 1736, 1740, Fort George Island, formerly called San Juan Island
Presidio Batton, 1567-1568, Batton Island, also called Vide Fort San Juan in 1700s
Presidio Piribiriba, 1703-1705, near Buccaneer Point
Presidio San Diego de Espinoza, 1730s tounknown, near Palm Valley, 20 miles north of St.
    Augustine
Garrison Guana, 1790s, near South Ponte Vedra Beach or nine miles north of St. Augustine
Presidio Santa Teresa de Mose, 1739-1763 1797-1821, St. Augustine
Garrison Ayachin, 1740-1763, St. Augustine
Garrison Quartel or Cartel, 1765, St. Augustine, St. John's County
Presidio Castillo de San Marcos, 1672-1900, St. Augustine
Garrison St. Frances, 1765-1900 1907-present, St. Augustine
Garrison Matanzas, 1740-1821, near Summer Haven
Blockhouse La Chua Ranch, 1703-1706, near Gainesville
Garrison Attapulgus, on Ochlockonee River, 1700-1704, Wakulla County
Presidio San Luis de Apalachee, 1656-1704, Tallahassee, mouth of Ocklokonee River

Also called San Matbo 1565, San Marcos de Apolache, and St. Mary de Apalache
Garrison and Asile Ranch, 1647-1651, near Lamont
Garrison Ayavalia, 1700-1704, near Blue Springs or Hampton Springs
Spanish fleet survivors at the Salvors Camp, 1715, Sebastian Inlet. 1500 soldiers
Presidio San Marcos de Apalache, 1679-1682 1718-1824 1861-1865, St. Marks
Harbor Fortress Tocobaga, 1567, near Safety Harbor
Harbor Fortress San Antonio de Padua, 1567-1568, Mound Key, also called Calos or Carlos
Presidio San Miguel de Panzacola (Pensacola). 1757, 1781
Presidio de Santa Maria de Galve, 1698, Barrancas of Pensacola Bay
Garrison San Carlos d'Austria, 1698, 1781, log fort on La Barrancas de San Tome
Stockade San Carlos Principe d'Asturias, 1719, three-gun battery, Santa Rosa Island at Point
    Siguenza
Presidio Santa Rosa Punta Siguenza, 1723, 1763, Santa Rosa Island. Eight guns
Garrison San Miguel, 1783, unknown location
Garrison San Bernardo, 1781, Pensacola
Garrison Sombrero, 1696, 1781, Santa Rosa Island, near the west end
Two Pensacola Blockhouses, 1780s, one near Plaza Ferdinand and second near Government
    and Main Streets
Garrison Bayou Chico, 1781, Bayou Chico
Garrison Montagorda, 1781-1796, also called Fuerte Arruinado, on Santa Rosa Island
Bay Garrison Ays or Ais, 1567, Oslo, East Florida coast
Stocado, prior to 1763, near Bluff Springs, 28 miles north of Pensacola
Bay Garrison Ayenlade, 1719, Santa Rosa Island
Bay Presidio San Jose, 1701-1704 1719-1723, St. Joseph Peninsula

Georgia
Garrison San Miguel de Gualdape, 1526-1527, St. Catherines Island
Presidio St. Catherines, 1566-1597 1605-1680, St. Catherines Island
Presidio Tolomoto, 1595-1597 1605-1684, near South Newport
Presidio Sapelo, 1605-1684, Sapelo Island
Presidio San Pedro, 1568-1684, Cumberland Island
Coweta Blockhouse, 1689-1691, Columbus
Garrison Santa Elena, 1566-1587,
Garrison Nuestra Senora, 1568
Garrison Santo Thomas, 1568
Garrison Guale, 1566-1570 1671-1680
Garrison Santa Catalina, 1680-1684

Kansas
Garrison Carvagnial/Fort de la Trinite, 1744-1760 (unknown)-1764, Kansas City

Louisiana
Garrison San Fernando, abt. 1766-1803, Beauregard Square, New Orleans
Garrison San Felipe de Borgona, abt. 1766-1803, North Rampart and Iberville St., New Orleans

23

Garrison San Luis, abt. 1766-1794, Canal and Decatur Streets, New Orleans. U.S. Customs House
Arsenal, 1769, Jackson Square, New Orleans
Garrison Tigouyou, 1766-1778, destroyed by a hurricane, New Orleans
Garrison San Juan del Bayo, 1770, near Alexandria
Garrison St. Jean, 1770, New Orleans
Garrison San Leon, abt. 1766-1780, near Belle Chasse, north of New Orleans
Garrison San Juan, 1766, New Orleans
Garrison Santa Maria, abt. 1766-1780, in ruins by 1780, at English Turn, north of New Orleans
Garrison San Carlos, 1766, New Orleans
Presidio Real Catolica, 1763, Madisonville
Garrison Petite Coquilles, 1766, 1793-1817, Shores of Rigolets
Garrison St. Phillip, 1761-1765 1792-1923, Triumph
Garrison Bourbon, 1793-1803, Triumph
Garrison Balize, 1722-1749 1766-1792 1794-1815, near Pilot Town
Garrison La Pointe Coupee, 1729-1780, near New Roads
Garrison Bute, 1764-1768 1778-1794, Bayou Manchac
Garrison San Gabriel, 1768-1769 1778-1781, Bayou Manchac
Garrison Galveztown, 1779-1794, south of Bayou Manchac

Michigan
Garrison and arsenal at St. Joseph, Michigan, 1691 French, English 1761, Spanish February 1781, Niles. After British attack at Presidio San Carlos, St. Louis, Rogers and Spanish went to St. Joseph to destroy the British arsenal.

Mississippi
The "Old Spanish Garrison," 1718-(unknown) 1775-1810
Garrison Ship Island, 1717-(unknown), Ship Island
Garrison Roche a Davion, 1781, near Natchez
Garrison Rosalie, 1716-1808, Natchez
Garrison Ecors Blanc, 1781, near Sibley
Garrison Portage des Sioux, 1799, Portage des Sioux
St. Charles Blockhouse, 1793, St. Charles
Garrison Old Round Stone, 1797-1805, St. Charles
Garrison Charette, 1790-1804, Washington
Garrison Don Carlos, 1767-1780, Spanish Lake

New Mexico
Presidio Santa Fe, 1610-1680 1692-1846, Santa Fe
First named La Villa Real de Santa Fe de San Francisco, 1692 rebuilt and renamed the Presidio de Nuestra Señora de los Remedios y la Exaltacion de la Santa Cruz. The Palace of Governors is part of the Presidio with fortified barracks behind the Governors Palace. Santa Fe is the oldest continuous capital in the U.S.
San Miguel Mission, fortified 1710
Puesto or Post Robledo, 1771, near Radium Springs

24

Garrison or post Santa Rita, 1804-1838, Santa Rita
Garrison or post Albuquerque, 1706, Albuquerque
Presidio El Paso del Rio Grande del Norte, 1683-1773, was in Juarez, Mexico. 1773 it was moved to Carrizal, in today's Mexico. Part of the settlement was in El Paso, U.S. today.

North Carolina
Garrison Santiago, 1567-1568, near Salisbury
Garrison San Juan de Xuala, 1567-1568, near Morganton
Cooweechee Blockhouse, 1567-1568, near Marshall

North Dakota
Garrison René Jusseaume's (1794 - 1795, 1796 - 1797), near Stanton. Stockade post built on the west bank of the Missouri River just below the mouth of the Knife River, between the Mandan and Hidatsa villages. It is also spelled Jusson or Gousseaume. The abandoned post was confiscated for Spain by explorer John Evans and renamed Fort Makay

Nebraska
Garrison Charles, 1795-1797, near Homer

North Carolina
Garrison San Juan, 1566-1568, near Morganton
Garrison at Cofitachequi, 1568-1570, Camden

South Carolina
Blockhouse Winyah Bay, 1526, near Georgetown
Garrison Santa Elena, 1565-1587, Parris Island
Garrison San Felipe or Carolina, 1565
Blockhouse Orista, 1568-1570, Seabrook Island
Garrison San Juan, 1566-1568, Piedmont, North Eastern S. C.
Garrison Santiago, 1567-1568
Garrison San Pablo, 1567-1568
Garrison San Pedro, 1567-1568
Garrison St. Louis, 1764-1768 Presidio San Carlos, 1778-1805, St. Louis
Garrison Genevieve, 1785-1804
Garrison Cape Girardot, 1733-(unknown) 1793-1808, Cape Girardeau
Garrison New Madrid, 1783 to (unknown) and 1789-1804, New Madrid
Garrison San Fernando, 1790s, near Caruthersville
Garrison Carondelet, 1787-1804, Vernon County, named after a Spanish Louisiana Governor

South Dakota
Garrison, 1794-1795, near Mobridge

Tennessee
Garrison Santa Elena, 1567, near Deep Springs
Garrison Barrancas, 1795-1799, Memphis

Texas
Garrison Caddos, 1711767 1770 (unknown) near Barkman
Presidio Nuestra Senora de los Dolores, 1716-1767 1770-(unknown) Nacogdoches
Garrison Old Stone, 1789-1836, Nacogdoches
Garrison Spanish Bluff, 1805-1813, Antioch
Presidio San Agustin de Ahumada, 1756-1771, Wallisville. Also called Presidio del Orcoquisac
Garrison Arkokisa, 1804-1805, Wallisville
Garrison Las Casas, 1819-1822, Port Bolivar
Garrison Maison Rough, 1817-1818, Galveston
Presidio name variations include Presidio Bajia, Presidio Nuestra Senora del Loreto de la Bahia
 de Espiritu Santo, and Presidio de Nuestra Senora de la Bahia del Espiritu Santo,
 1749-1836, Goliad.
Texas *(continued)*
It should be noted that initially there was a stockade, Port Lavaca in 1721. In 1726 it was moved
 to mission valley. In 1749 it was moved to its present site.
Presidio Refugio, 1807-1836, Refugio
Garrison Teodoro, 1750-1840, Spanish fort
Presidio San Xavier de Gigedo or Presidio de San Francisco Xavier de Gigedo, 1751-1755, near
 Rockdale
Garrison El Fuerte de Arroyo de Cibolo or El Fuerte Santa Cruz del Cibolo, 1771-1782, Karnes
 County
Presidio San Marcos de Neve, 1808-1812, near San Marcos
Presidio San Antonio de Bexar, 1718-1879, San Antonio
Presidio Julimes, formerly La Junta, 1777
Presidio Nuestra Senora Loreto, 1721
Garrison Lipantitlan, 1734, near San Patricio
Garrison Ramirez, unknown-1813, Live Oak County
Presidio Laredo, 1775-1846, Laredo
Presidio San Saba, 1752, Menard. It is also known as Presidio de San Luis de las Amarillas.
Presidio San Elizario or Presidio de Nuestra Senora del Pilar y Gloriosa San Jose, 1752-1746,
 Jimenez, Chihuahua, and moved to San Elizario, Texas, during 1760s

Virginia
Axacan, 1570-1571, York County, was close to present day Jamestown. It is unknown if a
 garrison existed. Spanish Mission Santa Maria was established. Five priests were later
 left at this location and all died from a local Native American attack.

Washington
Garrison settlement Nunez Gaona, 1791-1792, Neah Bay

Frontier of Today's Northern Mexico
Presidio El Paso del Rio Grande del Norte, 1683-1773, was in Juarez, Mexico. 1773 it was
moved to Carrizal, in today's Mexico. Part of the settlement was in El Paso, U.S. today
Presidio Fronteras, Soñora, 1692, 30 miles south of Douglas, Arizona

26

Presidio Santa Gertrudis Del Altar, 1755, Sonora, Mexico, South of Nogales
Presidio Terrente, Soñora, Mexico, 1742, east of Nogales
San Blas main Naval Base for the Pacific Ocean, Nayarit

Sources:
Arana, Luis R, and Manucy, Albert, *The Building of the Castillo de San Marcos*, Eastern National
    Park and Monument Association, 1977
Barnes Thomas C., Naylor, Thomas H. and Polzer, Charles W., *A Research Guide*, The University
    of Arizona Press, Tucson Arizona, 1981
Bense, Judith A., *Archaeology of Colonial Pensacola*, University Press of Florida, 1999
Bense, Judith A., *Pensacola*, University Press of Florida, 2003
Bolton, Herbert E., *Arredondo's historical Proof of Spain's Title to Georgia: A Contribution to the History of One of the Spanish Borderlands*, Anthropological Papers of the American
    Museum of Natural History, No. 68, 1990
Boyd, Mark F., Smith, Hale G., and Griffin, John W., *Here They Once Stood: The Tragic End of the Apalachee Missions,* University Press of Florida, reprint 1999
Brinckerhoff and Odie B. Faulk, *Lancers for the King, A study of the Frontier Military System of Northern New Spain, With A Translation of the Royal Regulations of 1772*, Arizona Historical
    Foundation, 1965
Brooks, A.M., and Averette, Annie, *the Unwritten History of Old St. Augustine*, the Record Co.,
    1909
Bushnell, Amy, *and the King's Coffer*: Proprietors of the Spanish Florida Treasury, 1565-1702,
    University Presses of Florida, 1981
Bushnell, Amy Turner, *Situado and Sabana, Spain's Support System for the Presidio and MissionProvinces of Florida*, American Museum of Natural history, University of Georgia Press,
    New York, 1994
Chatelain, Verne E., *the Defenses of Spanish Florida, 1565-1763*, Carnegie Institution of
    Washington, 1941
Coleman, Robert E., Arkansas *Post in the American Revolution: Spanish-Ruled Arkansas Post*,
    Chapter 10, Division of History, Southwest Cultural Resources Center, Nation al Park Service, Department of the Interior, professional Papers No. 12, Santa Fe, New Mexico,
    1987
Conner, Jeannette T., Translator, Colonial*Records of Spanish Florida: Letters and Reports of Governors and Secular Persons, Volume 1, 1570-1577*, the Florida State Historical
    Society, 1925
Deagan, Kathleen, and MacMahon, Darcie, *Fort Mose: Colonial America's Black Fortress of Freedom*, University Press of Florida, 1995
Geiger, Maynard, Translator, *The Martyrs of Florida (1513-1616)*, Joseph F. Wagner, Inc., 1936
Geiger, Maynard, *Biographical Dictionary of the Franciscans in Spanish Florida and Cuba, 1528-1841*, St. Anthony Guild Press, 1940
Gerald, Rex E., *Spanish Presidios of the late Eighteenth Century in Northern New Spain*,
    Museum of New Mexico Press, Santa Fe, 1968

Gonzalez de Barcia Carballido y Zuniga, Translator, *Ensayo cronologico, para la historia general de la Florida,* Madrid, 1723

Hadley, Diana, Naylor, Thomas H., and Schuetz-Miller, Mardith K., *The Presidio and Militia on the Northern Frontier of New Spain, Vol. Two, Part Two, The Central Corridor and the Texas Corridor, 1700-1765,* The University of Arizona Press, Tucson, 1997

Hann, John H., *Apalachee: The Land Between the Rivers,* University of Florida Press, 1988

Hann, John H., and McEwan, *The Apalachee Indians and Mission San Luis,* University Press of Florida, 1998

Hannings, Bud, *Forts of the United States; A Historical Dictionary, 16th through 19th Centuries,* McFarland and Co. Inc., 2006

Hoffman, Paul E., *Florida's Frontiers,* Indiana University press, 2002

Hudson Jr., Charles M., *The Juan Pardo Expeditions: Explorations: Exploration of the Carolinas' and Tennessee, 1566-1568,* University of Alabama Press, reprint 2005

Landers, Jane, *Black Society in Spanish Florida,* University of Illinois Press, 1999

Lewis, Clifford M., and Loomie, Albert J., *The Spanish Jesuit Mission in Virginia,* University of North Carolina Press, 1953

Lowery, Woodbury, *The Spanish Settlements Within The Present Limits of the United States,* Florida, 1562-1574, G. P. Putnam's and Son's, New York, 1911

Milanich, Jerald T., *Florida Indians and the Invasion from Europe,* University Press of Florida, 1995

Moore, David G., *Finding A Lost Spanish Fort (North Carolina's Real First Fort),* Tar Heel Junior Historian 47: 1, 2007

Moorhead, Max L., *The Presidio, Bastion of the Spanish Borderlands,* University of Oklahoma Press, 1975

O' Conner, Hugo, Translation, *The Defenses of Northern New Spain, Hugo O'Connor's Report to Teodoro de Croix,* Southern Methodist University Press, Dallas, 1994

Owen, Brad, Lt. Governor, *The Washington State Fact Sheet,* Fort Nunez Gaona (360) 786-7786

Polzer, Charles W., S.J., and Sheridan, Thomas E., Eds., *The Presidio and Militia on the northern Frontier of New Spain, Volume Two, Part One, The California's and Sinaloa-Sonora, 1700-1765,* University of Arizona Press, Tucson, Arizona, 1997

Serrano y Sanz, Translator, *Documentos Historicos de la Florida y la Luisiana, Siglos XVI al XVIII,* Biblioteca de los Americanistas, 1912

Smith, Buckingham, transcriber, *Coleccion de Varios Documentos para la Historia de la Florida y Tierras Adyacentes,* Trubner y Compania, 1857

Thomas, Alfred B., *Teodoro de Croix and the Northern Frontier of New Spain, 1776-1783,* University of Oklahoma Press, 1941

Thomas, David H., *The Archaeology of Mission Santa Catalina de Guale: 1. Search and Discovery,* Anthropological Papers of the American Museum of Natural History, No. 63, Pt. 2, 1987

Weber, David J., *New Spain's Far Northern Frontier, Essays on Spain in the American West, 1540-1821,* University of New Mexico Press, Albuquerque, 1979

Weber, David J., *The Spanish Frontier in North America,* Yale University Press, 1992

Worth, John E., Struggle for the Georgia Coast, University of Oklahoma Press, Revised 2007

28

By the KING.

A PROCLAMATION,

Declaring the Cessation of Arms, as well by Sea as Land, agreed upon between His Majesty, the Most Christian King, the King of *Spain*, the States General of the *United Provinces*, and the United States of *America*, and enjoining the Observance thereof.

GEORGE R.

WHEREAS Provisional Articles were signed at *Paris*, on the Thirtieth Day of *November* last, between Our Commissioner for Treating of Peace with the Commissioners of the United States of *America* and the Commissioners of the said States, to be inserted in and to constitute the Treaty of Peace proposed to be concluded between Us and the said United States, when Terms of Peace should be agreed upon between Us and His Most Christian Majesty: And whereas Preliminaries for restoring Peace between Us and His Most Christian Majesty were signed at *Versailles* on the Twentieth Day of *January* last, by the Ministers of Us and the Most Christian King: And whereas Preliminaries for restoring Peace between Us and the King of *Spain* were also signed at *Versailles* on the Twentieth Day of *January* last, between the Ministers of Us and the King of *Spain*: And whereas, for putting an End to the Calamity of War as soon and as far as may be possible, it hath been agreed between Us, His Most Christian Majesty, the King of *Spain*, the States General of the *United Provinces*, and the United States of *America*, as follows, that is to say,

That such Vessels and Effects as should be taken in the *Channel* and in the *North Seas*, after the Space of Twelve Days, to be computed from the Ratification of the said Preliminary Articles, should be restored on all Sides; That the Term should be One Month from the *Channel* and the *North Seas* as far as the *Canary Islands* inclusively, whether in the Ocean or in the *Mediterranean*; Two Months from the said *Canary Islands* as far as the Equinoctial Line or Equator; and lastly, Five Months in all other Parts of the World, without any Exception, or any other more particular Description of Time or Place.

And whereas the Ratifications of the said Preliminary Articles between Us and the Most Christian King, in due Form, were exchanged by the Ministers of Us and of the Most Christian King, on the Third Day of this instant *February*; and the Ratifications of the said Preliminary Articles between Us and the King of *Spain* were exchanged between the Ministers of Us and of the King of *Spain*, on the Ninth Day of this instant *February*; from which Days respectively the several Terms above-mentioned, of Twelve Days, of One Month, of Two Months, and of Five Months, are to be computed: And whereas it is Our Royal Will and Pleasure that the Cessation of Hostilities between Us and the States General of the *United Provinces*, and the United States of *America*, should be agreeable to the Epochs fixed between Us and the Most Christian King:

We have thought fit, by and with the Advice of Our Privy Council, to notify the same to all Our loving Subjects; and We do declare, that Our Royal Will and Pleasure is, and We do hereby strictly charge and command all Our Officers, both at Sea and Land, and all other Our Subjects whatsoever, to forbear all Acts of Hostility, either by Sea or Land, against His Most Christian Majesty, the King of *Spain*, the States General of the *United Provinces*, and the United States of *America*, their Vassals or Subjects, from and after the respective Times above-mentioned, and under the Penalty of incurring Our highest Displeasure.

Given at Our Court at *Saint James's*, the Fourteenth Day of *February*, in the Twenty-third Year of Our Reign, and in the Year of Our Lord One thousand seven hundred and eighty-three.

God save the King.

L O N D O N:
Printed by CHARLES EYRE and WILLIAM STRAHAN, Printers to the King's most Excellent Majesty. 1783.

British Print of Treaty of Paris 1783

30

Chapter VI
Treaty of Paris 1783

By the King A PROCLAMATION,

Declaring the Cessation of Arms, as well as by Sea as Land, agreed upon between His Majesty, the Most Christian King, the King of *Spain*, the States General of the United Provinces, and the United States of America, and enjoining the Observance thereof.

George R.

Whereas Provisional Articles were signed at *Paris*, on the thirtieth Day of *November* last, between Our Commissioner for treating of Peace with the Commissioners of the United States of *America* and the Commissioners of the said States, to be inserted in and to constitute the Treaty of Peace proposed to be concluded between Us and the said United States, when Terms of Peace should be agreed upon between Us and His Most Christian Majesty: and whereas Preliminaries for restoring Peace between Us and His Most Christian Majesty were signed at *Versailles* on the Twentieth Day of *January* last, by the Ministers of Us and the Most Christian King: and whereas Preliminaries for restoring Peace between Us and the King of *Spain* were also signed at Versailles on the Twentieth Day of January last, between the ministers of Us and the King of *Spain*: and whereas, for putting an End to the Calamity of War as soon and as may be possible, it hath been agreed between Us, *His Most Christian Majesty, the King of Spain*, the *States General of the United Provinces*, and the United States of *America*, as follows; that is to say.

That such Vessels and Subjects as should be taken in the *Channel* and in the *North Sea*, after the Space of Twelve Days, to be computed from the Ratification of the said Preliminary Articles, should be restored on all Sides; that the Term should be One Month from the *Channel* and the *North Seas* as far as the *Canary Islands* inclusively, whether in the Ocean or in the *Mediterranean*; Two months from the said *Canary Islands* as far as the Equinoctial Line or Equator; and lastly, Five Months in all other Parts of the World, without any Exception, or any other more particular Description of Time or Place.

And whereas the Ratifications of the said Preliminary Articles between Us and the Most Christian King, in due form, were exchanged by the Ministers of Us and of the Most Christian King, on the Third Day of this instant *February*; and the Ratifications of the said Preliminary Articles between us and of the King of *Spain* were exchanged between the Ministers of Us and of the King of Spain, on the Ninth Day of this instant *February*; from which Days respectively the several Terms, above mentioned, of Twelve Days, of One Month, of Two Months, and of Five Months, are to be computed: And whereas, it is Our Royal Will and Pleasure that the cessation of Hostilities between Us and the States General of the *United Provinces*, and the United States of *America*; should be agreeable to the Epochs fixed between Us and the Most Christian King:

We have thought fit, by and with the Advice of our Privy Council, to notify the same to all Our loving Subjects: and We do declare, that Our Royal Will and Pleasure is, and We do hereby briefly charge and command all Our Officers, both at Sea and Land, and all other Our Subjects whatsoever, to forbear all Acts of Hostility, either by Sea or Land; against His Most Christian Majesty, the King of *Spain*, the States General of the *United Provinces*, and the United States of *America*, their Vassals or Subjects, from and after the respective times above-mentioned, and under the Penalty of incurring Our highest Displeasure.

Given at Our Court at *Saint James's*, the Fourteenth Day of *February*, in the Twenty-third Year of Our Reign, and in the Year of Our Lord One thousand seven Hundred and Eighty-three.

God Save the King.

London:

Printed by Charles Eyie and William Straham, Printers to the King's most Excellent Majesty, 1783.

Spanish Halbert Lance

32

Spanish Frontier Soldado de Cuera (Leather Jacket Soldier)

Chapter VII

Arizona Presidio Tucson Records, 1776-1783

Partial Guadalajara Spanish archive

Arizona and Soñora
Military Names

Illegible, Juan Girado
Abate, Jose Maria
Abate, Josef Mario
Acosta, Joaquin
Acuna, Gregorio
Allande, Pedro
Allende y Saabedra, Pedro
Allende, Pedro Maria
Alvarado, Guadalupe
Alviso, Luis
Amesquita, Ramon
Amezquita, Loreto

Amezquita, Ramón
Anaya, Nicolas
Anza, Juan Bautista de
Arias, Ygnacio
Ayala, Jose Manuel
Baaneda illegible,
Francisco
Baldenegro, Jose
Balderama, Blas Antonio
Balderarain illegible, Juan
Baldez, Jose *see* Valdez
Bannona, Jose
Barreda, Francisco
Barrera, Jose
Berdugo, Joaquin

Berlugo illegible, Joaquin
Bustamante, Juan
Camacho, Sebastian
Cancio, Procopio
Canillo, Juan
Canno, Javier
Canoro, Cayetano
Carrillo, Juan Antonio
Castillo, Juan
Castillo, Juan Angel
Castro Francisco
Castro, Javier
Castro, Jose Francisco
Chamoino, Jose
Chamorro, Jose

35

Cruz, Domingo
Cruz, Francisco Xavier
Cruz, Javier
Currola, Juan
Cya, Diego
Dias, Antonio Reyes
Dias, Juan Miguel
Diaz, Francisco Xavier
Diaz, Juan
Escalante, Pasqual
Espinoza, Francisco Xavier
Espinoza, Ygnacio
Fernandes, Jose
Fernandes, Juan
Fernandez, Juan
Figueroa, Francisco Xavier
Fuentes, Jose Antonio
Gallardo, Joaquin
Games, Pedro
Gamunez, Joaquin
Gavino, Jose
Gongora, Joaquin
Gongora, Jose Joachin
Gonzales, Francisco
Granillo, Domingo
Granillo, Jose Domingo
Granillo, Jose Gerardo,
Granillo, Sebastian Ygnacio
Granillo, Sevastian
Gurrola, Javier
Gurrola, Juan
Hernandez, Manuel
Isnado, Juan
Lopez, Joaquin
Lopez, Juan Santos
Lugue, Juan
Lugue, Miguel

Marianero, Ysidro
Marquez, Francisco
Marquez, Francisco Xavier
Martinez, Jose Procopio
Martinez, Jose Ygnacio
Martinez, Juan Vicente
Mascareno, Maniero
Mascareno, Martin
Medina, Juan
Medina, Juan Jose
Medina, Roque
Mesa, Clemente
Mesa, Domingo
Mesa, Juan
Mesa, Jose Cayetano
Mesa, Luis
Mesa, Ygnacio
Minamata ?, Salvador
Miranda, Salvador
Morales, Fernando
Moreno, Juan Ygnacio
Ocovoa, Juan
Ola, Diego
Oliba, Juan Antonio
Oliva, Juan
Ortega, Joaquin
Ortega, José
Ortega, Juan
Ortega, Manuel
Oya, Diego
Pacheco, Vicente
Palomino, Jose
Palomino, Jose Antonio
Palomino, Juan
Palomino, Juan Miguel
Perez, Antonio
Ramirez, Jose Marcos
Ramirez, Juan
Ribera, Jose Francisco

Ribera, Pasqual
Rios, Gregorio
Rios, Juan Gregorio
Romero, Bautista
Romero, Francisco
Romero, Juan Bautista
Salazar, Andres
Santa Cruz, Mario
Santa Cruz, Modesto Hilario
Sena, Juan Simmon
Sosa, Jose Maria
Sosa, Josef Maria
Sosa, Manuel Vicente
Sosa, Vicente
Soto, Juan Jose
Soto, Simon
Tapia, Simon
Tisnado, Jose
Tisnado, Juan Jose
Tona, Jose or Toma
Trena, Jose Antonio
Unquito, Bautista
Urena, Armando Jose
Urena, Jose
Urquijo, Bautista
Urrea, Miguel
Usanaga, Ignacio Feliz
Usaraga, Francisco
Valdes, Jose
Vega, Juan
Vegas, Juan
Vera, Juan Simon
Villa, Juan Jose
Yguera, Agustin
Zamora, Jose Ygnacio
Zamora, Miguel

Tucson Presidio Individual Accounts in 1778

Light Troops	Credits (Pesos)	Debits (Pesos)
Juan Jose Tisnado	5	
Jose Francisco Ribera		32
Blas Antonio Balderrama	13	
Jose Gerardo Granillo	30	
Juan Miguel Dias	28	
Jose Procopio Martinez	5	
Sebastian Ygnacio Granillo		19
Francisco Xavier de la Cruz	61	
Jose Valdes	124	
Gregorio Acuna	62	
Pedro Gamez	59	
Juan Jose Soto	41	
Antonio Perez	26	
Sebastian Camacho	1	
Ramon Amezquita		9
Antonio Reyes Dias		17
Scouts		
Francisco Xavier Miranda*	33	
Ygnacio Soqui*	104	
Salvador Manuel Miranda*		20
Agustin de la Yguera		25

Totals:	2,414	Total: 445 Pesos
	1	5 reales
	24	04 maravelis

Sources: Medina 1779 and Oliva 18 de August of 1775. No. 3 and "Relacion"

Tucson Company Individual Accounts for 1778   (*1775 Tubac, Arizona Soldiers)

	Credits (Pesos) 1	Debits (Pesos)
1st Sgt. Jose de Tona		
1st Sgt. Juan de Vegas		3
1st Corporal Joachin Gamunez		1
1st Corporal Pasqual Ribera *	14	

2nd Corporal Francisco Xavier Figueroa *		50
2nd Corporal Jose Maria Sosa *	50	
3rd Corporal Jose Marcos Ramirez *	1	
3rd Corporal Francisco Xavier Espinoza *	1	
Soldiers:		
Luis Alviso *	1	
Jose Antonio Palomino*	107	
Juan Miguel Palomino*	82	
Juan Angel Castillo*	206	
Jose Caietano Mesa*	54	
Ysidro Martinez*		23
Francisco Xavier Marquez*		34
Francisco Xavier Diaz*		14
Juan Jose Villa*		
Ygnacio Arias*	17	
Juan Vicente Martinez*	95	
Modesto Hilario Santa Cruz*	46	
Andres Salazar*	6	
Jose Domingo Granillo*		2
Jose Manuel Ayala*	19	
Jose Ygnacio Martinez*		66
Miguel Zamora*	1	
Fernando Morales	61	
Jose Antonio Trena	165	
Juan de Mesa*	18	
Juan Antonio Oliba*	2	
Jose Ygnacio Zamora*	76	
Loreto Amezquita	55	
Juan Santos Lopez	30	
Guadalupe Alvarado	1	
Juan Ygnacio Moreno	22	
Juan Simon Vera	78	
Manuel Vicente de Sosa	73	
Pasqual Escalante	3	
Joachin Gallardo	123	
Simon Tapia	149	
Juan Baptista Romero	156	
Jose Joachin Gongora	7	

Juan Jose Medina*

Tucson Presidio for May 1779

Officers:

Captain Don Pedro de Allande	Present
Lt. Don Miguel de Urrea	In San Miguel
2nd. Lt. Don Diego de Ola	Present
2nd. Lt of Light Troops	
Don Jose Francisco de Castro	Present
Chaplain Friar Francisco Perdigon	Present

Armored Troops:

Sgt. Jose de Tona		1
1st. Corporals		2
2nd. Corporals		2
Soldiers	37	
Master Armorer		1

Light troops:

Sgt. Juan Vega	1
Corporals (paid the same as armored troops)	2

Drummer	vacant
Soldiers	17

Indian (Native American) Scouts

Corporal	1
Scouts	9

5 Officers, 4 present, and   Troops 73

Source: Medina 1779

Tucson Presidio for November 1782

Captain Don Pedro de Allande	Present
Lt. Don Josef Maria Abate	Present
First 2nd. Lt. Don Ygnacio Usarraga	Present
Second 2nd Lt. Don Juan Antonio Carrillo	Present
Chaplain Don Gabriel Franco	Present
Sgt. Juan Fernandez	1
Another, Josef Maria Sosa	1

Drummer Juan Gregorio Rios	1
Corporals	4
Carbineers	4
Master armorer	1
Soldiers	55
5 Officers	67 men

Source: Neve (Gov) 30 November 1782

Tucson Presidio 1783 Inspection

Men	Appeared on 1775 Roll	1779 Roll	May 1782 Act.	Credit	Debit
Sgt. Juan Fernandez					
Sgt. Josef Maria Sosa					
Drummer Juan Gregorio Rios					
Corporals					
Francisco Usarraga				17	
Luis Alviso	*	*	26		
Francisco Marquez	*	*	25		
Ygnacio Arias	*	*	24		
Carbineers					
Mario Santa Cruz			4		
Domingo Granillo					
Juan Ramirez			48		
Domingo Granillo	*	*	55		
Juan Oliva	*	*	22		
Armorer Jose Urena	*		41		
Soldiers					
Cadet Don Pedro de Allande				48	
Juan Simon Vera		*	16		
Vicente Sosa		*	40		
Bautista Romero		*	9		
Joaquin Gongora		*		33	
Juan Medina	*	*	8		
Juan Tisnado	*		81		
Juan Diaz	*		54		
Sevastian Granillo	*		91		
Javier Cruz	*		14		

Men Debit	Appeared on 1775 Roll	1779 Roll	May 1782 Act.	Credit
Ramon Amesquita	*	*		125
Agustin de la yguera	*		72	
Clemente Mesa				27
Miguel Luque				54
Jose Chamorro				209
Salvador Miranda		*		54
Francisco Romero				31
Cayetano Canoro				73
Joaquin Berdugo				83
Luis Messa				64
Francisco Castro		*	62	
Ygnacio Espinosa				9
Domingo Mesa				150
Juan Ocovoa			15	
Juan Currola				18
Javier Castro, I				27
Manuel Ortega				8
Bautista Urquijo				10
Javier Castro, II			10	
Distinguished Don Juan Beldarrain	*	*	17	

Men Debit	Appeared on 1775 Roll	1779 Roll	May 1782 Act.	Credit
Javier Gurrola				67
Procopio Cancio			*	85
Vicente Pacheco			*	44
Martin Mascareno			*	123
Francisco Barreda				24
Francisco Gonzales				63
Juan Ortega			*	86
Jose Baldenegro			*	43
Joaquin Acosta				122
Nicolas Anaya				60
Joaquin Lopez				140
Juan de Ortega				18
Simon Soto				104
Manuel Hernandez				108

Jose Barrera					95
Jose Ortega					126
Ygnacio Mesa					127
Juan Palomino		*			110
Juan Luque					116
Domingo de la Cruz					53
Juan Castillo		*			62
Juan Bustamante					52
Joses Tisnado		*			62
Total men reported: 62	7	20	11	205	3,835

Sources:

Abate 24 December1783; Medina 1779; Oliva 13 August 1775

Spanish Colonial Tucson by Henry F. Dobyns, University of Arizona Press, Tucson, Az.

Arizona State Museum Archives

Tucson Presidio soldier rosters and records.

1777 Annual report AGI, GUAD (Guadalajara) 515

1778 Dobyns 1976:155; AGI , GUAD (Guadalajara) 271

1779 3 May Dobyns 1976:154; AGI , GUAD (Guadalajara) 277

1782 30 November Dobyns 1976:157; AGI, GUAD (Guadalajara) 284

1783 roster, service records Dobyns 1976:157-158; AGI GUAD (Guadalajara) 285; AGI, GUAD 286

Dedication to the Tuscon Presidio Spanish Soldiers

42

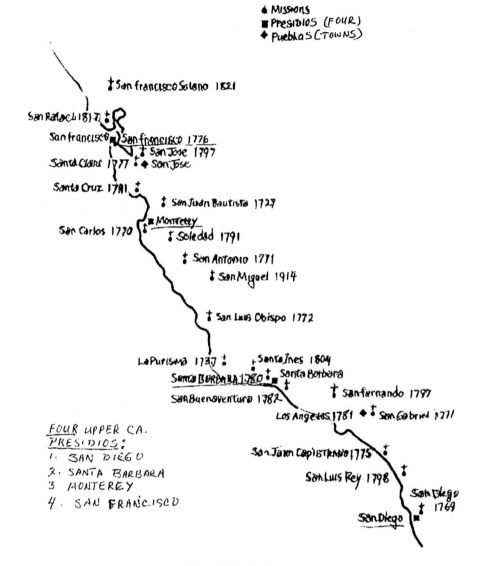

Map of Alta California

44

Chapter VIII

California Presidio Records, 1776-1783

Archive partial copy of November 5, 1781, San Francisco Presidio roster

Spanish California Military Names from 1776-1783

Note: Only the names of soldiers and officers in the author's Bancroft Library microfilm copies are listed. Other soldiers, during this period, may be omitted due to lack of archival records.

Acabedo, Francisco Francisco   *see* Acevedo,

Acebedo, Francisco Antonio

Acebedo, Julian   *see* Acevedo,

Acevedo, Francisco

Acevedo, Julian

Aceves, Antonio Antonio   *see* Areves,

Aguias, Francisco

Aguilar, Javier

Alamo, Maximo

Alanis, Maximo

Albiso, Domingo

Alegre, Antonio

Altaminaro, Justo

Altamirano, Justo Roberto

Alvarado, Ignacio   *see* Alvarado,

Ygnacio

45

Alvarado, Javier
Alvarado, Ygnacio
Alvares, Joaquin
Alvarez, Ascencio
Alvarez, Juan or Alvares
Alvarez, Luis
Amador, Pablo
Amarillas, Jose Angel
Amesineta, Juan Antonio   *see*
Amezquita, Juan Antonio
Amezquita, Juan Antonio
Antuna, Manuel
Arana, Josef Carmen Parra   *see* Arana,
Josef Carmon
Arana, Josef Carmon
Arangura, Jose
Arangure, Josef Prudencio   *see* Aranguro,
Prudencio; Aranure, Josef Prudencio
Aranguro, Josef Prudencio
Aranure, Josef Prudencio
Arce, Gabriel de
Arellano, Manuel
Areves, Antonio
Arguello, Josef Dario
Armenta, Joaquin or Armensa
Aseves, Antonio Quiterio
Ayala, Josef Calizto

Barela, Casimiro or Varela
Bariasa, Salvador
Barra, Juan Antonio y
Bartelo, Augustos
Beltran, David
Beltran, Javier
Beltran, Joaquin
Beltran, Nicolas
Beltran, Xavier
Bernal, Dionicio
Bernal, Juan Francisco

Bernal, Manuel
Bernal, Ramon
Billela, Marcos or Varela
Bojorques, Pedro
Bojorques, Ramon
Botilles, Juan
Bravo, Marcelino or Mariano
Briones, Marcos
Briones, Vicente
Bruno, Francisco
Buelna, Antonio
Butron, Manuel
Bustamonte, Manuel

Calinos, Nicolas
Calvo, Francisco
Calvo, Francisco Xavier
Camacho, Jose Anastacio
Camacho, Juan
Camacho, Tomas Maria
Cantica, Ignacio
Cantua, Ygnacio
Canuelas, Francisco   *see* Cayuelas,
Francisco
Carero, Manuel
Cariaga, Salvador
Carrillo, Guillermo   *see* Carrillo,
Guillo
Carrillo, Guillo
Carrillo, Josef Raymundo   *see* Carrillo,
Joseph Raymundo; Carriollo, Raymundo
Carrillo, Joseph Raymundo
Carrillo, Mariano
Carrillo, Raymundo
Castelo, Augustin
Castro, Augustin
Castro, Antonio
Castro, Francisco

Castro, Ignacio de — see Castro, Ygnacio
Castro, Joaquin de
Castro, Ygnacio
Cayuelas, Francisco
Cervantes, Victoriano
Cordero, Francisco
Cordero, Marciano — see Cordero, Mariano
Cordero, Mariano
Corets, Josef Antonio
Cortes, Jose Antonio — see Cortes, Josef Antonio
Cortes, Josef Antonio
Cota, Antonio
Cota, Mariano
Cota, Pablo Antonio
Cota, Roque
Crus, Juan de la — see de la Cruz, Juan

De la Cruz, Juan
De la Luz, Mariano
De la Vega, Mathias
De la Vega, Ramon Lasso
Diaz, Joaquin
Diaz, Manuel
Domingues, Ildefonso — see Dominguez, Ildefonso
Domingues, Jose — see Joseph Dominguez
Dominguez, Dolores — see Dominguez, Jose Dolores
Dominguez, Ildefonso
Dominguez, Jose Dolores — see Dominguez, Joseph Dolores
Dominguez, Josef Maria
Dominguez, Joseph
Dominguez, Joseph Dolores

Dominguez, Juan Jose
Dominguez, Juan Joseph
Duarte, Alejandro

Espinosa, Jose Miguel — see Espinosa, Josef Miguel
Espinosa, Josef Miguel
Espinoza, Antonio
Espinoza, Jose Joaquin
Espinoza, Salvador
Estrada, Bonifacio

Fages (Priest)
Felis, Victorino — see
Feliz, Victoriano
Felix, Anastasio — see Feliz, Anastasio Maria; Feliz, Anastasio Marin; Feliz, Anastasio
Felix, Claudio
Felix, Francisco
Felix, Vicente — see Feliz, Vicente
Feliz, Anastasio Maria
Feliz, Anastasio Marin
Feliz, Anastasio
Feliz, Vicente
Feliz, Victoriano
Fernandez, Rosalino
Figueroa, Joaquin
Figueroa, Manuel
Flores, Hermanegildo — see Flores, Hermongildo
Flores, Hermongildo
Flores, Jose Miguel — see Flores, Josef Miguel
Flores, Josef
Flores, Josef Miguel
Frias, Vicente

47

Galindo, Nicolas
Gallego, Carlos
Galvo, Francisco
Garcia, Felipe
Garcia, Francisco de Parela
Garcia, Francisco de Paula
Garcia, Joseph Antonio
Garcia, Luis
Garcia, Phelipe   *see* Garcia, Philipe
Garcia, Philipe
Gerardo, Rafael
Gil, Pedro   *see* Gil, Rafael de Pedro y
Gil, Rafael de Pedro y
Gloria, Jose Maria   *see* Gloria, Joseph Maria
Gloria, Joseph Maria
Gomes, Francisco Villa
Gongora, Jose Maria
Gonzales, Alejo
Gonzales, Diego   *see* Gonzalez, Diego
Gonzales, Felipe
Gonzales, Jose Antonio
Gonzales, Josef
Gonzales, Rafael Gerado
Gonzales, Tomas
Gonzalez, Alejandro Anastasio
Gonzalez, Alejandro Antonio
Gonzalez, Diego
Gorman, Isidro
Grijalba, Pablo
Guerrera, Joaquin   *see* Guerrero, Joauin
Guerrero, Joaquin
Guerrero, Joseph Maria or Jose
Guerrero, Julian
Guijas, Josef

Gutierrez, Ignacio
Guzman, ...foribis or Guzman, Toribio

Heredia, Bernardo
Hernandez, Justo
Herrera, Bernardo   *see* Herrera, Josef Bernardo
Herrera, Josef Bernardo
Higuera, Ignacio   *see* Hiquera, Ignacio
Higuera, O
Hiquera, Ignacio

Ibarra, Juan Antonio
Ibarra, Ramon
Iguera, Ignacio Anastacio
Iguera, Joseph
Iguera, Manuel

Juares, Francisco

Lara, Josef Antonio   *see* Lara, Josef de
Lara, Josef de
Lauro, Ygnacio
Leon, Diego de
Leon, Josef Monte de
Leyba, Agustin   *see* Leyva, Agustin
Leyba, Francisco
Leyba, Joseph Antonio
Leyva, Agustin
Linares, Ignacio   *see* Linares, Ygnacio
Linares, Ygnacio
Lisalde, Pedro
Lobo, Jose   *see* Lobo, Josef
Lobo, Josef

48

Lopes, Francisco
Lopes, Gaspar   *see* Lopez,
Gaspar
Lopez, Gaspar
Lopez, Joaquin
Lopez, Jose Maria
Lopez, Joseph Maria
Lopez, Juan Bautista
Lopez, Juan Francisco
Lopez, Luis
Lopez, Prudencio
Lopez, Sebastian
Lugo, Francisco
Lugo, Francisco Salvador de
Lugo, Luis
Lugo, Luis Gonzaga
Lugo, Manuel Ignacio
Lugo, Seferino
Lugo, Ygnacio

Marquez, Rafael
Martines, Andres
Martines, Jose Maria   *see* Martinez,
Joseph Maria
Martines, Juan Ignacio   *see* Martinez,
Juan Ygnacio
Martinez, Josef Maria
Martinez, Juan Ygnacio
Martinez, Torivio
Mejia, Francisco Xavier   *see* Mejia,
Francisco Javier
Mejia, Francisco Javier
Mejia, Juan Norberto
Mejia, Pedro Jose   *see* Mejia,
Pedro Joseph
Mejia, Pedro Josef
Mejias, Pedro
Mesa, Antonio

Mesa, Valeno   *see* Mesa,
Valerio
Mesa, Valerio
Miranda, Alejo
Miranda, Juan Maria
Miranda, Pedro
Molina, Pedro
Montano, Antonio
Montano, Valentin
Montiel, Juan Andres
Moraga, Jose   *see* Moraga,
Joseph
Moraga, Joseph
Moreno, Felipe Santiago
Moreno, Josef
Morillo, Julian

Navarro, Antonio
Neve, Governor
Nieto, Jose Manuel Perez
Nieto, Manuel
Noriega, Joseph Ramon

Ochoa, Custodio
Ochoa, Felipe
Oliveras, Jose
Olivares, Jose Miguel
Olivas, Juan Matias   *see* Olivas,
Matias
Olivas, Matias
Olivera, Ignacio   *see* Olivera,
Ygnacio, Olivera, Jose Ygnacio; Olivera,
Josef Ygnacio
Olivera, Jose Ygnacio
Olivera, Josef Ygnacio
Olivera, Juan Maria…
Olivera, Ygnacio
Olivera, Ygnacio II
Olivera, Ygnacio Narciso

Ontiveras, Francisco
Ontiveras, Jose   *see* Oniveras,
Josef
Ontiveros, Josef
Ontiveros, Jose Antonio
Orchaga, Manuel
Ortega, Francisco   *see* Ortega,
Jose Francisco; Ortega, Joseph Francisco
Ortega, Jose Francisco
Ortega, Jose Maria   *see* Joseph
Maria
Ortega, Josef Francisco
Ortega, Josef Maria
Ortega, Ygnacio Maria
Osono, F C Alvarez

Pacheco, Juan Salvio
Pacheco, Miguel
Padilla, Juan Francisco
Pardo, Antonio
Parra, Jose Antonio   *see* Parra,
Josef; Parra, Josef Antonio
Parra, Josef
Parra, Josef Antonio
Patinio, Josef Victorino *see* Patino,
Jose
Patino, Jose
Patron, Jose Antonio
Patron, Ignacio Maria
Pena, Francisco
Pena, Gerardo
Pena, Jose Antonio or Joseph
Pena, Joseph Antonio
Pena, Lin...
Pena, Luis
Peralta, Gabriel
Peralta, Juan Jose   *see* Peralta,
Juan Joseph
Peralta, Juan Joseph

Peralta, Linero
Perez, Cristian
Perez, Jose Ignacio   *see* Perez,
Joseph Ignacio or Ygnacio
Perez, Joseph Ignacio
Pico, Jose Maria
Pico, Santiago
Pina, Antonio or Pena
Pinto, Juan Maria
Pinto, Pablo
Polanco, Jose Maria

Quijada, Vicente
Quintero, Luis

Ramirez, Francisco
Reyes, Francisco
Reyes, Marin
Rios, Julian
Rivera y Moncada, Fernando de
Robles, Antonio
Robles, Juan Jose   *see* Robles,
Josef
Robles, Juan Josef
Robles, Manuel
Robles, Manuel Anastasio
Robles, Manuel Antonio
Rocha, Juan Estevan
Rochin, Ygnacio
Rodrigues, Ignacio   *see* Rodrigues,
Ygnacio; Rodriguez, Ignacio; Rodriguez,
Ygnacio
Rodrigues, Joaquin   *see* Rodriguez,
Joaquin
Rodrigues, Pablo
Rodrigues, Ygnacio
Rodriguez, Antonio Miranda
Rodriguez, Ignacio
Rodriguez, Joaquin

Rodriguez, Jose Antonio
Rodriguez, Ygnacio
Romero, Jose Estevan   *see* Romero, Josef Esteban
Romero, Josef Esteban
Romero, Juan Maria
Rosalio, Eugenio or Rosales
Rosas, Alejandro
Rosas, Basilio
Rubio, Marco
Ruis, Efigenio   *see* Ruiz, Efeginio
Ruis, Fructuoso Maria   *see* Ruiz, Fructuoso
Ruiz, Alejandro Ruiz or Ruis
Ruiz, Efeginio
Ruiz, Francisco Maria   or Ruis
Ruiz, Fructuoso
Ruiz, Juan Maria   *see* Juan Maria
Ruyz
Ruyz, Diego
Ruyz, Juan Maria

Saez, Justo
Saez, Nazario
Sal, Ermenegildo   *see* Sal, Heremegildo; Sal Hermangildo
Sal, Heremegildo
Sal, Hermangildo
Salazar, Jose Loreto
Salvador, Jose
Salvador, Loreto
Samaniego, Jose Maria
Sanches, Francisco or Sanchez
Sanches, Jose Antonio   *see* Sanchez, Joseph Antonio
Sanches, Jose Fades
Sanchez, Jose Tadeo   *see* Sanchez, Josef Tadeo

Sanchez, Josef Tadeo
Sanchez, Joseph Antonio
Sandoval, Antonio
Sarracino, Pedro
Sepulveda, Francisco
Sepulveda, Francisco Xabier *see* Sepulveda, Javier
Sepulveda, Javier
Serrano, Francisco
Serrano, Rafael
Silvas, Jose Miguel or Silva
Soberanes, Jose   *see* Soberanes, Joseph; Soberanos, Jose Maria; Soveranos, Jose Maria
Soberanes, Joseph
Soberanos, Jose Maria
Sojo, Jose or Joseph
Solis, Alejandro
Solis, Jose
Soso, Justo
Sotelo, Francisco or Soselo
Sotelo, Jose Antonio
Soto, Alejandro de
Soto, Guillermo
Soto, Ignacio   *see* Soto, Ygnacio
Soto, Mateo de
Soto, Regis de
Soto, Ygnacio
Sotomayor, Alejandro de
Soveranos, Jose Maria

Tapia, Felipe   *see* Thapia, Phelipe
Thapia, Phelipe

Valarde, Jose Maria
Valdes, Eugenio   *see* Valdez, Eugenio

Valdes, Melicio   *see* Valdez,
Melesio
Valdez, Eugenio
Valdez, Melesio
Valencia, Jose Manuel   *see* Valencia,
Joseph; Valencia, Manuel
Valencia, Joseph
Valencia, Juan Ignacio
Valencia, Manuel
Valenzuela, Augustin
Valenzuela, Josef Maria
Valenzuela, Juan Segundo
Valenzuela, Manuel
Valenzuela, Pedro
Vallejo, ... Ignacio
Vallejo, Juan Joseph
Vanagas, Josef
Varelo, Marcelino
Vargas, Manuel
Vasques, Nacio
Velarde, Jose Maria   *see* Velardo,
Josef
Velardo, Josef

Velasques, Jose   *see* Velasquez,
Josef
Velasquez, Josef
Verdugo, Anastasio Javier
Verdugo, Florencio
Verdugo, Jose Maria or Juan Maria Verdugo
Verdugo, Leonardo
Verdugo, Marciano
Villa, Jose
Villagomez, Francisco   or Villagomes
Villasenor, Juan de
Villavicencio, Feliz
Villavicencio, Rafael
Villela, Marcos

Ybarra, Juan Antonio
Ybarra, Ramon
Yorba, Antonio

Zeloyal, Juan Jose
Zuniga, Jose   *see* Zuniga,
Josef
Zuniga, Josef
Zuniga, Pio Quinto or Quinto

Evening of April 1775 of the San Diego Mission

1775 March 14 San Diego
Rafael de Pedro y Gil   Paymaster
Settling accounts for all.
Missions
Fray Vicente Fuster=Administrator of San Diego
Fray Antonio Paterna with San Gabriel
...... Joseph Davila this 26 July until Oct. 2 in
Monterey

52

Lt. Commander D. Joseph Francisco Ortega
Paymaster   Don Rafael de Pedro y Gil
Sgt.   Don Mariano Carrillo
Corporal   Don Guillermo Carrillo
Corporal   Don Mariano de la Luz Verdugo
Corporal   (Escort to San Gabriel) Juan Joseph Robles

1775 March 14 San Diego (con't)

Corporal (Mission of San Diego) Josef Manuel de Leon
Soldiers=

Juan Estevan Rocha	Nicolas Gonzalez	Manuel Bernal
Alejandro de Soto	Joseph Bonifacio Estrada	Jose Mariano Yepiz
Alejandro Antonio Gonzalez	Martin Reyes	Juan Alvarez
	Manuel Antonio Robles	Ignacio Vallejo
Josef Maria Soberanes	Josef Antonio Leyba	Antonio Joseph Patron
Mariano Antonio Cordero	Gerardo Pena	Ignacio Alvarado
Luis Lugo	Antonio Cota	Nicolas Beltran
Juan Francisco Lopez	Francisco Rafael Marquez	Joseph Dominguez
Francisco Maria Ruiz	Joseph Raymundo Carrillo	

1775 March 14 San Diego (con't)

Soldiers: Joaquin Beltran
             Joaquin de Armenta
             Juan de Ortega
             Francisco Sotelo
             Josef Maria Ortega
             Deserted and imprisoned in San Gabriel-Anastasio Camacho
1Lt. – 1 Sgt. – 4 Corporals – 31 soldiers-inactive services
Carpenter   Joseph Lorenzo Esparza
Black Smith Phelipe Romero
             Joseph Manuel Arroyo

Muleteers	Francisco Bernal
	Manuel Virjan
	Luis Contreras
	(San Gabriel) Cristobal de Cardenas

| Salary | Lt. 700 Pesos per year |
| | Paymaster 1000 Pesos per year |

Sgt. 450 Pesos per year
Corporal 400 Pesos per year
Soldiers 365 Pesos per year

Corporal Guillermo Carrillo...1775
...in Monterey

1775 March 14 San Diego (con't)
Soldiers

Alejandro de Soto	Jose Maria Soberanos	Manuel Anastasio Robles
Alejandro Anastasio	Francisco Maria Ruiz	Manuel Bernal
Gonzalez	Martin Reyes	

...this is...............
Of 1775...................of Monterey.

Presidio 1774.......................
...also.....of the Monterey Company.
Sgt. Don Jose Maria Gongora...this
    28 July to 2 Oct.

Soldiers
Antonio Espinoza
Anastasio Feliz 11 Feb. to 18 Sept.
Alejandro Ruiz 23 Sept. ....
Francisco Antonio Acebedo 6 Aug. –Sept.
Francisco Lugo 28 Sept. ....
Joseph Antonio Pena 3 Aug. to 28 Sept.
Joseph Antonio...... 28 Sept. to

Luis Pena 12 Aug. to ....
Seferino Lugo 28 Sept. to..........
Xavier Beltran 28 Sept. to ...
Manuel Iguera (wife and family) 19 Sept.
Josef Bernardo Herrera wife and family 19 Sept.
Phelipe Garcia-married and family 19 Sept.
Joaquin Espinoza-8 of fam. 19 Sept.

Nazario Saez- wife and fam. 19 Sept.

Manuel ..... Wife and FAM. 19 September

Also received ...in the royal store of San Diego

1775 March 14, San Diego (con't)

The soldiers
Francisco Cordero
Ignacio Olivera
Exists in.....
     PP 360-424

Julian ....
Matheo Ignacio Soto

1775 Dec. 25 San Diego
Rafael de Pedro y Gil

1775 Dec. 25 San Diego
Pedro y Gil

1777 Dec. 31, San Francisco
Hermenegildo Sal, inhabited-personnel
And money/assets of the company of the presidio (fort) on this date=servants
Of the presidio and of the missions of
San Francisco and Santa Clara=missionaries
Settlers=

Lt. Joseph Moraga=
Sergeant Pablo Grijalba=
Corporals
Domingo Albiso

Valerio Mesa
Pablo Pinto

Gabriel Peralta

Ramon Bojorques

Soldiers
Juan Antonio Amezquita

Ignacio Gutierrez
Ignacio Soto

55

Justo Roberto Altamirano
Carlos Gallego
Juan Salvio Pacheco
Ignacio Linares
Luis Alvarez
Joseph Antonio Garcia
Antonio Quiterio Aseves

Manuel Valencia
Pedro Bojorques
Joseph Antonio Sanchez
Manuel Arellano
Joaquin de Castro
Phelipe Thapia

Workers of the presidio (San Francisco)
Phelipe Otondo
Salvador Espinoza
Juan Espinosa
Pedro Lopez
Total 9

Pedro Fontes
Juan Sanchez
Melchor Cardanas
Thomas de la Cruz
Miguel Belen

Workers for the Mission San Francisco
Diego Olbera
Alejo Feliciano
Joseph Giol (?)
Victorano Torres
Total 8

Joaquin Molina
Angel Segundo
Joseph Rodriguez
Joseph de Castro

Workers of Mission Santa Clara
Francisco Ibarra
Christobal Armenta
Augustin Soberano
Antonio Romero 1-o
Antonio Romero   2-o
Total 9

Joaquin Molina
Angel Segundo
Joseph Rodriguez
Joseph de Castro

Their destination intended=
Domingo Albiso for the presidio S.F (San Francisco)
Valeno Mesa for the town of San Jose
Pablo Pinto for the presidio (SF)
Gabriel Peralta for the Santa Clara Mission
Ramon Bojorques for the San Francisco Mission

1777 Dec. 31 San Francisco
Hermianegildo Sal-account manager

Account information on this page is not transcribed into English

Total 44, 208.5.3

1778 Jan. 10 San Diego
Pedro Gil-personnel of the presidio and
missions defending it. Adjustment of
salaries and rations.

Lt. Josef Francisco Ortega..........	31 Dec. 1777	$188.3 (pesos)
Guard...Rafael de Pedro y Gil	"	742.5
Sergeant Mariano Carrillo	"	137.
Corporal Guillo Carrillo	"	226.2 ¼
Corporal Mariano Verdugo	"	31.5
Corporal of Mission San Diego Alejo Gonzales	"	48.5 ¾
Corporal of Mission San Gabriel Jose Ignacio Olvera	"	176.7
Corporal San Juan Capistrano Mission Juan Estevan Rocha	"	731.5
¾		
Corporal Nicolas Beltran	"	150.4 ¾
Soldiers		
Alejandro de Sotomayor	"	141.2 ½
Jose Maria Verdugo	"	88.1
Luis Lugo	"	50.?
Juan Francisco Lopez	"	40.0
Anastasio Felix	"	36.1
Martin Reyes	"	539.2 ¼
Manuel Antonio Robles	"	208.0
Joseph Antonio Leyba	"	446.7 ¼
Antonio Cota	"	448.3 ¼
Rafael Marquez	"	59.7 ¼

Manuel Bernal	"	251.7 ½
Francisco Pena	"	475.2 ¾
Joseph Antonio Pena	"	87.5 ¼
Juan Alvarez	"	643.6 ½
Ignacio Alvarado	"	98.1 ¼
Joseph Iguera	"	287.5 ¾
Joseph Dolores Dominguez	"	436.3
Juan Joseph Dominguez	"	147.3 ¼
Joaquin de Armenta	"	536.
Francisco Sotelo	"	376.2 ¾
Juan Angel Amarillas	"	22. ¾
Rafael Serrano	"	361. 1/?
Mathias de la Vega	"	17.4
Hermanegildo Flores	"	40.4
Francisco Acevedo	"	59.1 ½
Vicente Felix	"	123.6 ¼
Santiago Pico	"	88.1 ½
Pedro Lisalde	"	102. ?
Ignacio Maria Patron	"	16.3 ¾
Pio Quinto Zuniga	"	35.2
Pedro Molina	"	164.1 ½
Mateo Ruby (?) My opinion is Rubio Re: other records	"	60.4 ¼
Antonio Alegre	"	49.2 ¾
Francisco Ramirez	"	41.0 ½
Joaquin Guerrero	"	95.2
Antonio de Castro	"	165.44
Joseph Maria Lopez	"	24.3 ¼
Pedro Sarracino	"	222.3 ¾
Joseph Ignacio Perez	"	63.1 ½
Alejandro Solis	"	87.6 ¼
Julian Rios	"	54.4 ¼

Joseph Miguel Olivares	"	52.5 ¾
Juan Joseph Vallejo	"	97.6 ¼
Francisco Bruno	"	137.7 ¾
Joseph Maria Gloria	"	137.2 ¼

Joseph Maria de Ortega	"	77.1 ¼
Francisco de Parela Garcia	"	50.1 ½
Augustos Bartelo	"	32.4 ¾

Lt. 1=Armorer 1=Sergeant 1
Corporals 6=soldiers privates 48=

(Note: civilian workers were added as part of the military posts)

Carpenter Joseph Esparza	31 Dec. 1777	117.3 ½
Blacksmith Felipe Romero	"	142.6 ¾
Service to Mission San Gabriel ….. Antonio Sandoval	"	11.0 ¼
……………… of the presidio Tades Rivera	"	79.0 ½
Service to San Juan Capistrano Joseph Manuel Silva	"	57.3 ¼
…………….. Isidro Joseph Leal	"	65.4 ¼

……………… 7 soldiers who were of presidio.
……………… 26 Nov. 1777 from Monterey ordered by
Governor Neve
Soldiers

Torribio Martinez	26 Nov. 1777	50.0 ¾
Joseph Maria Guerrero	"	13.5 ½
Joaquin Lopez	"	87.7 ¾
Francisco Villa Gomes	"	119.7 ½
Ignacio Cantica	"	85.3 ¾
Joseph Antonio Rodriguez	"	83.1 ¾
Julian Acevedo	"	178.7 ¾

The soldiers who stayed

Passing ……… Monterey ………………………
Armorer of San Diego ……………………………………..
Corporal Juan Jose Robles …………………………… 25.7 ¾
Soldier
Joseph Raymundo Carrillo 1777 95.6 ¼

Francisco Maria Ruiz		"	155.2
.... Florencio Verdugo	Oct.	"	84.0 ½
Joaquin Beltran	Dec.	"	294.0 ½
.... Ignacio Vallejo	20 Oct.	1776	397.3 ¼
Gerardo Pena	31 Oct.	"	208.
Josef Monte de Leon	28 Feb.	1776	96.2

.... that left the Mission of San Diego
Soldier   107.4 ¼

In 1777 summation ....
Of San Diego....................................troops
Of Loreto

Sergeant Francisco Aguias	Luis Lopez
Soldiers	Pablo Amador
Ignacio Anastacio Iguera	Julian Morillo=Joseph Ramon
Juan Camacho	Noriega=Joaquin Diaz=
Claudio Felix	Phelipe Moreno=servant of presidio Juan
Juan Botilles	Ignaci
Javier Aguilar	
Joseph Manuel Nieto	

Total Imported Supplies   (Pesos) $309. 3 ¾

In the year...
...of Monterey
Corporal Juan Josef Robles
Soldiers
Seferino Lugo
Sebastian Lopez
Juan Maria Ruiz
Value of Supplies   129.0 0 ¼
Soldier discharged Joseph Mariano...
...   308.1 ½
...of San Diego...
Following individuals
Soldiers

Jose Maria Soberanes	308.6 ¼
Mariano Cordero	202.3
Discharged Jose Anastacio Comacho	148.1 ½
Carpenter who died Joseph Urselino	94.1

Total   803.3 ¾

San Diego Mission...

...

...in 1777-
Also rations were given to the priests
O
of San Juan Capistrano.

...of San Diego...

1777 Supplies had an extraordinary cost
For the troops that...Lt. Coronel
Juan Batista de Anza, for the Indians
That...at Monterey,

For the presidio workers

1778 Jan. 10 San Diego
Pedro y Gil, War...

...
Of San Diego in 1777...
...value total   37,635.5.

1777 March 11   San Diego
Pedro y Gil, war....inventory of supplies
And ...existing in the "R" store.

18 fanegas corn grain=town
17 swords=16 hats of ...=
Thread, hide travel case,
13...

...of Lt. Gov. of Loreto Captain Don
Fernando de Rivera y Moncada...

...

Don F C Alvarez Osono ...
The book of the accounts of Fages,
...leather jacket troops, blacksmiths, carpenters and

..

...of San Diego and inventory.

1784 Dec. 31   San Francisco
Joseph Moraga commander of the presidio
...of the individual troops.

Corporals:

Juan Joseph Peralta

Justo Altaminaro

Mariano Cordero

Antonio Areves

Nicolas Galindo

Augustin Valenzuela

Ignacio Higuera

Ignacio de Soto

Soldiers

Pedro Bojorques

Ramon Bojorques

Joseph Valen

Ignacio Linares

Juan Bernal

Manuel Figueroa

Manuel Arellano

Salvador Espinoza

Felipe Ochoa

Alejo Miranda

Ignacio Castro

Nicolas Berreyesa

Joseph Gonzalez
Miguel Pacheco

Pedro Peralta
Gabriel Moraga

To each person was a discount of 12.50
For the fund levied.   870

1795 Jan. 1   San Francisco
Jose Perez Fernandez-the Gov. Borica

1780 = Jan. = San Diego
Jose Francisco Ortega, Rafael de Pedro y Gil

Account of corresponding individuals
From the year 1779

	Pages
Francisco Ortega	381-384
Rafael de Pedro y Gil (paymaster)	385-386
Mariano Carrillo, Sgt.	387-389
Corporals	
Guillermo Carrillo	390-391
Ma...Verdugo	392-393
Juan Estevan Rocha	394-395
Alejandro Antonio Gonzalez	396-397
Jose Ygnacio Olivera	398-399
Soldiers	
Alejandro de Soto	400-401
Nicolas Beltran	402-404
Jose...Verdugo	405-406
Luis Lugo	407-408
Juan Francisco Lopez	409-410
Anastacio Feliz	411-412
Martin Reyes	413-414
Manuel Antonio Robles	415-416

Francisco Leyba	417-418
Antonio Cota	419-420
Rafael Marquez	421-422
Manuel Bernal	423-424
Francisco Pena	425-426
Jose Antonio Pena	427-428
Juan Alvarez	429-420
Ygnacio Alvarado	421-432
Joaquin Figueroa	433-444
Juan Jose Dominguez	445-446
Joaquin Armenta	447-448
Jose Angel Amarillas	449-450
Rafael Gerardo	451-452
Francisco Acevedo	453-454
Vicente Feliz	455-456
Santiago Pico	457-459
Marco Rubio	460-461
Joaquin Guerrera	462-463
Antonio Castro	464-465
Jose Maria Lopez	466-467
Pedro Garracino	468-469
Augustin Castelo	470-471
Alejandro Solis	472-473
Jose Miguel Olivares	474-475
Salvador Cariaga	476-477
Francisco Bruno	478-479
Jose Maria Gloria	480-481
Jose Maria Ortega	482-483
Francisco Paula Garcia	484-485
Antonio Sandoval	486-487
Pedro Lisalde	488-489
Jose Miguel Flores	490-491
Tomas Maria Camacho	492-493
Pio Quinto Zuniga	494-495
Juan Maria...Olivera	496-
Francisco Sotelo	497-499
Hermenegildo Flores	500-501
Jose Ignacio Perez	502-503
Jose Lorenzo Esparza, Carpenter	504-505

Juan Bautista Lopez	"
Juan Maria Romero	"
Felipe Santiago Moreno	"
Regis de Soto	"

Extraordinary Costs   530-532

1781, October 4, San Gabriel, without signatures. List of recruits, with the jacks and jennies, that have perished and those that have been assigned.

Juna Ygnacio Valencia
Josef Villa
Manuel Valenzuela
Manuel Orchaga
Josef Tadeo Sanchez
Ramon Ybarra
Josef Maria Martinez
Josef Maria Velardo
Josef Esteban Romero
Juan Maria Romero
Manuel Ignacio Lugo
Ygnacio Rodrigues
Francisco Xavier Mejia
Josef Loreto Salazar
Pedro Josef Mejia
Juan Antonio Ybarra
Francisco Xavier Calvo
Josef Patino
Felipe Gonzales
Josef Maria Polanco
Josef Prudencio Arangure
Maximo Alanis
Julian Guerrero
Pedro Valenzuela
Matias Olivas
Josef Ontivero
Josef Antonio Parra
Josef Carmen Parra Arana

Justo Hernandez
Josef Lobo
Josef Migu Espinosa, Josef Miguel
Josef Antonio Cortes
Gaspar Lopez
Joaquin Rodriguez
Lujan Andres Montiel
Ildefonso Dominguez
Francisco Juarez
Fructuoso Maria Ruiz
Francisco Ontiveras
Melesio Valdez
52 soldiers in above list
Oct. 28, 1781 – Account for 52 sent to Croix
Recruits who deserted:
Ygnacio Rochin
Prudencio Lopez
Isidro Gorman
Recruits who were killed (at Yuma)
Francisco Castro
Antonio Pardo
Manuel Diaz
Josef Guijas
Ascencio Alvarez
Soldiers from the Sonora Presidios:
Ygnacio Lauro
Mateo de Soto
The presidios of Loreto, San Diego,

Josef Maria Samaniego
Rosalino Fernandez
Vicente Quijada
Juan Norberto Mejia
Juan Ygnacio Martinez
Efigenio Ruiz
Francisco Xabier Sepulveda
Agustin Leyba
Victorino Feliz
Guillermo Soto
Juan Segindo Valenzuela
Eugenio Valdez

Monterey and San Francisco.
Officers:
Captain Fernando de Rivera y Moncada
Lieutenant Ramon Lasso de la Vega
Lieutenant Josef de Zuniga
Lieutenant Diego Gonzales

1781, October 24, San Gabriel, List of recruits, etc. continued
There follows a list of the Pobladores:

Feliz Villavicencio
Antonio Mesa
Josef de Lara
Josef Vanegas
Pablo Rodriguez
Manuel Camero
Antonio Navarro
Josef Moreno
Rasilio Rosas
Alejandro Rosas
Alejandro Rosas
Antonio Rodriguez
Luis Quintero
The following names appear without any
caption:
Juan de dios Murietta

Andres Lojorquez
Mateo de Soto
Xavier Romero
Guadalupe Alvarado
Josef Domingo Mesa
Josef Chamorro
Josef Acuna
Valentin Montano
Vicente Frias
Andres Martinez
Gustodio Ochoa
Diego de Leon
Juan ygnacio Valencia
Juan de dios Villasenor
Juan Josef Zelayal

There are 16 names, probably members of the Sonora escort, or those who formed the guard for the missions on the Colorado that were attacked July, 1781.

Total present: 54, animals that perished:
Horses 10
Mules 53
Jacks 28   Total 91
Animals distributed: horses 72

Mules 161
Jacks 158   Total: 392
62 pack mules arrived plus   Colorado 14 July, 1781 San Gabriel

1781, October 30, San Gabriel, Lieutenant Josef Francisco Ortega. The company that is at this Garrison the Presidio and Missions of the Santa Barbara Channel.

Lieutenant: Josef Francisco Ortega (Commander – 1769)

2nd. Lt.: Josef Dario Arguello (1781)

Sergeants

Pablo Antonio Cota (1769)

Ygnacio Olivera (1769)

Heremegildo Sal (in place of Mariano Carrillo) 1775

Corporals

Alejandro Sotomayor 1769

Josef Maria de Ortega (1774)

Soldiers

Luis Lugo (S.D.)

Alejandro Ruiz (MR)

Luis Pena (MR)

Josef Gonzales (Rafael Gerardo y (MR)

Martin Reyes (S.D.)

Anastacio Maria Feliz   (MR)

Francisco Salvador de Lugo (1774)

Joaquin Higuera   (S.D.)

Ygnacio II Olivera   (MR)

Francisco de Paula Garcia   (S.D.)

Josef Miguel Flores   (S.D.)

Josef Lobo

Melesio Valdez

Ygnacio Lugo

Josef Maria Valenzuela

Manuel Orchaga

Josef Esteban Romero

Francisco Xavier Mejia

Juan Andres Montiel

Loreto Salvador

Ildefonso Dominguez

Francisco Galvo

Victoriano Feliz

Agustin Leyba

Josef Velardo

Josef Ontiveros

Josef Prudencio Aranure

Francisco Maria Ruiz (MR)

Juan Matias Olivas

Julian Guerrero bur 10 July 1782

Felipe Gonzales

Justo Hernandez

Josef Parra

Francisco Ontiveros

Josef Maria Polanco

Francisco Juarez

Eugenio Valdez

Josef Antonio Corets

Guillermo Soto

Josef Maria Samaniego

Fructuoso Ruiz

Joaquin Rodriguez

Juan Ygnacio Valencia

Ygnacio Rodriguez

Josef Victorino Patinio   Rosalino Fernandez
Josef Carmon Arana   Vicente Quijada
Ygnacio Maria Ortega (S.D.)   Juan Ygnacio Martinez
Mariano Cota (S.D.)   Efigenio Ruiz
Tomas Gonzales   Jose Villa.
Total: 1 Lieutenant, 12nd. Lieutenant, 3 Sergeants, 2 corporals, 54 soldiers.
On July 1, 1782 there were the same ones with the exception of the soldiers:
Francisco Ontiveros
Francisco Juarez (buried 1 Mar. 1782 at S.G.)
Jose Antonio Cortes (difunto)
Josef Prudencio Aranguro.   50 soldiers
Gaspar Lopez (buried 2 Mar. 1782 at S.D.)

1781, September 8, San Gabriel. Neve, without signature
Lt. of the company of new formation of Presidio of Santa Barbara, of Josef Francisco de Ortega,
Lt. of the presidio of San Diego, and forgiven successor of Josef de Zuniga, who was named Lt.
of one of the Presidios of the peninsula for superior title of Teodoro de Croix, Field Marshal.
1781, October 26,   San Diego. Military record of soldiers
Juan Maria Romero, of the company of Monterey.
Francisco Xavier Sepulveda item
Juan Segundo Valenzuela   "
Pedro Josef Mejia   "
Juan Antonio Ybarra   "
Gaspar Lopez   "
Maximo Alanis   "
Pedro Valenzuela   "

1781, October 8,   San Gabriel.   Neve (Gov.)
For the New Company of Santa Barbara to commission of San Diego, to the
Corporal Josef Ygnacio Olivera (1769)
Soldiers
Alejandro de Sotomayor (Later made a corporal)
Josef Maria Ortega (1774)
Luis Gonzaga Lugo
Francisco de Paula Garcia
Joaquin Figueroa
Marin Reyes
Josef Flores, replacement for the recruits, sup:
1781 October 26, San Diego. Registration of Soldiers

Juan Maria Romero, company of Monterey

Francisco Xavier Sepulveda	Item
Juan Segundo Valenzuela	"
Pedro Joseph Mejia	"
Juan Antonio y Barra	"
Gaspar Lopez	"
Maximo Alanis	"
Pedro Valenzuela	"

1783, Dec. 3 Santa Barbara. Ortega.

Extract from the record of presidio of Santa Barbara.

Lt. Josef Francisco Ortega

2nd. Lt. Josef Arguello

Sergeants: Pablo Antonio Cota, Josef Ygnacio Olivera, Josef Raymundo Carrillo.

Corporals: Alejandro de Sotomayor, Josef Maria Ortega

Soldiers: 51   Total 58 men.

2 leather jacket soldiers: Josef Maria Dominguez and Josef Calizto Ayala:

Their affiliations and certifications, starting with 10 years of volunteers.

1784, Aug. 2. Monterey. Diego Gonzales. List of individuals of this presidio.

Lt: Diego Gonzales

2nd. Lt.: Ermenegildo Sal

Sergeants: Mariano de la Luz Josef Maria Dominguez

Corporals: Vicente Briones, Rafael Villanvicencio, Antonio Yorba

Soldiers: Francisco Cayuelas

Carpenter: Manuel Rodriguez   Black Smith: Gregorio Segura

1781, December 31. San Gabriel, without signature.

Settlement of wages of the settlers, termination of their contract, and date of their enlistment:

Settlement in favor of settler's $2302 p. 5 r 9g.

They enlisted for three years at $10p a month, drawing a real a day for the period of 10 years.

They started their contract in 1780-1781.

Feliz Villavicencio	at Los Alamos	enlisted	on	May 30, 1780.
Antonio Mesa	" " "			June 4, 1780
Josef de Lara	" Cosala, Sonora	"		August 11, 1780
Josef Vanagas	" Rosario	"		August 11, 1780
Pablo Rodrigues	" " "			August 13, 1780
Manuel Carero	" " "			August 19, 1780
Antonio Navarro	" " "			August 21, 1780

Josef Moreno	"	"	"		Sept. 2, 1780
Basilio Rosas	"	"	:		Sept. 6, 1780
Alejandro Rosas		"	"	"	November 7, 1780
Antonio Miranda Rodriguez	"	"			Nov. 17, 1780
Luis Quintero		" Los Alamos "			Feb. 3, 1781

They began to draw rations from their arrival at San Gabriel (August 18, 1781)
1782, June 18, Santa Barbara. Copy made by Ortega.
Neve (Governor) on February 19, 1782, decrees that the pobladores should draw a real daily, since their arrival or said mission, San Gabriel, on said date. P. 15
1781, Jan. 30. Monterey. Alferez Josef Velasquez at Loreto and Sergeant Gabriel de Arce were ordered to bring up the pack animals and supplies from the frontier of Baja California. P. 121-2

(to San Diego)
1781, March 24, Monterey.   Neve gives orders to Alferez Josef Velasquez on the manner of conducting the pobladores to the frontier. . 142-5
1781, November 10, Monterey. Presidial Company.
1 Lt.
1 2nd Lt.
2 Sergeants
2 Corporals
51 soldiers.
1782, April 15, Monterey, Presidio Company, Hermangildo Sal,
Hapilitado. The following troops had passed to San Diego and the Santa Barbara Companies:
Francisco Maria Ruiz

Sergeants: Antonio Cota	Hermongildo Flores
Soldiers: Alejandro Ruiz	Josef Antonio Lara
Luis Pena	Francisco Acabedo
Rafael Gerado Gonzales	Julian Acebedo
Francisco Salvador Lugo	
Anastacio Marin Feliz	
Ygnacio Narciso Olivera	

October 1781 24, San Gabriel
Without signature – List of recruits and he-mules, she-mules etc. which have died on them and which have been distributed. Note: For convenience, I have rearranged the names alphabetically. RSW.

| Alamo, Maximo | Parra, Jose Antonio |

Arana, Jose Carmen
Patino, Jose
Arangura, Jose Prudencio
Polanco, Jose Maria
Calvo, Francisco
Quijada, Vicente
Cortes, Jose Antonio
Rodrigues, Joaquin
Domingues, Ildefonso
Rodrigues, Ignacio
Espinosa, Jose Miguel
Romero, Jose Estevan
Felis, Victorino
Romero, Juan Maria
Fernandez, Rosalino
Ruis, Efigenio
Frias, Vicente
Ruis, Fructuoso Maria
Gonzales, Felipe
Salazar, Jose Loreto
Guerrero, Julian
Samaniego, Jose Maria
Hernandez, Justo
Sanchez, Jose Tadeo
Ibarra, Juan Antonio
Sepulveda, Javier
Ibarra, Ramon
Soto, Guillermo
Juares, Francisco

Valarde, Jose Maria
Leon, Diego de
Valdes, Eugenio
Leyva, Agustin
Valdes, Melicio
Lobo, Jose
Valencia, Juan Ignacio
Lopes, Gaspar
Valenzuela, Juan Segundo
Lugo, Manuel Ignacio
Valenzuela, Manuel
Martines, Andres
Valenzuela, Pedro
Martines, Jose Maria
Villa, Jose
Martines, Juan Ignacio
Villasenor, Juan de
Mejia, Francisco Javier
Zeloyal, Juan Jose
Mejia, Juan Norberto
Mejia, Pedro Jose
Montano, Valentin
Montiel, Juan Andres
Ochoa, Custodio
Olivas, Matias
Ontiveras, Francisco
Ontiveras, Jose
Orchaga, Manuel

Total animals 54horses, she-mules and he-mules
Dead 10, 53 and 28
Allotted 72, 196 and 158
Value $8115

1781 = Oct. 31 (San Gabriel)
(No signature) =…settlers…
Of contract and day of entry
Not transcribed into English

1781 = Nov. 5 = San Francisco
Hermenegildo Sal, copy for Moraga
Arrived from Mexico in 1779, 51 swords, pistols and lances
565-7

1781 = Nov. 5 = San Francisco
Sal = copy for Moraga names of the military company and of the settlers.

Lt. Jose Moraga
Sgt. Pablo Grijalba
Corporals
Pablo Pint
Valerio Mesa
Gabriel Peralta
Joaquin Alvares
Soldiers

Juan Antonio Amesineta	Manuel Arellano	Jose Antonio Gonzales
Ramon Bojorques	Ignacio de Castro	Miguel Pacheco
Mariano Cordero	Felipe Tapia	Manuel Figueroa
Justo Roberto	Juan Francisco Bernal	Salvador Espinoza
Ygnacio Linares	(Yg)nacio Vasques	Felipe Ochoa
Antonio Aceves	Augustin Valenzuela	Ygnacio Castro
Ygnacio Soto	Ignacio Hiquera	Jose Antonio Sotelo
Jose Manuel Valencia	Nicolas Calinos	Ignacio Gutierrez
Pedro Bojorques	Jose Miguel Silvas	Alejo Miranda
Jose Antonio Sanches	Juan Jose Peralta	

P.54. Without date (1781) Without Place (Santa Barbara)
Without signature (Neve) A copy
Note: The words in parenthesis above were put there by the scribe who copied this material. If the 1781 is correct, Santa Barbara is incorrect since it was not founded until 1782. This is not a

complete list of those sent to Santa Barbara. Names have been rearranged alphabetically by writer for convenience in reference. RSW

Mounts supplied to soldiers and their value

P.55 Name	Horses	She-mules	He-mules	Values
Jose Arangura	1	2	1	$63
Francisco Calvo	1	2	1	63
Ildefonso Dominguez	1	2	1	63
Victorino Feliz	1	2	1	63
Rosalino Fernandez	1	2	1	63
Feliipe Gonsales	1	3	-	68
Julian Guerrero	1	1	2	58
Justo Hernandez	1	1	2	58
Francisco Juarez	1	3	-	68
Agustin Leyba	1	2	1	63
Jose Lobo	1	2	2	58
Manuel Ignacio Lugo	1	3	-	68
Juan Ignacio Martines	1	2	1	63
Francisco Javier Mejia	1	1	2	58
Juan Andres montiel	1	2	-	48
Francisco Ontiveras	1	2	1	63
Manuel Orchaga	1	1	2	58
Jose Patino	1	2	1	63
Jose Polanco	1	1	2	58
Vicente Quijada	1	-	3	53
Ignacio Rodriguez	1	3	1	68
Joaquin Rodriguez	1	2	1	63
Jose Estevan Romero	1	2	1	63
Efeginio ruiz	1	3	-	68
Fructuoso Ruiz	1	2	1	63
Jose Loreto Salazar	1	2	1	63
Jose Samaniego	1	2	1	63
Guillerrmo Soto	1	2	1	63
Eugenio Valdes	1	2	1	63
Melecio Valdes	1	3	-	68
Juan Ignacio Valencia	1	1	2	58
Manuel Valenzuela	1	2	1	63
Jose Maria Velarde	1	1	2	58
Jose Villa	1	-	2	30

What is left, not distributed	1	8	3	213
What was sent to Jose Cortes	1	3	-	68

Charge to the Presidio, one
Dead and another lost.

Total   39   80   48 $2632
For allotment to the Presidios and armament 30 pesos 7 reales 4 4/5 granos
Decrease on the general?   238 "   2   "   4 "
Net receipts   15303   "   6   "   8 "
There is included here that of the previous document

4-6

1782 April 15   Monterey
Hermengilde Sal, Diego Gonzales
Company adjustments to Oct...

Lt.   Diego Gonzales
2nd. Lt. Mariano Carrillo
Sgt.   Marciano Verdugo
Corporals:
Vicente Briones
... Raymundo Carrillo
Antonio Yorba
Rafael Villavicencia
Jose Domingues
Soldiers:

... Maria ...	Juan de la Crus	Bernardo Herrera
Marcelino Varelo	Bonifacio Estrada	Justo Soso
(illegible)	Diego ...	Manuel A...
Jose Soberanes	Severino Lugo	David Beltran
Juan Maria R...	Felipe Garcia	

Antonio Buelna	Marcos Briones
Manuuel Butran	Antonio Montano
Francisco Cayielas	Joaquin Beltran

75

Domingo A...
Eugenia Rosales
Manuel Vargas
...foribis Guzman
Julian Rios
Ygnacio Can...
Jose Antonio Rodriguez
...casimiro Varela
Sebastian Lopez
Juan Maria Pinto
Jose Sojo
Marcos Villela
Juan Maria Verdugo
... Felis
Linero Peralta
Dionicio Bernal

Francisco Villagomes
Antonio Alegre
Francisco Sanches
Jose Fades Sanches
Ramon Ybarra
Jose Maria Martinez
Norberto ...
Jose Miguel Espinoza
Leonardo Verdugo

Troops that passed San Diego and Santa Barbara
Sgt.   Antonio Cota
Soldiers

Alejandro Ruis
Lins... Pena
Rafael Geraldo
Francisco Lugo
Anastacio Feliz
Ygnacio Olivera

Francisco Maria Ruis
Hermenegildo Flores
Jose Antonio Pena
Francisco Acevedo
Julian Acevedo

(YDEM) were...discharged
        Jose Antonio Ontiveros
        Jose Antonio Patron
Were Deceased
Sgt.   Juan Jose Robles
Corporal   Alejandro Duarte
Soldiers: Francisco Pena
        Jose Maria Guerrero
        Joaquin Lopez
        Victoriano Cervantes
        Jose Joaquin Espinoza
Workers... of the Presidio

```
            Jose Davila
Carpenter   Manuel Rodrigues
Black Smith Gregorio Segura
            Fernando ...
Workers who left the Presidio
            Gabriel Espinoza
            Marciano Soto
            Ramon Buelna
            Jose Maria Gonzales
            Fades Rivera
Carpenters: Jose Orsulino
            Manuel Davila
```

```
Summary of credits              12, 767 pesos ($)
Summary of Debits                1,305 pesos
                        Total   11, 462
```

1781 Jan. 20   Monterey
Without signature

1782 July 17 Arispe
Noble person Teodoro de Croix, Commander of the Internal Provinces (Caribbean, Florida to California)
Killed was Captain Rivera y Moncada.

Note: Captain Rivera y Moncada was killed in battle with the Yuma Native American crossing the Colorado River with settlers to California.

1782 Dec. 31 Monterey
Diego Gonzalez, Commander of Presidio
Lt.   Diego Gonzalez
Paymaster   Hermenegildo Sal
Corporals
Vicente Briones

Joseph Raymundo Carrillo
Joseph Dominguez
Antonio Yorba
Rafael Villavicencio
Soldiers:

Antonio Alegre	Bonifacio Estrada	Eugenio Rosalio
Antonio Buelna	Casimiro Varela	Francisco Cayuela
Antonio Montano	Diego Ruyz	Joseph Antonio Rodriguez
Bernardo Heredia	Domingo Anir(?)	Joseph Soberanes
Francisco Reyes	Javier Beltran	Juan de la Cruz
Francisco Sanchez	Joaquin Beltran	Mareos Billela
Francisco Villagomez	Josef Sojo	Philipe Garcia
Juan Maria Pinto	Manuel Antuna	Sebastian Lopez
Juan Maria Ruyz	Manuel Butron	Severino Lugo
Juan Maria Verdugo	Manuel Iguera	Toribio Guzman
Julian Rios	Manuel Vargas	Ygnacio ...cantis
Justo Saez	Marcelino Bravo	
Leonardo Verdugo	Marciano Briones	

1 Lt. = 1 Paymaster
5 Corporals = 27 soldiers
   Total 44 men

1803=March 9=Loreto, Baja Cal(ifornia)
...of Santa Barbara

Received the Royal treasury account from the ranch that corresponds to the 2nd. Semester.
109-11

1796=December 31, San Francisco
Pedro de Albemi

Reduction of Artillery, ordinance and ammunition that exist
In the battery of San Joaquin

1783=September 10=San Diego
Jose Zuniga=presidio (fort) company

Lt. Jose Zuniga
2nd. Lt. Jose Velasques
Corporals
Juan Estivan Rocha
Ygnacio Alvarado
Francisco Acevedo
Jose Maria Verdugo

July 1784
Company of the Royal Presidio of Santa Barbara

Corporal= Juan Maria Olivera
Soldiers=

Juan Jose Dominguez	Julian Acevedo
Manuel Nieto	Agustin Castro
Antonio Pina	Jose Maria Lopez
Francisco Lopes	Francisco Bruno
Juan Alvares	Jose Olivares
Manuel Robles	Jose Solis
Antonio de Cota	Quinto Zuniga
Joaquin de Armensa	Pedro ...
Ramon Bernal	Salvador Bariasa
Santiago Pico	Antonio Sandoval
Vicente Felix	Roque de Cota
Marco Rubio	Francisco Felix
Jose Maria Gloria	Francisco Sepulved
Juan (illegible) Valensuela	Francisco Soselo (Illegible)
Pedro Mejias	Hermenegildo Flores
Juan Antonio Ibarra	Cristian Perez
Ramon B...	Ygnacio Perez
Maximo Alanis	Juan Francisco Padilla
Luis Garcia	Jose Maria Pico
Francisco Serrano	Jose Manuel Silva
Manuel Bustamonte	Jose Miguel Silva
Pedro Valensuela	

Summary

Lt.   1
2nd Lt.   1
Corporal   5
Soldiers   43
      Total 50

Reserve

?... =   armaments, 35 pair of pistols, 1 sword, and
         2 strong mares; medicine,

(Note: Lt. Felipe Goycoechea replaced 1 Jan. 1784 by Lt. Ortega

Rank	Names	illegible illegible illegible
Lt.	Don Phelipe Goycoechea	
2nd. Lt.	Don Joseph Arguello	
Sgt.	Pablo Cota	
"	(illegible) Olivera	
"	Raymundo Carillo	
Corp.	Alexandro (illegible)	
"	Jose (illegible) Ortega	

Soldiers:

(Illegible) Amador	Francisco (illegible) Soto
Luis (illegible)	Jose (illegible)
(Illegible) Ruis	(Illegible) Rubio
	(Illegible) Miro
Luis Pena	Jose Valenzuela
Jose (illegible)	(Illegible) (illegible)
(Illegible) Aceves	Jose (illegible) (illegible)
	Jose (illegible) (illegible)
(Illegible)	Francisco Mejia
Francisco Lugo	Juan Mancias
Anastasio (illegible)	
Joaquin Figueroa	
Ignacio (illegible)	

1783 Oct. 10-Arispe
Cristobal Carvalon

1781 Feb. 5-Mexico
Gutierres

1785 April 12 San Francisco
Jose Moraga-names of this company (S.F.)

Lt. Jose Moraga
2nd. Lt. Ramon Sazo

Sources:

The Bancroft Library, University of California, Berkeley, CA 94720-6000, Archives
Archives of California:Vol. 1   Provincial State Papers. Tomos I-II, 1767-1780
Vol. 2   Provincial State Papers. Tomos III-IV, 1781-1784
Vol. 15 Provincial State Papers. Benicia. Military. Tomos I-XIX, 1767-1793
Vol. 21 Provincial State Papers. Presidios. Tomos I-II, 1780-1821
Vol. 22 Provincial Records. Tomos I-II, 1775-1794

Salamanca, Spain Archive: LEG, 7278, EXP,9,70 San Diego Presidio; LEG,7275,EXP,7,82
San Francisco Presidio; Leg,7275,EXP,6,84 Monterey Presidio.

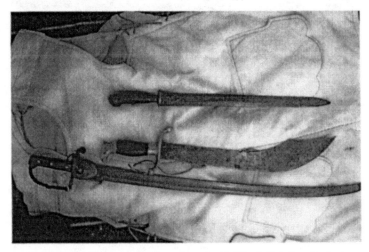

Buffalo Knife, Machete, Sword, and a Soldier's Leather Jacket

Bernardo Galvez Governor of Spanish Louisiana

A Bernardo Galvez portrait by Agustin Berlinero.
Original is in the Museo Naval,Madrid From Raparaz, Yo Solo, 92

Chapter IX

Louisiana Records, 1776 –1783

Honor and Fidelity
Standard used by Bernardo Galvez
In Louisiana

Louisiana 1776-1783 (Spanish and French Soldiers)

A

Abalos, Francisco
Abbadie, Jacques (Santiago)
Abiles, Jose
Abiles, Manuel Xptobal
Abilla, Joseph
Abrego, Josef
Abres, Nicolas
Acebedo, Pedro
Acosta y Herrera, Jose de
Acosta y Rey, Carlos

Acosta y Sousa, Ygnacio de
Acosta, Ignacio de
Acosta, Jose
Acosta, Manuel
Acosta, Thomas de
Adam, Francisco
Adam, Jean Baptiste
Adam, Luis
Adamville,
Adan, Ebariato

Adeva, Ramon
Agraus, Joseph
Aguado, Antonio,
Aguado, Jose
Aguiard, Antonio
Aguilar, Agustin
Aguilar, Juan de
Aguilar, Lucas
Aguilera, Gavino

Aguilera, Jose
Aguillera, Agustin
Aguirre, Juan
Aguirre, Miguel
Agustin (Grevenbert)
Agustino, Julian
Aidler, Juan Luiz
Aigre, Juan Louis
Ail, Baltazar
Ailhaud, Ste. Anne, Juan
Bautista
Alamo, Jose Del
Alarcon, Cristobel
Alarcon, Manuel
Alard, Luis
Alaric, Joseph
Alary, Francisco
Alauar, Vicente
Albanil, Lazaro
Albarado, Francisco
Machado
Albert, Andre
Albert, George
Albuquelquel, Francisco
Alcala, Jose
Alcan (illegible), Sebastian
Alcantara, Fernando
Alcantara, Pedro
Alcazar, Felipe
Alcazar, Juan
Alcazar, Juan Ignacio
Alcoceba, Antonio
Alcolado, Juan
Aldana, Pedro
Alderete, Miguel
Aleman, Blas
Aleu, Magin
Alexia, Joseph
Alfonso, Bernardo Luis
Alfonzo, Antonio
Alfos, Mariano
Align, Batiste
Allain, Agustin
Allain, Francisco
Allain, Juan Francisco
Allain, Pedro

Allan (Alain), Jean Baptiste
Allan, Agustin
Allan, Bourg
Allan, Francisco
Allan, Juan Francisco
Allan, Juan Francisco Jr.
Allan, Pauline
Allan, Pedro
Allan, Zeon
Allard, Luis
Allot, Aruban
Almeida, Jose Enrique
Almeida, Lazar
Almeida, Simon
Alonso, Francisco
Alonso, Isidro
Alonso, Pedro
Alonzo, Estefan
Alonzo, Jose Antonio
Altars, Manuel
Alture, Miguel
Alva, Narcissi de
Alvarez Bergara, Jose
Alvarez Campania, Jose
Alvarez, Baltasar
Monte (Monfe), Jacinto
Alvarez, Felix
Alvarez, Fernando
Alvarez, Jose
Alvarez, Jose Luis
Alvarez, Julian
Alvarez, Manuel Marques
Alvarez, Miguel
Alvarez, Rafael
Alverto, Cayetano
Amado, Francisco
Ambros, Domingo
Amiot, Juan
Amoros, Vicente
Ana, Manuel
Anaya, Joachin de
Andrada, Josef
Andrade, Juan
Andrade, Pedro
Andrea, Matias
Andres, Pedro
Andry, Gilberto

Andry, Luis
Andry, Manuel
Anfray, Francisco
Anstibe, Baptiste
Antaya, Jacobo
Antaya, Pedro
Antoine, Claudio
Antonio, Carlos
Antonio, Juan Bartolome
Aparicio, Francisco
Aquin, Thomas
Aragon, Manuel
Aragon, Tomas
Aragon, Vicente
Aranda, Josef
Arango, Juan
Araujo, Antonio
Araujo, Josef
Arbre, Abelle
Arduen, Andres
Arenas, Juan de
Arenas, Martin
Argote, Antonio
Argumosa, Teodico
Arias, Martin
Arion, Pedro
Arjona, Manuel
Armad, Luis
Armand, Louis
Armas, Christobal de
Arnal, Juan Bautista
Arnau, Charles
Arnault, Joseph
Aroenau, Jean
Aroenau, Joseph
Aroenau, Pierre
Arregui, Juan
Arriola, Jose
Arriola, Mateo
Arroyo, Jose
Arteta, Juan
Asma, Paul
Aspiazu, Francisco
Aspitia, Rafael
Audibert, Miguel
Aueonne, Bernardo
Aufpan, Thomas
Aurillon, Joseph

Aury, Batiste
Aury, Jans
Auteman, Federico
Avart, Roberto
Avart, Valentin Robert
Aveliano, Joaquin
Avendano, Josef
Aventrano, Jose Francisco
Aviles, Manuel
Ayala, Bruno
Ayala, Manuel de
Azelin, Joseph
Azivar, Bicente
Aznar, Antonio
Azur, Luis Francisco
B
Baamonde, Jose
Babain, Siperien
Babin (Babain), Ignace
Babin (Babien), Joseph
Babin Laine, Joseph
Babin, Charles
Babin, Efrain
Babin, Etienne
Babin, Paul
Babin, Siprien
Babin, Amant
Babin, Jacques
Bachoni, Jose
Badeau, Domingo
Baeseterre, Antonio
Bahot, Pierre
Baillet, Carlos
Baillie, Laurento
Balaguer, Alberto
Balderas, Ignacio
Balderrama, Miguel
Balet, Baptista
Balet, Jacinto
Balet, Joachin
Baleta, Josef
Balier, Antonio
Ballancur, Joseph
Balle, Jaime
Ballesteros, Francisco
Ballesteros, Rafael
Balloestero, Francisco
Balmacedo

Baloira, Domingo
Baloyra, Doming
Balquet, Jean Baptiste
Balza, Baltazar
Banegas, Cayetano
Banegas, Jose
Baptiste, Etienne
Baptoiste, Manuel
Baputista, Antonio
Barat, Juan Bautisa
Barat, Vicente
Barberon, Etienne
Barbin, Prosper Casimiro
Barca, Gabriel
Bare, Francisco
Barea, Antonio
Barea, Gabriel
Bargas, Antonio Francisco
Bargas, Christobal de
Bargas, Jose
Bargas, Luis
Bargas, Mariano
Bargas, Miguel
Baron, George
Barrat, Antonio (Antoine)
Barrat, Viincente
Barraves, Jose
Barre, Juan Bautista
Barre, Richard
Barreda, Hermenegildo
Barrera, Francisco
Barrera, Jose Nicolas
Barrera, Josef
Barrios, Diego de
Barrios, Mariano Antonio
Barrios, Pierre
Barrise, X
Barrutia, Juan
Bas, Manuel
Basarte, Jose
Basedon, Loran
Basedonio, Lorenzo
Basor, Basilio
Basquez, Benito
Basquez, Jose
Bassain, Janbatiate
Bassot, Juan Antonio de
Batvin, Jean Baptiste

Baudouin, Francisco
Baudouin, Pedro
Baugine, Francisco
Baurain, Santiago Baurain
Baurele, Roberto
Bautista, Juan
Bayu,
Bazquez, Nicolas
Bazquez, Pedro
Bazqus, Nicolas
Beancur, Joseph
Bearegard, Elias
Beaufort, Francisco
Beaulieu
Beaumont Livaudais, Juan
Enoul
Beaurepos
Beguinet, Jose
Bekers, Jose
Belan, Joseph
Belasquez, Juan
Belasquez, Manuel
Belazques, Juan
Belhumor, Pedro
Bellachasse de Ville
Bellair (Jacques Hubert
Bellair)
Bellard, Antoine
Bellefontaine, Jean
Bellerose, Antonio
Bellestre, Francisco
Bellet, Baltazar de
Bellio,
Belllu, Pedro
Bello, Donato
Bello, Matio
Belly, Pedro
Belome, Gregoire Gaspar
Belpeche, Antonio
Beltran, Amador
Beltran, Francisco
Beltran, Manuel
Beltran, Tomas
Beltremieux, Luis
Beluc, Valentino
Beluche, Renaldo
Beluche, Rinaldo
Belzome, Enrique

85

Benitez, Juan
Benito, Jose
Benois Etiene
Benois, Jane Charlle
Benois, Maturin
Benoist de Ste. Clere, Juan
Bautista
Benpiere, Berthelleme
Bentanour, Luis
Benzan, Antonio
Bepeccher, Antonio
Bequendorf, Enrique
Bequet, Andres
Bequet, Juan Baptista
Bequet, Pedro
Bequete, Baptista
Bequeted, Gabriel
Berard, Jean
Berde, Francisco
Berdet, Juan
Berdinos, Julian
Berdon, Joseph
Bergara, Jose Euxenio de
Bergara, Miguel
Berge, Pedro
Bergeron, George
Bergeron, Germain
Bergeron, Joseph
Bergeron, Juan Bautista
Bergeron, Louie
Bergeron, Pierre
Bergoi, Francisco
Berlucho (Bertucho),
Francoise
Berlucho, Simon
Bermeo, Jose
Bermeo, Josef
Bermudes, Bartholome
Bermudes, Diego
Bermudez, Francisco
Bermudez, Jose
Bernard, Andres
Bernabeu, Gregorio
Bernal, Jacinto
Bernal, Luis
Bernard, Jean Baptiste
Bernard, Michel
Bernard, Pierre
Berne, Francisco

Berne, Pedro
Bernie, Francisco
Bernie, Luis
Bernie, Pedro
Bernoudy,
Beron, Andres
Beron, Francisco
Berret, Luis
Bertaud, Augutin
Bertaud, Pierre
Bertendona, Ramon
Berthelemy, Gaspar
Bertoule, Bertrand
Bertran, Pierre
Bertran, Amable
Bertran, Juan Bautista
Bertrand, Alezis
Bertrand, Amable
Bertrand, Antonio
Bertrand, Juan Luis
Bertrand, Thomas
Bertucat, Luis
Bertuoart, Luis
Bespen, Matias
Betes, Jose
Betiste, Enselme
Bibaren, Baptisa
Bible, Joseph
Bienbenido, Baptista
Bienenu, Juan Bautista
Bienvenu, Antonio
Bienvenu, Juan
Bienvenu, Roberto
Bigodet, Juan
Bigraud, Juan
Bilacha, Juan
Bilet, Louis
Billalba, Mariano
Billegas, Jose
Binay, Antonio
Birot, Francisco
Bisitte, Francois
Bivaren, Baptiste
Bizat, Joseph
Bizonet, Pedro
Blais, Antonio
Blan, C. Luis
Blan, Valentin

Blanchard, Aimable
Blanchard, Andres
Blanchard, Anselmo
Blanchard, Anselmo
(Enselme)
Blanchard, Firmain
Blanchard, Geronimo
Blanchard, Gui
Blanchard, Joseph
Blanchard, Victor
Blanchart, Pierre
Blanchet, Luis
Blanco, Balentin
Blanco, Bonifacio
Blanco, Diego
Blanco, Juan
Blanco, Miguel
Blanco, Pedro
Blanco, Vicente
Blas, Francisco
Blasco, Joaquin
Blondeau, Luis
Bo..dat, Joseph
Bocanegra, Rafael
Bochoni, Jose
Bodaille, André
Bodry, Joseph
Boduen, Joseph
Boduen, Juan
Boduen, Luis
Bofarull, Casimiro
Bofrer, Pedro
Bogeneau, Nicolas
Boirier, Joseph
Bois Dore, Antoine
Boisdore, Joseph
Boisdore, Luis
Boisseron (Beauceron),
Etienne
Boisseron, Jean
Bolac, Luis
Bolling, M
Bona, Antonio
Bonain, (Bonin), Antoine
Bonain, Jean Luis
Bonain, Paul
Boner, Pedro
Bonet, Antonio

Bonet, Francisco
Bonet, Juan Bautista
Bonilla, Manuel
Boniquet, Antonio
Bonnavauliere, Endre
Bonnet, Pierre
Boojenio, Nicolas
Borbone, Carlos
Borde, Jaques de
Bordel, Jean
Bordelon,
Bordelon, Antoine
Bordon, Jose
Bordon, Roque
Bore
Borel, Pierre
Boret, Andres
Borman, Antonio
Borme, Louis
Borme, Luis
Borne, Francisco
Borne, Sebastian
Borne, Simon
Borocie, Francisco
Borras, Francisco
Borry, Luis
Bosseau,
Bossie, Francisco
Bossier, Pedro
Botin, Francisco
Bouai, Rafael
Boudrot, Augustin
Bouillon, Jean
Boulard, Luis
Boulay, Noel
Bouligney, Francisco
Bouligni, Francisco
Bouligny, Francisco
Boullery, Nicolas
Bouniquet, Josef Antonio
Bourasn, Charle
Bourbon, Jean
Bourdelon, Antoine
Boure, Joseph
Boure, Pierre
Bourg, Joseph
Bourgeoin, Joseph
Bourgeois, Baptiste

Bourgeois, Michel
Bourgeois, Pierre
Bourgeois, Saul
Bourgeoiz, Jean
Bourgevis, Francisco
Bourlis, Nicols
Bourussu, Charles
Boutet, Antoine
Boutet, Baptiste
Boutet, Francois
Boutet, Philippe
Boutin, Joseph
Boutin, Paul
Bouvie, Pedro
Boyer, Andres
Brabo, Francisco
Bradnet, Agustin
Braguier, Francisco
Brand, Armand
Brand, Joseph
Brand, Saul
Brande, Andres de
Braseau, (Brazeau) Carlos
Braseur, Piere
Brasse, (Brasset) Blaise
Brasset, Pierre
Brasso (Brazau), Carlos
Brau, (Brand) Jean
Brauer, Jens
Braur, Charlle
Braur, Joseph
Braur, Josephe Mari
Braur, Lejeune, Pierce
Braur, Michelle
Braur, Pieran
Braux, (Brand) Firmin
Braux, Jausephe
Braux, Piere
Bravo, Jose
Bravo, Josef
Brazo, Carlos
Breau (Brand) Charles
Breau (Brand) Honore
Breda, Luis
Brigida, Manuel
Brignau, (Brinac) Michel
Brimieau, Saturnin
Bringier, Marius

Brinoly, Francisco
Brisset, Juan
Brofils, Juan
Bron, Francisco
Broquedis, Pierre
Brougue, Lange
Broum, Guillaume
Brounner, Juan
Brounner, Rodolph
Broupart, Benez
Brouque, Joseph
Broussard, Amand
Broussard, Augustin
Broussard, Claud
Broussard, Firmain
Broussard, Francisco
Broussard, Jean Baptiste
Broussard, Joseph
Broussard, Luis
Broussard, Maturin
Broussard, Pierre
Broussard, Silvain
Broussard, Simon
Broutin, Andre Francisco
Narcesse
Brouyar, Estevan (Etiene)
Brucieras, Baptista
Bruella, Pedro
Brunet Noel
Brunet, Agustin
Brunet, Andres
Brunet, Antonio
Brunete, Antonio
Brunete, Antonio, Jr.
Bruno, Saturin
Bruntaud, Pierre
Bucareli, Antonio
Buche, Baptista
Buden, Antonio
Buebalta, Antonio
Bueno, Vicente
Bujean, Augustin
Bujean, Mathurin
Bujean, Pierre
Bulli,
Bulliers, Alexandro
Burg, Thomas
Busain, Etiene

Buscaban, Bertrand
Bustamante, Antonio
Bustamante, Jose
Bustos, Andres
Bustos, Jose
Butler, Tomas
Butron, Rafael
Buyer, Juan Bautista
C
Caballero, Antonio
Caballero, Juan
Caballerro, Angel
Cabaret, Alexandro
Cabello, Antonio
Cabello, Manuel
Cabera, Joseph
Cabezas, Juan
Cabo, Jose
Cabral, Juan
Cabrera, Domingo
Cabrera, Francisco
Cabrera, Mateo
Cacedo, Francisco
Cadet, Pedro
Caduc, Juan
Cagigal, Felip Jado
Cagigal, Felipe
Cagigal, Juan Francisco
Cagigal, Juan Manuel
Cahier, Joseph
Cahieux, Nicolas
Caignard, Santiago
Cailloux, Dominique
Calbe, Antonio, Jr.
Calbe, Antonio, Sr.
Calbo, Juan
Calderon, Francois E
Calderon, Marcos
Caldona, Lucas
Calfa, Carlos
Calfa, Simon
Callejas, Juan
Callier, Joseph
Calonge, Juan
Calonge, Mariano

Calvo, Juan
Calvo, Juan Miguel
Calvort, Josef
Camacho, Juan
Camarsac, Martin
Cambas, Juan Baptista
Camderosse
Camer, Ambrosio
Camiel, Joaquin
Caminge, Jean
Camino, Manuel
Campana, Jose
Campbell, Juan
Campderos, Juan
Campeau, Francoise
Campo, Manuel del
Campo, Pablo
Campo, Santiago del
Campos, Andres Do
Campos, Blas
Campos, Francisco
Campos, Juan Jose Ramon
Camus, Manuel
Canadas, Ramón
Canal, Antonio
Canberque, Santiago
Candado, Francisco
Canelly, Emond
Cano, Vicente
Canouay, Mauricio
Cansell, Pedro
Cansiles, Pedro
Cantara, Baptista
Cantelmi, Francisco
Cantrelle, Miguel
Cantrelle, Miguel
Cantrelle, Santiago (Jacques)
Cantrelle, Miguel
Canzzel, Pedro
Capderos, Juan
Capetillo, Joseph
Capilla, Sebastian
Capitan, Baptista
Capotillo, Josef Garcia
Caraballo, Bartolome
Caraby, Juan Bautista

Caraby, Pedro (dit Dubois)
Carache, Juan
Carbajal, Pedro
Carco, Luis
Carco, Nicolas
Card, Joseph
Carierre, Michel
Carlin, Joseph
Carmarsaque, Martin
Carmouche, Juan Bautista
Carmouche, Pedro (Pierre)
Carnes, Antonio
Carnicer, Francisco
Carnicer, Manuel
Caro, Juan
Caron, Joseph
Carondelet, Baron
Carpentier, Enrique
Carrasco, Manuel
Carrasco, Rugino
Carreau, Joseph
Carredondo, Francisco
Carrera, Miguel
Carrera, Nicolas
Carreras, Manuel
Carrier, Pierre
Carriere, Francisco
Carriere, Juan
Carrillo, Antonio
Carrillo, Joseph
Carrizosa, Felipe Lopez
Carsoule, Armault
Cartabona, Francisco
Cartgavona, Francisco de
Casa, Jose
Casamayer, Jose
Casanova, Juan
Casas, Francisco
Casas, Juan de las
Case, Joseph
Caseberque, Santiago
(Jacques)
Casimiro, Simon
Casorla, Francisco
Castaned, Francisco
Castaneda, Francisco

Castanoz, Francisco
Castellanos, Manuel Maria
Castese, Domingo (Dominique)
Castillo, Antonio del
Castillo, Felipe
Castillo, Gregorio del
Castillo, Jose Anselmo
Castillo, Joseph
Castillo, Manuel del
Castillo, Pedro
Castillon, Andres
Castillon, Pedro
Castonge, Baptista
Castro, Domingo
Castro, Gabriel
Castro, Juan de
Castro, Ramon
Castyell, Eudaldo
Catan, Mauricio
Catani, Mauricio
Caumon Jens Charles
Caurera, Jose
Cavalier, Luis
Cavallero de Cluet (Clouet), Alejandro
Cavallero, Antronio
Cavee, Francisco
Cavelier Laine ..
Cavelier,
Cavelier, Anto.
Cavelier, Antonio
Cavelier, Juan Ba.
Cavelier, Juan Bautista
Cavezas, Joseph
Cavorla, Francisco
Caxigas, Francisco
Cayado, Josef
Cayole, Francisco
Cayuetas, Francisco
Cazorla, Antonio
Cazorla, Antonio Lorenzo
Cazorla, Diego
Cazorla, Jose Augustin
Cazorla, Joseph
Cdhery, Antoine
Cerro, Francisco del

Cerro, Ramon
Certainriche, Jorge
Cervantes, Melcor
Cervera, Matias
Cespedes, Fernando
Cevallos, Sebastian
Chabaud, Juan Joseph
Chabert, Pedro
Chacon, Francisco
Chacon, Jose
Chaise, Carlos
Chaldebert, Guillermo
Chaler, Francisco
Chalmet Delino, Ygnacio
Champagne, Juan Bautista
Champignolle, Jean Pierre
Champini, Luis
Chanbon, Estevan
Chanchelier, (Chancielleir), Louis
Chaneto, Luis
Chanrrion, Carlos
Chapelle, Jeronimo
Chaperon, Joseph
Chaperon, Santiago
Chapion
Chapuz, Miguel
Charante,
Charlanneau,
Charlesenith, Christian
Charmar, Agustin
Chartran, Joseph
Chatelero, Luis
Chaunier, Joseph
Chausler, Luis
Chauvin Deleri Desillets, Francisco
Chavert, Pedro
Chaves, Pedro Lopez Jose
Chaves, Rafael
Chavez, Rafael
Chenie, Juan Bautista
Cher, Juan
Cherbrier, Estevan (Etine)
Cherret, Nicolas
Chester, Governor
Cheval, Vicente

Chevalier, Demorand Vincent
Chevalier, Jean
Chevalier, Joseph
Chiazon, Paul
Chico, Gregorio
Chile, Luis
Chiloque, Bernardo
Chinchilla, Antonio
Chinchillo, Jose
Chip, Pedro
Chistian, Santiago
Chitabre, Martin
Choisi, Juan Joseph
Chorret, Pedro
Chouvin, Juan Maria
Chovin, Pablo
Chozas, Domingo
Chretien, Joseph
Cidillo, Josef
Cilo, Francisco
Ciriel, Luis
Cirnolle, Pablo
Clairtaud, Pedro
Clarisen, Antonio
Clark
Clauatre, Piere
Clazen, Pedro
Clemente, Francisco
Clos, Francisco
Cloustre, Jauseph
Cloutier, Gabriel
Cluet, Jose Maria
Clumb, Jacobo
Cobarrurias, Jose
Cobo, Francisco
Cocu, Pierre
Codero, Bizente
Codonan, Antonio
Coffigny, Claudio
Colas, Antonio
Coho, Jose
Col, Juan
Colas, Antonio
Colbert, Manuel
Colet, Paul
Colin,
Colinas, Francisco

Collado, Simon
Collell, Francisco
Colomb, Claud
Colon, Francisco
Colon, Valentin
Comau, Jean
Comau, Miguel
Commeau, Charle
Common, Etiene
Common, Firmin
Common, Piere
Comon, Jauseph
Concha, Juan de la
Conde, Manuel
Conde, Jose
Conget, Pascual
Conpare, Francisco
Conti, Manuel
Conti, Silvio
Contreras, Jose Ignacio
Contreras, Vicente
Copado, Agustin
Coquelin, Santiago (Jacques)
Corasol, Juan
Corbato, Cosme
Corbet, Manuel
Corbo, Francisco
Cordero, Manuel
Cordero, Vicente Ferrer
Cordoves, Juan
Cormien, Joseph
Cormien, Michel
Cormier, Baptiste
Cornalle, Pablo
Cornijo, Manuel
Corno, Francisco
Cornon, Charles
Cornon, Firmain
Corona,
Coronel, Jose
Corral, Carlos
Corro, Francisco
Cortes, Diego
Cortes, Jose
Cortes, Nicolas
Cortez, Cayetano
Cortez, Juan

Corusseau, Charles
Cosset, Joseph
Cosset, Juan
Cote, Alexandro
Cote, Joseph
Coudaugnan, Antonio
Couder, Pedro
Coumot, (Coumeaux) Joseph
Counard, Antoine
Counille, Salvador
Courege, Juan
Couronne, Juan Francisco
Courray, Jean Bautiste
Courtableau, Santiago
Cousot, Alexandre
Coussot, Francisco
Coussot, Henri
Cozan, Juan Bautista
Crebanches, Florian
Crepo, Luis
Crespillo, Felipe
Crespo, Antonio y Nove
Crespo, Sebastian
Cristian, Jacobo
Cristian, Juan
Croc, Jose
Croiset, Francisco
Croiset, Simon
Croisillon, NoCroit, Conrado
Croizet, Simon
Crooks, William
Croquer, Vicente
Cros, Baldivio de
Croslot, PedroCroue, Jacque
Cruz, JuanBauptista
Cruzat, Frandcisco
Cruzat, Jose
Cruzat, Jose Maria
Cruzom, Juan Jose
Csanueba, Juan
Cuadroche, Pedro
Cuba, Alonzo de
Cubas, Ramon de
Cuellar, Juan
Cuellar, Manuel Vicente
Cuerda, Francisco
Cuesta, Rafael
Cueto, Pascual

Cuetos, Diego
Culmene, Juan
Cura, Antonio
Cure, Jean
Cusot, Pedro
Cusot, Simon
D
D'Arensbourg, Pedro
D'Hauterive, Bernardo
D'Hommer
D'Orbanne, Juan
D, Luis
Daigle, Alexis
Daigle, Estevan
Daigli, Josef
Dalby, Juan
Dalcourt, Pedro
Dallemand, Pierre
Daltaresee, Jean
Dambaises, Jean Baptiste
Damour, Jean Baptiste
Danelson, James
Daniel, Niculas
Danile, Nicolas
Darby, Juan
Darby, Pedro
Dardenne, Athanase
Darenbourg
DarenbourgLaine,
Dario, Paul
Dartigaux, Juan Bautista
Daublin, Noel
Daunois
Daunois La Tonchere
DaunoisDe la Jonchere
Dauphin, Joseph
Dauphin, Juan
Dauphin, Pedro
Dauphin, Santiago (Jacques)
David, Andres
David, Etiene
David, Francois
David, Jean Jacques
Davide, Augustin
De Acosta, Tomas
De Alba, Narcissa
De Ayola, Manuel

90

De Belleisle, Francisco Simars
De Bertendona, Ramon
De Cagigal, Manuel
De Camos, Fernando Perez
De Cartabona, Silvio Francisco
De Castillo, Antonio
de Elouja, Bernardo
de Ezpeleta, Josef
de Flores, Josef
de Flores, Santhiago
de Guevara, Marcos Antonio
de Kessel, Baron
de la Chaise, Carlos
de la Chaise, Honorato
de la Cruz, Antonio
de la Cruz, Josefa Avocha
de la Cruz, Maria
de la Cruz, Salvador
de la Luz, Rafael
de la Mata, Josef
de la Morandier, Estevan Roberto
de la Paz, Antonio
de la Pena, Josef Antonio
de la Pena, Josef Lopez
de la Puente, Juan Eligio
de la Ronde, Pedro
de la Villebeuvre, Juan
de Lara, Miguel
de Lassize, Juan
De Lassized, Nicolas Lorant (Lorenzo)
De Leon, Lorenzo
De los Remedios, Juan
De los Rios, Francisco
De Luna, Andrew
De Mezieres, Antonio Maria
De Navarro, Josef Suarez
De Navas, Francisco
De Navas, Juan
De Oca, Miguel Montes
De Pineda, Manuel
De Quinones, Josef
De Quinones, Manuel
de Salles, Lluis
de Soto, Antonio (Antonio de Soto y Vaillant)

De Soto, Jose Rafael
De Tineo, Pedro
De Toro, Josef
de Verges de St. Sauveur, Francisco Xavier
de Ville de Goutin Bellechasse, Joseph
de Ville de Goutin, Carlos
de Ville de Goutin, Francisco
de Villiers, Carlos
de Villiers, Luis
de Villiers, Marcos
Debien, Pedro
deBlanc y St. Denis, Luis Carlos
Debo, Pedro
Deborde, Juan
Debrander, Francois
Dechan, Baptista, Jr.
Dechan, Baptista, Sr.
Dechene, Joseph
Declouet, Alejandro
deClouet, Alejandro JR.
deClouet, Alexandro, Caballero de Clouet
Declouet, Baltazar
deClouet, Luis
Decluet, Carlos
Decoouz, Pierre
Decoursel, Achille
Decuir, Francisco
Decuir, Jean Paul
Decuir, Josef
Decuir, Josef de la Chaise, Carlos
Decuir, Joseph
Decuire, Pierre
Decuix, Joseph
Deflandre, Juan Bautista
Defourd, Charles
Degran, Andres
Dejan, Antonio
Del Pozo, Jose
Del Pozo, Vicente
Del Rey, Francisco
Del Toro, Salvador
Del Villar, Angel
Del Villar, Nicolas
Delabarre

Delaca, Jean Bautiste
Delande, Santiago
Delaney, Guillermo
Delano, Francisco
Delasaire
Delassize, Nicolas
Delatte, Claud
Delery Desillete
Delery, Francisco
Delery, Francisco I
Delgado, Antonio
Delgado, Juan Jose
Delhommer, Joseph
Delille Dupard, Francisco
Delille, Nicolas
Delino, Luis Xavier
Delmas, Juan Bautista
Delome, Jose
Deloniers, Louis
Delorie, Francisco
Deluvigny, Andres
Deluvigny, Carlos
Demarais, Jean Baptiste
Demarre, Luis Amable
Demeaux, Felipe
Demorand
Demorud, Pierre
Denoye, Quiery
Depo, Joseph
Depre, Baptista
Depre, Rene
Derruen, Esteban
Desbordes, Santiago
Deslandes, Jorge
Despres, Henrique's
Desprez, Henriques
Deveron, Juan
Devilliers, Baltasar
Dezprez, Enrique
Dhollande, Jean
Diar
Dias, Andres
Dias, Blas
Dias, Jose Justo
Dias, Josef
Dias, Manuel
Diaz, Agustin
Diaz, Antonio

91

Diaz, Bartholome
Diaz, Donozo Melchor
Diaz, Fernando
Diaz, Jose
Diaz, Josef Antonio
Diaz, Juan
Diaz, Pablo
Diaz, Placida Faxardo
Diez, Francisco
Diez, Tomas
Dinempina. X
Dios, Manuel
Doblen, Francisco
Doblin, y Del
Dodie, Augustin
Dodie, Gabriel
Dofusat, Guido
Dolet, Pedro
Domingo, Santiago
Dominguez, Antonio
Dominguez, Domingo
Antonio
Dominguez, Josef
Dominguez, Juan
Dominguez, Matheo
Dominguez, Pablo
Domour, Charles
Donozo, Melchor
Donzel, Pedro
Dorgenois, Lebreton
Doricourt, Antonio Maria
Doricourt, Francisco
Dorion, Pedro
Dortolan, Bernardo
d'Ortolant, Bernardo
d'Ortolant, Bernardo
Dorvint, Alfonzo
Dorvint, Antonio
Doublin, Valentino
Doucet, Joseph
Doucet, Juan
Doucet, Michel
Doucet, Paul
Doucet, Pedro
Doucet, Saul
Doucette, Bautista
Douet, Guillermo
Douguer

Dozac, Antoine
Doze, Antoine
Dragon, Miguel
Dreax, Guido
Dresenmeyer, Juan Federico
Dreux, Gentilly
Dreux, Guido
Driole, Luis
Droi, Francisco
Dronet, Francisco
Drouet, Juan Luis
Drousin, Joseph
Duan, Francisco
Duan, Jean
Duant, Charle
Duant, Claud
Duarte, Jose
Dube, Joseph
Duberge Sensober, Francisco
Dubertrand, Gabriel
Dubnisson, Francisco
Dubois, Antonio
Dubray, Luis
Dubreuil, Jacobo
Dubrevil, Raymando
Dubuclet
Duchene, Pedro
Duchessing, Diego
Duchoguet, Enrique
Duchoguet, Francisco
Ducournean, Simon
Ducrest, (Louis) Armand
Ducret, Luis
Ducros
Dufo, Baptista
Duforest
Dufour, Charles
Dufrene, Lluis Berna
Duga, Jausephe
Dugan, Athanase
Dugan, Charles
Dugan, Francois
Dugas, Jean
Dugas, Pierre
Dugat, Athanaze
Dugat, Charles
Dugat, Francois
Dugat, Jean
Dugat, Pierre

Dugue Livandais
Dulino Chalmet, Ignacio
Dumontiers, Felix
Duoote, Pierre
Duoret (dit Belhumeur),
Nicolas
Dupin, Pedro
Duplantier, Armand
Duplesix, Martin
Duplessis, Francisco
Duppuis, Joseph
Dupre, Antonio
Dupre, Derbonne
Dupre, Francisco
Dupre, Laurent
Dupre, Santiago (Jacques)
Dupuis, Baptiste
Dupuy, Andres
Dupuy, Joseph
Duran, Antonio
Durand, Juan Bautista
Durant au, Pedro
Durantan, Pedro
Durbus, Pedro
Durel, Francisco
Durel, Juan Bautista
Durel, Juan Bautista
Durel, Ursino
Durell, Juan Bta.
Durell, Urein
Duroche, Pedro
Duroche, Simon
Durocher, Pedro
Duruy, Andres
Dussean
Dutiene, Louis
Dutille, Francisco
Dutillet, Francisco
Duval, Pierre
Duvernais, Andres
Duvernay, Francisco
E
Ebert, Amand
Ebert, Batiste
Ebert, Casiden
Ebert, Charles
Ebert, Joseph
Ebert, Pierre
Ebert, Prosper

Edelmeyer, Enrique
Eduardo, Miguel
Eguia, Francisco
Eguiarreta, Vicente
Elfe, Jacques
Elias, Pedro
Elices, Santiago
Elisa, Francisco
Emend, Charles
Emme, Francisco
Emont, Charles
Emont, Francisco
Emoul Livandais
Enriques, Joseph
Equia, Francisco
Equier, Ambroise
Eras, Francisco
Errier, Santiago (Jacques)
Escales, Miguel
Escobar, Joseph
Escot, Juan Antonio
Escudero, Jose
Esmeraldo, Antonio
Esnayder, Pedro
Espino, Miguel
Espinosa, Jose
Espinoza, Pedro
Espitra, Rafael
Estamp, Juan
Esteban, Dionisio
Estebes, Antonio
Estelle, George
Esten, Agustin
Estevan, Manuel
Estevan, Tomas
Esteves, Pablo
Estrada, Ignacio
Estrada, Manuel
Estrasheim, Juan Pedro
Estruquit, Guillermo
Estun, Luis
Etie, Pedro
Eugeni, Angel
Evert, Maturin
Evia, Ramón
Ezpeleta, Jose

Ezpeleta, Josef
F
Fabre, Agustin
Fabre, Horore
Fabre, Jaque
Fache, Joseph
Fache, Luis
Facini, Joseph
Fago (Fagot), Andres
Fainette, Oleman
Fait, Jacobo
Fajardo, Juan
Fala, Juan
Falgoust, Luis
Faller, Joseph
Fanguy, Vicente
Farggasse, Philipert
Fasiny, Josef
Faucheux, Francisco
Fauque, Andre
Faures, Joseph
Faures, Piere
Favre, Haycnthe
Favrot, Pedro
Faxardo, Josef
Federico, Josef
Federico, Luis
Feilagos, Marcelino
Felipe, Matias
Feneto, Luis
Feran, Joseph
Ferez, Agustin
Fernandez de Ruiloba, Vicente
Fernandez Trebejo, Antonio
Fernandez, Alonso
Fernandez, Andres
Fernandez, Antonio
Fernandez, Benito
Fernandez, Carlos
Fernandez, Diego
Fernandez, Domingo
Fernandez, Francisco
Fernandez, Ignaio
Fernandez, Javier Francisco
Fernandez, Josef
Fernandez, Juan

Fernandez, Manuel
Fernandez, Miguel
Fernandez, Nicolas
Fernandez, Santiago
Ferran, Martin
Ferrand, Francisco Joseph
Ferrand, Juan
Ferrand, Santiago (Jacques)
Ferrer, Jaime
Ferrer, Ramon
Ferrerio, elligible
Ferrero, Juan
Ferret, Jean Pierre
Ferret, Joseph
Ferrnandez, Diego
Fiax, Andres
Fidecharme, Andres
Fides, Jose
Figuer, Isidro
Figueroa, Christobal
Figueroa, Jose
Figueroja, Joaquin
Figuerola, Joauin
Fily, Jacobo
Firsps, Pablo
Fischelchvein, Andres
Fischer, Federico
Flaidel, Jorge
Flandre, Pedro de
Flandres, Juan Bautista de
Flon, Manuel
Florencio, Andres
Flores, Celestino
Flores, Joseph
Flores, Juan Antonio
Florez, Agustin de
Fmina, Pedro
Foche, Baptista
Foche, Pedro
Focie, Alphonso
Fointenu (Fontenot), Luis
Folch y Juan, Vicente
Folganes, Fernando
Gonzales, DiegGonzales, Domingo
Gonzales, Gregorio

Gonzales, Jose
Gonzales, Jose Maria
Gonzales, Jose Mariano
Gonzales, Juan
Gonzales, Manuel
Gonzales, Matias
Gonzales, Ramon
Gonzales, Rogue
Gonzalez, Baltasar
Gonzalez, Bruno
Gonzalez, Domingo
Gonzalez, Francisco
Gonzalez, Jose
Gonzalez, Josef Manzano
Gonzalez, Juan
Gonzalez, Juan Maria
Gonzalez, Luis
Gonzalez, Manuel
Gonzalez, Sebastian
Goon, Pedro
Gordo, Manuel
Gosson, Antonio
Gotie, Baptista
Goycochea, Miguel
Gracia, Tomas
Granados, Jose Maria
Granados, Josef
Grand-Pre, Carlos de
Granenigo, Joseph
Grange, Joseph
Gran-Pre, Carlos de
Granssone, Charle
Grape, Francois
Gravelle, Alexandro
Gravois, Joseph
Gravois, Paul
Gremillon, Joseph
Grene, Francisco
Grevembert, Francisco
Grevembert, Louis
Greven Bert, Jean Bautiste
Grevenbert, Barthelemy
Grevenbert, Francois
Grever, Ambriosio
Grezar, Santiago
Grezat, Santiago (Jacaques)
Griffon, Antonio

Griffon, Carlos
Grifon, Daniel
Grille, Juan
Grillo, Domingo
Grillo, Jose
Grimarest, Enrique
Grine, Bartolome
Grouque, Jacques
Gruy, Juan Bautista
Gudiel, Ysisdro
Guebara, Marcos
Guebedewaux, Francois
Guehaut, Pierre
Guenard, Joseph
Guenon, Pedro
Guerbois
Guerencio, Jose
Guerin, Pedro
Guerra, Rafael
Guerrero, Agustin
Guerrero, Jose Bicente
Guerrero, Juan
Guest (Ghessy), Francisco Xavier
Guiddy, Domingo
Guiderie, Pierre
Guidry, Joseph
Guignan, Guillermo
Guignan, Pedro
Guijarro, Pedro
Guilbaut, Joseph
Guillama, Domingo
Guillan, Juan
Guillemar, Guillermo
Guillemard, Gilberto
Guillermo, Jeronimo
Guillori, Gregorio
Guillori, Juan
Guillorie, Bautista
Guillorie, Claud
Guillorie, Joseph
Guillorie, Louis
Guillory
Guillot, Joseph
Guimberto, Jacques
Guio, Pierre
Guion, Amable
Guion, Nicolas

Guirola, Ventura
Guitar, Pedro
Guitros, Abraham
Gusman, Antonio
Gutierres, Joaquin
Gutierres, Juan
Gutierrez, German
Gutierrez, Manuel
Gutierrez, Pablo
Gutierrez, Silverio
Guziel, Juan
H
Haidel, Jorge
Halendais, Belie...
Haler, Jose Jacobo
Harang, Alexandre
Harddouin, Honore
Haverchy, Guillermo
Haydel, Jorge
Hazem
Hazur Delarme, Luis Xavier
Heber, Agustin
Heber, Joseph
Hebert, (Hever) baptiste
Hebert, Alexandre
Hebert, Cazidans
Hermoso, Cabo Juan
Hermoso, Juan
Hernandez Claro, Diego
Hernandez Trujillo, Domingo
Hebert, Etienne
Hebert, Jean
Hebert, Jean Baptista
Hebert, Josef Nicolas
Hebert, Mathurin
Hebert, Pierre
Hebert, Prostet
Hebert, Ygnace
Heiniman, Juan
Helabbre, Jacobo
Helfrig, Jose Jorge
Helias, Pedro
Henet, Baptista
Henry, Jacques
Henry, Jean
Herbert, Amand
Herbert, Josef
Herbert, Josef Nicolas

Heredia, Alonso
Herera, Sebastian
Herman, Cristian Federico
Hernandez, Antonio
Hernandez, Antoni
Hernandez, Antonio Agustin
Hernandez, Domingo Manuel
Hernandez, Francisco
Hernandez, Gerronimo
Hernandez, Jose
Hernandez, Jose Luis
Hernandez, Juan
Hernandez, Lorenzo
Hernandez, Manuel
Hernandez, Mariano
Hernandez, Matias
Hernandez, Vicente
Hernandez, Ysidro
Herold, Coronado
Herrando, Domingo
Herrera y Beloquin, Agustin
Herrera, Francisco
Herrera, Francisco Antonio
Herrera, Jose
Herrera, Josef
Herrera, Juan
Herrera, Manuel
Herrera, Maximo de
Herrera, Miguel
Herrera, Pedro
Herrera, Sebastian
Herrero, Manuel
Herrero, Matio
Herrnandez, Lorenzo
Hervouet, Juan
Heuer, Joseph
Hibon, Pedro
Hidalgo, Cristoval
Hiedra, Domingo
Hindenberger, Francisco
Hochman, Andres
Hochman, Antonio
Hochman, Philipe
Hollier, Luis
Hollier, Santiago
Homs, Miguel
Honore, Francisco

Honore, Luis
Honore, Luis, Sr.
Hortez, Juan Baptista
Hortiz, Joseph
Horuo, Luis
Hot, Carlos
Hoz, Jose
Hubardeau, Guillaume
Huberdau, Simon
Hubert, Antonio
Hubert, Francisco
Hudet, Antonio
Huerta, Lorenzo
Huet, Louis
Hugon, Joseph
Huno, Luis
Hurracca, Sebastian
Hurtado Mendoza, Mariano
Hurtado, Francisco
Hurtado, Lorenzo
Hurtado, Lorenzo
Huval, Jean
I
Ibanez, Juan
Ibarra, Luis
Iglesias, Pedro
Iglesias, Ramon
Illegible, Jorge
Illegible, Senaris
Imbaut, Juan Bautista
Infante, Francisco
Ingle, Simon
Inhavrige, Lorenzo
Iturriaga, Ignacio
Ixart, Francisco
Izquierdo, Manuel
J
Jaillot, Antonio
Jalbro, Jacques
Jamina, Pedro
Jamudo, Jose
Janes
Janes, Evam
Janise, Michel
Jannis, Joseph
Jannot, Juan Bautista
Janraine

Janson, Carlos
Jansonne, Joseph
Jaquier, Josef
Jaramillo, Antonio
Jardelat, Pedro
Jaulin, Jean
Jeansonne, Charle
Jeansonne, Jean
Jeansonne, Paul
Jeoffroy, Ambroise
Jesus, Lorenzo
Jetrus, Louis
Jimenez, Jose Domingo
Jobert, Pedro
Joffrion, Joseph
Joffryon, Jason
Joffryon, Pierre
Jolganes, Fernando
Jones, Evan
Jorda, Jaime
Jorge, Agustin
Jotre, Louis
Jourdan, Pedro
Juan Bautista, Manuel
Juarez, Calixto
Juarez, Ramon
Judice, Luis
Judice, Luis Jr.
Judice, Luis Sr.
Judice, Miguel
Julia, Ignacio
Jung, Andre
Junquera, Pedro
Jurado, Pablo
Justiz, Santiago
K
Kaiser, Enrique
Keinler, Santiago
Kelly, James
Kessel, Baron
Kien, Juan
Kion
Kirov, Josef
Kolberg, Juan Federico
L
L 'Homme, Alexandro de
L'espine, Jacque

95

L'Ynfortune, Pierre
La Barre, Francisco Renato de
La Barre, Pedro Volan (Bolant)
La Baure, Baptiste
La Beau, Carlos
La Branche, Alexandro
La Casse, Carlos
La Chaise, Carlos
La Costa, Juan Bautista
La Criz, Antonnio de
La Cruz, Nicolas de
La fantecia, Baptista
La Fleur, Joseph
La Fleure (Santiago) Jacques
La fleure, Bautiste
La Fleure, Jean
La Flor, Manuel de
La Fonte, Nicolas
La fosse (La Fauce) Romain
La Landa Ferriere, Luis
La Landa, Luis
La lande Dapremont
La Lllulippe, Augustin
La Luz, Jose Miguel de
La Miranda, Joseph
La Mone, Pierre
La Morandiere, Estevan Roberto de
La Porte, Juan Pedro
La Puente, Francisco
La ronde, Pedro
La Rosa, Juan
La Soude
La Topilet
La Torre, Francisco
La Torre, Marciano de
La tour
La tournelle, Santiago
La vagne, Pierre
La Vega, Francisco
La verge, Pedro
La vergne, Francisco
La vergne, Juan
La vergne, Miguel
La vigne, Honore
La vigne, Pedro

La Villa real, Tomas de
La ville, Antoine
La ville, Pedro
La Villebeure, Juan de
La violette, Juan
La viqueur, (Levigneur) Prise
Labadia, Silbestre
Labadores, Jose
Labarre
Labe, Jacobo
Labee, Jean
Laberge, Pedro
Labergne, Alain
Lable, Baptiste
Lable, Jean
Labrie, Pedro
Labro, Juan
Labros, Joseph
Labuciera (Labusciere), Joseph
Lacarda, Jose
Lachaise Novilliere, Honarato de
Lachaise, Carlos
Lachaise, Honorato de
Lachanese, Bautista
Lachapela, Juan
Lachapella
Lachar, Diego
Lachar, Juana
Lachar, Maria
Lacomba, Salvador
Lacomble, Agustin
Lacosta, Claudio
Lacou, Juan Bautista
Lacour, Baptista
Lacour, Nicolas
Lacourse, Joseph
Laderruta, Pablo
Ladueor, Antonio
Lae, Antonio
Laflanbuza, Joseph
Laflor, Luis
Lafores, Josef
Laforma, Baptista
Laframbueze, Baptista
Lafranchies, Francisco
Lafranco, Baptista
Lafuente, Jose

Lagautrais
Lagrenade, Antonio
Lagrenade, Lichel
Lagrenade, Miguel
Lagron, Carlos
Laine, Bodaille
Laine, Lagron
Lajoy, Antonio
Lalanda, Luis
Laloirfe
Lalonde, Baptiste
Lalonnier, Luis
Lamarque, Reneau
Lamarre, Francisco
Lamathe, Louis
Lambert, Luis
Lambert, Pedro
Lamirande, Constant
Lamoneda, Joaquin
Lamorandiere, Juan
Lamotte, Pedro Juan
Lanbromon, Pedro
Lancheben, Luis
Lancon, Juan Bautista
Landa, Fernando
Landa, Luis
Landaverde, Anastacio
Landeros, Josef
Landreaux, Francisco
Landrie, Alanuze
Landrie, Alexandre
Landrie, Enselmo
Landro, Francisco
Landry Francois
Landry, Jens Athanaze
Landry, Agustain
Landry, Armand
Landry, Athanaze
Landry, Baptiste
Landry, Bazile
Landry, Charles
Landry, Etienne
Landry, Firmin
Landry, Hiacinte
Landry, Jacques
Landry, Jans Yasainto
Landry, Jean
Landry, Josef
Landry, Joseph

Landry, Joseph Ignacio
Landry, Joseph Marie
Landry, Marin
Landry, Mathurin
Landry, Olivier
Landry, Paulle Mari
Landry, Pierre
Landry, Saturnine
Landry, Simon
Lange, Antonio
Langele, Joaquin
Langlois (Petit)
Langlois, Antoine
Langlois, Auguste
Langlois, Francisco
Langlois, Joseph
Langrer, Enrique
Langurand, Dominique
Lanlois, Philipe
Lannue, Joseph
Lanolo, Baptista
Lanzos, Manuel de
Laperle, Pierre
Lapierre, Joseph
Lapierre, Juan Baptista
Laplanta, Francisco
Laplanta, Luis
Laporta, Joseph
Lapuente, Luis
Lapuente, Pedro
Lara, Jose
Lara, Josef
Larabanne, Pedro
Larcheveque, Santiago
Lardueza, Antonio
Lardueza, Joseph
Lardueza, Luis
Lardueza, Pedro
Larespere, Francois
Larien, Juan
Larieux, Estevan
Laroche, Charles
Larrey, Manuel
Larrivee, Eustache
Larroche, Todas Santos
Larroque, Mariano
Larrose, Todos Santos

Las Cagigas, Francisco
Manuel de
Las Heras, Geronimo de
Lasis, Alexandro
Lasis, Juan
Lasise, Juan
Lasonda, Joseph
Lassblonera, Jacobo
Lasterra, Jose
Lasudray, Luis
Latre, Francisco
Laugurand, Domingo
Lauraque, Juan Bautista
Laurent, Gabriel
Laurent, Joseph
Lauve, Nicolas (dit Colin)
Lavallee, Simon
Laveau Trudeau, Carla
Lavega, Fra ncisco
Lavergne, Luis
Lavergne, Nicolas
Lavigne, Santiago
LaVille, Pedro
Law, Nicolas (dit Colin)
Laysard (Layssard), Estevan
(Eteinne Macaffries)
Lazaro, Juan
Lazo, Pedro (Pedro Lazo de
la Vega)
Le Blan, Gerome
Le Blanc de Villaneuve, J.
Le Blanc, (Etienne) Estevan
Le blanc, Desire
Le Blanc, Jean
Le blanc, Jerome
Le Blanc, Marselle
Le Blanc, Octavio
Le Blanc, Pablo
Le Blanc, Peaul
Le Blanc, Pierre
Le Blanc, Rene
Le Blanc, Silvian
Le Blanc, Simon
Le bleu, Berthelemy
Le Bleu, Francois
Le Blon, Juan Bautista
Le bourgeois, Pedro
Le Breton Dorgenois,
Francisco Jos.

Le Brun, Guilleaume
Le Chevalier de Villiers
Le Compte, Louis
Le Conte, Francois
Le Cour, Pierre
Le Gran
Le Jeune, Blaise
Le Jeune, Charles
Le Jeune, Jean Baptiste
Le Jeune, Michel
Le Norman, Martin
Le Peltier, Julian
Le Sassier, Alexandro
Le Sassier, Julian
Leal, Jose
Leblac, Balentine
Leblan, Jean baptiste
LeBlanc De VIllenuene,
Pablo Luis
Leblanc St. Denisa, Carlos
LeBlanc, Alexandro
Leblanc, Batiste
LeBlanc, Esteban
LeBlanc, Isac
LeBlanc, Joseph
Leblanc, Juan Pierre
LeBlanc, Valentin
Leblanc, Ysaac
LeBourgeois, Pedro
LeBreton, Bartholome
Lebrun, Guillermo
Leconte, Guillermo
Leconte, Joseph
Leconte, Nicolas
Ledoux, Francisco
Ledoux, Juan Pedro
Ledoux, Pierre
Lefleau, Juan Bautista
Leger, (Legee) Simon
Leger, Francois
Legre, Jean Baptiste
Legros, Baptiste
Legros, Francois
Leiba, Fernando de
Leland Dalcourt
Lelis, Federico
Leman, Juan
LeMelle, Francisco

Lemer, Luis
Lemere, Luiz
Lemineur, Pierre
Lendreneaux, Juan Pierre
Leon, Jose
Leon, Jose Fablo de
Leon, Juan
Leonard (or Renaud) Estevan
Leonard, Juan
Leonare, Jean Baptiste
Leper, Joseph
Leroy, Luis
Lesasier, Vicente Joseph
Lessasier (Sassier) Julian
Lessasier (Sassier) Luis
Lessassier Laine
Lessassier, Jose
Lessassier, Julian
Lessassier, Vizente Joseph
Lestage, Guillaume
Lestrade, Pedro
Lettre, Jean
Leybba, Fernando de
Licteau, Esprit
Liebana y Pazuengos,
Ambrosio de
Liero, Manuel
Lilliers, Luis de
Limier, Antonio
Limourt, (Lincourt) Joseph
Limourt, Charles
Lincouv, Charles
Lindsay, Josef
Linkeran, Jose
Lionnois, Juan
Lioteau, Francisco
Liquete, Clemente
Liret, Pedro
Lisoro, Fernando
Lisoro, Fernando
Litago, Sebastian
Litago, Sebastian
Livandais, Balthazar
Livandais, Laine
Llamosas, Thomas
Llanes, Diego
Llano, Antonio
Llanos, Josef Gonzalez

Llonca, Pedro
Lluch, Francisco
Loeches, Manuel
Loise, Tomas
Lolier
Lomar, Michel
Lomme, Alejandro de
Loms, Alejandro de
Longinos, Josef
Longoria, Francisco
Lopez Carrizosa, Felipe
Lopez de la Pena, Jose
Lopez, Andres
Lopez, Antonio
Lopez, Barolome
Lopez, Bernabe
Lopez, Blas
Lopez, Casimiro
Lopez, Cristobal
Lopez, Francisco
Lopez, Gabriel
Lopez, Jacinto
Lopez, Javier Miguel
Lopez, Jose
Lopez, Josef
Lopez, Josef Lorenzo
Lopez, Juan
Lopez, Manuel
Lopez, Nicolas
Lopez, Pedro
Lopez, Romualdo
Lopez, Sebastian
Lopez, Simon
Lopez, Tomas
Lopez, Vicente
Lorain, Jean bautiste
Lorain, Nicolas
Lorain, Pierre
Lorain, Santiago
Loran, Felisberto
Lorene, Joseph
Lorenze, Baptista
Lorenzo, Domingo
Lorenzo, Thomas
Lorenzo, ysidoro
Loriel, Pedro
Lormier, Pierre

Los Reyes, Antonio de
Los Reyes, Diego de
Los Reyes, Juan de
Los Reyes, Pedro de
Los Santos, Alejandro de
Losa, Francisco
Loubie Pellerin
Loubie, Manuel
Louriere, Charles
Loysel, Francisco
Lozano, Fernando
Lozano, Juan
Lubuciera, Joseph
Luby, Pedro
Lucas, J. L. (dit La trousse)
Lucas, Pedro
Lucere, Antonio
Luez, Alexo
Lugar, Juan Antonio
Lumbreros, Juan
Luque, Felipe
Luz, Rafael de la
M
Macarty, Agustin
Macarty, Eugenio
Macarty, Jacob
Macarty, Juan Bautista
Macarty, Luis
Macau, Joseph
MacDonnell, Enrique
Macias, Matio
Macnemara, Bartolome
Macnemara, Patricio
MacNemorney, John
Madrid, Benito
Madrid, Gil de la
Madrid, Mariano
Madrigal, Bernardo
Madrigal, Jose
Magnon, Arnault
Maicanague, Jose
Maicas, Antonio
Maichar, Antonio
Mala, Luis
Malagon, Jose
Malbef, Luis
Malbo, Baptista

Maldonado, Antonio
Maldonado, Jose
Malette, Antonio
Mallar, Luis
Mallet, Pedro
Malpef, Luis
Mamano, Tomas
Manc, Francisco
Mandeville
Mane
Manglar, Juan
Manrrique, Martin
Mans, Michel (Maux)
Mansano, Thomas
Mansebo, Jose
Manuel, Pedro
Manzanera, Jose
Manzanilla, Dionisio
Manzano, Crispulo
Marchan, Joseph
Marchan, Luis
Marchand, Pedro
Marchand, Simon
Marchauf, Joseph
Marche, Endre
Marchena, Jose
Marcil, Antonio
Marcizo, Joseph
Marco, Manuel
Marcollay, Pablo
Marcos, Luis
Mareantelle
Margotan, Jacobo
Marichar, Francisco
Marichar, Joseph
Marichard, Jacobo
Marichard, M Nicolas
Marie, Alexas
Marie, Jean
Marie, Paulle
Marigni, Pedro
Marigny Mandeville
Marigny, Pedro
Marillom Pedro
Marin, Joaquin
Marion, Francois
Marioneau, Louis

Marioneaux, Louis
Marmilloon, Pedro
Marmillou, Pedro
Marotan, Juan Luiz
Marotan, Pedro
Maroto, Manuel
Marquez, Basilio
Marquez, Joseph
Marquez, Juan
Marquez, Juan Christian
Marquez, Nicolas
Marrero, Jose
Marrero, Juan
Marrero, Juan Ramon
Marrian, Barthelemy
Mars, David
Marshall, Guillermo
Martel, Jose
Martelo, Jose
Martigny, Juan Bautista
Martin Buenaventura
Martin, Ambrosia
Martin, Andres
Martin, Anselmo
Martin, Bernardo
Martin, Bruno
Martin, Casimiro
Martin, Claude
Martin, Estevan
Martin, Francisco
Martin, Jacobo
Martin, Josef
Martin, Juan
Martin, Nicolas
Martin, Pedro
Martine, Francisco
Martinez (Martini), Juan
Baptisa
Martinez Rubio, Josef (Jose
Rubio)
Martinez, Antonio
Martinez, Cirilo
Martinez, Francisco
Martinez, Francisco II
Martinez, Geronimo
Martinez, Jose Diaz
Martinez, Josef

Martinez, Juan
Martinez, Juan Manuel
Martinez, Manuel
Martinez, Matias
Martinez, Santiago
Martinez, Vicente
Martini, Joseph
Martiny, Juan
Martiny, Juan Bautista
Marx, Juan Christian
Masa, Jose
Masia, Jose
Masicot, Carlos
Masicot, Santiago
Masicot, Santiago (Jacques)
Mason, Pedro Ganon
Masse, Louis
Mataranz, Jose
Mateo, Jose
Mateos, Francisco
Mateos, Juan Alonso
Materne, Andres
Materne, Nicolas
Materne, Santiago
Mateus, Francisco
Matheo, Jose
Matheos, Manuel
Mathurin, Jacques
Mathurin, Joseph
Maureau, Joseph
Mauriac, Jean Baptiste
Maxent, Antonio
Maxent, Gelberto Antonio
Maxent, Giberto
Maxent, Maximiliano
Maxent, Onorato
Mayeus, Baptiste
Mayeux, Joseph
Mayone, Joaquin
Mayordomo, Pedro
Mayorquin, Antonio
Mazorra, Agustin
Medina, Bartolome
Medina, Josef
Medinero, Antonio
Medinero, Antonio

Medranda, Andres
Meiller, Jacob
Meilleur, Juan Bautista
Meilleur, Miguel
Mekens, Pedro
Melancon, Charles
Melancon, Jacques
Melancon, Jean Baptiste
Melancon, Josef
Melancon, Josef
Melancon, Olivier
Melancon, Paul
Melancon, Pierre
Melancon, Saul
Melayen, Jacques
Melo, Domingo
Melo, Manuel
Melo, Patricio
Mena, Francisco
Mena, Jose
Mena, Xavier de
Menar, Pedro
Menard, Francisco
Menard, Louis
Menard, Pedro
Menchaca, Joaquin
Mendez, Cayetano
Mendez, Jose
Mendez, Josef
Mendez, Matheo
Mendieta, Francisco
Mendizavall, Francico
Mendoza y Argueda, Juan
Mendoza, Christobal
Mendoza, Ja e
Mendoza, Josef Antonio
Mendoza, Juan de
Mendoza, Pedro
Menen, Juan
Menen, Juan
Menendez, Antonio
Mentzinger, Enrique
Mentzinger, Juan Bautista
Menudo, Juan
Mercantel, Francisco
Mercier, Juan
Meredit, Thomas

Merino, Andres
Mesias, Jose
Mesier, Antonio de
Mesier, Diego
Meson, Jose
Metalie, Jacque
Metode, Jacobo
Metoyer, Pierre
Metzinger, Enrique
Meuillon
Meuillon, Juan Bautista
Meullion, Aime
Mexias Juan
Mexias, Alonso
Mexias, Jose
Mexis, Alonso
Meyer, Francisco
Meyer, Jose
Mezieres, Diego
Michavila, Jose
Michel, Pierre
Michon, Alexo
Michon, Lorenzo
Mideingle, Juan Bautista
Mier, Leonardo de
Miguel, Josef
Miguel, Manuel
Migueles, Domingo
Miguet, Juan
Mildon, Juan
Miler, Juan
Milg, Vilhem
Millam, Jean
Millan, Jose
Millan, Manuel
Martinez, Manuel
Millan, Mateo
Millanes, Joaquin
Millon, Mauricio
Millon, Santiago
Mingau, Piere dan
Minor, Stephen (Estevan)
Mir, Jans
Miralles, Antonio
Miramon, Pedro
Miranda, Francisco
Miranda, Jose

Miranda, Josef de la
Mire, Betonny
Mire, Joseph
Mire, Simon
Mirke, Jacque
Miro, Estevan
Miztre, Jacques
Moisineaur, Louis
Moizan, Pedro
Molay, Maro
Mole, Nicolas
Molere, Josef
Molina, Domingo
Molina, Francisco
Molina, Jose
Molina, Sebastian
Molinero, Mathias
Molon, Santiago (Jacques)
Mondion, Joseph
Mondion, Pedro
Mondon, Andres
Monfil, Felipe
Monfilis, Felipe
Monge
Monget, Francisco
Monget, Juan Luis
Monje, Manuel
Monpleusir
Monroy, Josef
Montagut, Rafael
Montal (illegible), Gabriel
Montalvo, Francisco
Montanary, Josef
Montardy, Pedro
Montauban, Arnand
Montecinos, Blas
Monteduc, Michel
Montegut, Manuel
Montenegro, Jose
Montero, Antonio
Montero, Bartolome
Montero, Carlos
Montes, Domingo
Monteserin, Pedro
Montesinos, Juan Jose
Montoliu, Cristoval
Montreuil, Francisco
Montrevil, Francisco

Monzon de Pena, Gregorio
Moon, Juan
Moquin, Jacques
Morain, Francisco
Moral, Francisco del
Morales, Domingo
Morales, Estanislao
Morales, Fernando
Morales, Josef
Morales, Juan de
Morales, Manuel
Morales, Nicolas
Morales, Xabier
Moran, Antonio
Moran, Martin
Morand, Carlos
Morandiere, Estevan de la
Morant, Carlos Sr.
Morant, Francois
Morata, Rafael
Moreaux, Martin
Morenne, Agustin
Moreno, Francisco
Moreno, Gabriel
Moreno, Joseph Estevan
Moreno, Juan
Moreno, Lucas
Moreno, Manuel
Moreno, Narciso
Moreno, Nicolas
Morin, Agustin
Morin, Christophe
Morin, Francisco
Moriton, Charles
Moro, Baptista
Moro, Carlos
Moron, Pierre
Motardy, Pedro
Mote, Jose
Mountin, Jean
Mounton, Joseph
Mounton, Salvador
Mouton, Louis
Mouton, Marrin
Moutte, Francoise
Mouy, Mauricio de
Mulle

Mune, Juan
Munez, Francisco
Munoz, Agustin
Munoz, Alfonso
Munoz, Antonio
Munoz, Fernando
Munoz, Francisco
Munoz, Juan
Munoz, Mariano
Munuera, Antonio
Murillo, Fernando
Muro, Jose
N
Naizai, Pierre
Narbone, Antonio
Natau, Samuel
Nava, Francisco
Nava, Joseph Antonio
Navarro, Bizente
Navarro, Blas
Navarro, Diego Josef
Navarro, Francisco
Navarro, Jose
Navarro, Joseph
Navarro, Julian
Navarro, Martin
Navas, Francisco
Navas, Jose
Navas, Jose Francisco
Navas, Jose Manuel de
Navas, Rafael
Navasques, Facundo
Navasques, Jazinto
Neda, Lorenzo
Negler, Juan
Negro, Andres
Negron, Gabriel Alberto
Negron, Jose Alberto
Negron, Pedro
Nepomuzeno, Palomi Juan
Neris, Juan
Nicolas, Antoine
Nicolas, Bertrand
Nicolas, Francisco
Nicolas, Jean
Nicolas, Joseph
Nicolas, Juan

Nicolas, Juan Bautista
Nicolas, Santiago (Jacques)
Nicolson, Henry
Nicolson, James
Nitar, Pierre
Nogueira, Domingo
Nolet, Pedro
Noriega, Jose
Norman, Martin
Norman, Simon
Notario, Bartolome
Nourry, Francisco
Nova, Manuel de
Noye,
Nuelet, Pedro
Nuese, Alexo
Nugent, Eduardo
Nunez, Jose
O
O' Reilly, Alexandre
O'Coner, Hugo
O'Conor, Dionisio
O'Reilly, Felipe
O'Relly, Guillermo
Obero, Manuel
Obiedo, Andres
Obregon, Jose
Obregon, Pedro
Ocarol, Benito
Ochagarria, Liberato
Ocharan, Francisco
Ochoa, Pedro
Oconor, (O'Coner), Mauricio
Ogan, Juan
Oglesbey, Daniel
O'Hara, John
Ojeda, Cristobal
Ojeda, Juan de
Ojeda, Silbestre
Olaya, Francisco
Olayo, Lazaro
Olazabal, Jose
Olazo, Jose Maria
Olcoz, Andres
Olibares, Jose
Olibien, Nicolas

Olier,
Oliva, Gines
Olivares, Estevan
Olivares, Jaime
Olivares, Josef Antonio
Olivares, Marcos
Olivier Forstall, Carlos
Olivier, Carlos
Olivier, Honore
Olivier, Juan Bautista
Olivier, Nicolas Godupaoy
Olivier, Pedro
Olivo, George
Ollier, Jacques
Ollier, Luis
Ollier, Santiago
Olmo, Juan del
Olmo, Manuel del
Olvera, Manuel
Oms, Miguel
O'Neill, Arturo
Oneylli, Eugenio
Onoro, Domingo
Onoro, Francisco
Onoro, Martin de
Onoro, Martin Jose
Ontanaya, Francisco
Ontanon, Juan
Orande, Diego
Orat, Simon
Ordonez, Joseph
Ordonez, Manuel
O'Reilly, Arturo
Orilion, Joseph
Orion, Joseph
Oro, Antonio
Orozco, Manuel
Orrego, Francisco
Orrueta, Ventura
Ortado Mendoza, Joseph
Ortega Ramos, Francisco
Ortega, Pedro
Ortega, Vicente
Ortiz, Diego
Ortiz, Francisco
Ortiz, Jose Antonio

Ortiz, Joseph
Ortiz, Pedro
Ortiz, Vicente
Ortolant, Jean
Ortotanto, Jean
Orueta, Buena Ventura
Osorio, Jose Antonio
Osorio, Josef
Osorio, Mariano
Osorno, Joaquin
Osorno, Joaquin Maria Angel
Sebastian
Osorno, Juan
Otero, Pascual
Otin, Ramon
Otondo, Miguel
Otonere, Luis Sr.
Outar, Mathien
Owen, Ismaheel
Ozcariz, Josef
Ozeune, Francois
P
Paber, Juan Cristian
Pablo, Francisco
Pabon, Jose
Pabrot, Pedro Jose
Pacheco, Dionisio
Pacheco, Jose Domingo
Pacquet, Louis
Padilla, Miguel
Padilla, Pedro
Padrino, Andres
Paez, Cristoval
Paez, Joaquin
Pagara, Juan
Paille, Juan
Paillet, Juan
Pain, Francisco
Pajarero, Manuel
Pajes, Manuel
Palacias, Francisco
Palao y Pratz, Antonio
Palao y Pratz, Martin
Palermo, Juan
Palomino, Antonio
Pampalon
Pan y Agua, Ramon

Panadero, Santiago
Pando, Manuel de
Paniagua, Josef Ramon
Paniagua, Ramon
Panis, Jacinto
Pantoja, Pedro
Papen, Joseph
Pardo, Benito
Pardo, Cristoval
Pardo, Jose
Pare, Francois
Pare, Joseph
Paredes, Andres
Paredes, Josef
Paredez, Josef
Parisigny, Domingo
Paron, Antonio N.
Parra, Calixto
Parra, Cayetano
Parrilla, Francisco
Part, Francois
Part, Olivier
Part, Pierre
Pascal, Mathieu Antonio
Pasqual, Joaquin
Pastor, Alexo
Pastor, Andres
Pastor, Antonio Pastor,
Manuel
Patin, Alejandro
Patin, Antoine
Patin, Jayme
Patin, Joseph
Patino, Francisco
Patut, Luis
Paul, Jean
Pauly, Joseph
Pavie, Joseph
Paytre, Cristofe
Paz, Bernardo de la
Pecheret, Francisco
Pecheret, Miguel
Pedres, Bernardo
Pedrosa, Jose
Pedrosa, Juan Jose
Peinado, Geronimo

Pek, Francisco Carlos
Pelaez, Miguel
Pellerin Laine
Pellerin,
Pellerin, Gregoire
Pelletier de la Houssaye, Luis
Pellot
Peltie, Pedro
Peltier, Julien
Pena, Antonio
Pena, Francisco de la
Pena, Ysidro
Penalver, Ignacio
Penalvex, Manuel
Penaranda, Gabriel
Penaza, Salvador
Penel, JosepPenelle, Pierre
Pepen, Francisco
Pepin, Pedro
Peralta, Agustin
Peralta, Antonio
Peralta, Juan
Peramas, Joaquin
Peraza, Manuel
Percina, Andres
Percirabas, Josef
Perdomo, Bentura
Perdomo, Jean
Pereda, Jose
Pereira, Blas Jose
Pereira, Joaquin
Peres de Campos, Fernando
Peres Roque, Ygnacio
Peres, Bartolome
Peres, Luis
Peret, Francisco
Pereyra, Juan
Perez Cavallero, Luis
Perez, Andres
Perez, Benito
Perez, Domingo
Perez, Felipe
Perez, Francisco
Perez, Francisco Antonio
Perez, Gabriel
Perez, Jose Eustaquio
Perez, Juan

Perez, Lucas
Perez, Luis
Perez, Manuel
Perez, Mariano
Perez, Miguel
Perez, Santiago
Perez, Vicente
Perez, Ysidoro
Periz, Luis
Perne, Ygnace
Peron, Joseph
Perosillo, Juan Domingo
Peroux, Henry
Perrau, Pedro
Perrault, Miguel
Perret, Alfonso
Perret, Alphonse
Perret, Manuel
Perret, Noel
Perret, Pedro Pujol
Persil, Santiago Antonio
Pertierra, Santos
Pertuit, Nicolas
Pery, Alexis
Pestano, Juan
Petely, Jose
Pety, Joseph
Pety, Salomon
Peyrin, Pedro
Peyrin, Pedro
Phaifer, Samuel
Pheyfer, Samuel
Philibert, Arnaud
Piboto, Santiago
Picard, Juan
Pico, Tomas
Piconfreras, Jose
Picou
Pielgan, Francisco
Piernas, Luis
Piernas, Pedro
Pierre, Huillaume Jean
Pierrnas, Joseph
Pihoto, Santiago
Pilet, Antonio
Pinan, Antoine
Pincau, Vincent

Pineda, Manuel
Pineda, Pedro
Pineda, Salbodor
Pinillos, Antonio
Pinillos, Manuel Antonio
Pino, Francisco del
Pino, Juan del
Pinot, Vincent
Pinto, Francisco
Piquery, Antonio
Piquery, Nicolas
Piris, Geronimo
Pita, Pedro
Pitre, Francois
Pitre, Miguel
Piutana, Josef
Pizarro, Ignacio
Plaisance, Mathieu
Plaise, Christophe
Plancha, Pedro
Plaseres, Jose
Platille, Mathieu
Plauche, Estevan (Etienne)
Plaza, Juan
Plechin, Phelipe du
Plest, Juan Bautista
Ploser, Antonio
Pober, Juan
Pochet, Francisco
Pogy, Antonie
Poiret, (Boiree) Jean
Poiret, Joseph (Poiriee)
Poirier, Michel
Poirrier, Flourantin
Pokhe, Martin
Polo, Josef Francisco
Polo, Joseph
Polo, Thomaspole, Pedro
Polock, Olibero
Pomares, Francisco
Ponce, Ignacio
Pontalba, Joseph
Ponzie, Jaime
Popewits, Vicente
Porcel, Juan
Porche, Augustin
Porche, Baptiste

Porche, Jean Baptiste
Porche, Jean Francois
Porche, Joseph
Porche, Michel
Porche, Pierre
Porche, Simon
Poree, Carlos
Poree, Eugenio
Poree, Thomas
Porell, Thomas
Porras, Jose de
Porrero, Gabriel
Porsely, Juan Pedro
Portal, Pedro
Portillo, Francisco
Portuit, Francisco
Postigo, Fernando del
Postigo, Juan Garcia del
Potestad, Andres
Potie, Luis
Poulle, Juan
Pourciaux, Baptiste
Pozadae, Josef
Pradie, Gabriel
Prado, Antonio
Prados, Joseph de
Prados, Juan de
Pratte, Jean Baptiste
Praun, Juan
Prejaean, Basille
Prejean, Charles
Prejean, Joseph
Prejean, Marrin
Pretely, Joseph
Prevost, Joseph
Prevost, Pablo
Prevost, Salomon
Prevot, Baptiste
Prevot, Francois
Prevot, Joseph
Prevot, Nicolas
Priestman, Thomas
Prieto, Gaspar
Prieto, Juan
Prieto, Pedro
Prieto, Tomas
Primeau, Pierre
Primo, Andres
Probanche, Baptista

Proffit, Carlos
Proto, Luis
Prudhomme, Michel
Puches, Blas
Puchet, Pedro
Puello, Simon
Puente, Francisco
Puente, Juan
Puerta, Nicolas
Puig, Felix
Pujol Perret, Pedro
Pulgar, Francisco
Punzada, Juan
Punzano, Jose
Pure, Eugenio
Purre (Pouree), Euginio
Q
Quainbidan, Charles
Quare, Francois
Quenel, Pedro
Queres, Antonio
Querry, Luis
Query, Antoine
Quesada, Antonio
Quevedo, Miguel
Quienel, Antonio
Quienel, Pedro
Quierdero, Gregorio
Quigli, Edvard
Quinones, Estevan
Quintana, Domingo
Quintana, Jose
Quintero, Christobal
Quintero, Jeronimo
Quiros,Fernando
Quitar, Pablo
R
Raballet, Jean Baptiste
Raballet, Joseph
Rabasa, Antonio
Rabelle, Antonio
Racle, Jacobo
Rafa, Juan
Rafaeles, Felix
Rafales, Felipe
Rafan, Jose
Raitre, Michel

Rambau, Alexis
Rambiu, Antoine
Ramires, Antonio
Ramirez, Francisco
Ramirez, Gregorio
Ramirez, Josef
Ramirez, Juan
Ramirez, Pedro
Ramirez, Veremundo
Ramise, Antonio
Ramon, Antonio
Ramon, Jose Antonio
Ramon, Santiago
Ramos, Blas
Ramos, Fabien
Ramos, Francisco
Ramos, Jose
Ramos, Melchor
Ramos, Simon
Ransan, Louis
Rapen, Andres
Rapen, Pedro
Raquet
Ravelos, Antoine
Reamis, Antonio
Rebel, Juan
Reberon, Juan
Rebollono, Antonio
Rebolloso, Pedro
Rechard, Simon
Recio, Rafael
Recuron, Guillaume
Redondo, Francisco
Reggio, (Rexio) Carlos
Reggio, Luis
Reine, Pedro
Reiter, Michel
Remedios, Juan de los
Renaud, Luis
Renne, Estevan
Renne, Pedro
Requena, Nicolas
Resel, Vicente
Resev, Andre
Revellon, Francisco
Revet, Michel

104

Revidiego, Gregorio
Revoil, Antonio
Revoille, Pedro
Revolo, Luis
Rexis, Juan
Rey, Francisco Juan
Rey, Roque
Reyes, Antonio
Reyes, Francisco
Reynaud, Juan
Riano, Francisco
Riano, Francisco de
(Francisco Reano Guemes)
Riano, Juan
Ribar, Joseph
Ribas, Francisco
Ribera, Antonio, Sr.
Ribera, Baptista, Jr.
Ribera, Jose Bartholome
Ribera, Miguel
Ribero, Sebastian
Ribet, Joseph
Ribiera, Antonio, Jr.
Ribiera, Antonio, Sr.
Ribiera, Baptista
Ribiera, Phelipe
Richard
Richard, Amanas
Richard, Amant
Richard, Baptista
Richard, Fabiean
Richard, Jean
Richard, Joseph
Richard, Luis
Richard, Mathurin
Richard, Pierre
Richard, Polle
Richard, Victor
Riche, Federic
Rico, Juan Jose
Rico, Juan Josef
Ride, Lorenzo
Ride, Luis
Riesch, Joaquin
Rigoche, Ignacio
Rilleux, Vincent
Rillieux, Louis
Rillieux, Pedro

Rincon, Antonio
Rio, Francisco
Rio, Domingo
Rios, Blas
Rios, Francisco
Rios, Juan
Rios, Manuel
Rios, Ramon de los
Risel, Vicente
Riter, Andres
Rivar, N.
Rivar, Paul
Rivare, Francisco
Rivart, Juan Bautista
Rivas, Bernardo
Rivas, Francisco
Rivera, Hermenegildo
Rivera, Jaime
Rivera, Jose
Rivera, Miguel
Riveras, Marcos
Rivero, Silbestre
Rivet, Blaise
Rivet, Civille
Rivette, Etiene
Rivette, Francois
Rivette, Pierre
Rivette, Sirille
Rivette, Teidore
Rixner, Jorge
Rixner, Juan Luis
Rober, Jacobo
Rober, Luis
Robert, Bartholome
Robert, Louis
Robico, Effreme
Robiehot, Firmin
Robiera, Mariano
Robin, Roberto
Robin, Roberto (Roberto
Robin de Laugni, Sr.),
Robinde Logny, (Langin),
Pedro
Robineon, David
Robinet, Louis
Robira, Diego
Robles, Juan

Robles, Nicolas
Roc, Dominique
Roca y Juan, Jose
Roca, Luis
Roch y Cirona, Miguel
Rocha, Ambrosio
Roche, Henrique
Roche, Simon de
Rocq, Maurice
Rodriguez,
Rodriguez Moreno, Pablo
Rodriguez Suares, Juan
Rodriguez, Agustin Garcia
Rodriguez, Andres
Rodriguez, Antonio
Rodriguez, Bartolome
Rodriguez, Bernardo
Rodriguez, Esteban
Rodriguez, Fernando
Rodriguez, Francisco
Rodriguez, Jose
Rodriguez, Juan
Rodriguez, Manuel
Rodriguez, Miguel
Rodriguez, Pablo
Rodriguez, Salvador
Rodriguez, Tomas
Rodriguez, Victor
Rodriguez, Xptoval
Roge, Louis
Roger, Jean
Roger, Joseph
Roig y Girona, Miguel
Roig y Xirona, Miguel
Rojas, Juan de
Rojas, Manuel
Rolaan, Agustin
Roland, Bautista
Roldan, Enrique
Romagsa, Jose
Roman, Manuel
Romano, Diego
Romano, Juan
Romero, Antonio
Romero, Bartholome
Romero, Bernabe
Romero, Diego

Romero, Francisco
Romero, Joaquin
Romero, Juan
Romero, Manuel
Ronde, Pedro de la
Roquerol, Salvador
Roquigny, Paul
Rosabach, Nicolas
Rosier, Luis de
Ross, Eduardo
Ross, Estevan
Rota, Ysidro
Roubieu, Gaspar
Rousseau, Nicolas
Rousseau, Pedro
Roussel, Juan Bautista
Rousseve, Juan Bautista
Roustan, Francisco
Routixe, Michel
Rouvier, Francisco
Roxas, Jose Joaquin
Roy, Abraham
Roy, Carlos
Roy, Francisco
Roy, Jacinto
Roy, Joachin
Roy, Joseph
Roy, Nicolas
Roy, Noel
Roy, Pedro
Roye, Nicolas
Rubidu, Joseph
Rubieau, Gaspar
Rubio, Antonio
Rubio, Caspar
Rubio, Jines
Ruby, Salvador
Rucerbe, Bautista
Rucher, Simon de
Ruesta, Esteban
Rui, Antonio
Rui, Domingo
Rui, Vicente
Ruiz, Angel
Ruiz, Calixto
Ruiz, Julian
Ruiz, Manuel

Ruiz, Pedro
Runi, Francisco
Russell, Luis
Rutisor, Antonio
Rutisor, Juan
Ruvio, Juan
Ruvio, Leon
S
Saavedra, Manuel
Sabadon, Juan
Sabatier, Jerome
Sabe, Pedro
Sabedra, Diego Martin
Sabedra, Jose
Sabinac, Cade
Sabourin, Luis
Sabua, Baptista
Sael, Gregorio
Saes, Pedro
Saez, Juan
Saez, Miguel
Saez, Pedro
Saint Amant, Miguel
Saint Amant, Pedro
Saint Eloy, Daniel
Saint Germain, Renaldo de
Saint Laurent, Santiago
Saint Mount,
Saintpe, Pedro
Salado, Juan
Salas, Joaquin
Salazar, Diego
Salazar, Jose
Salazar, Manuel
Salcedo, Ignacio
Salcedo, Juan
Salcedo, Leon
Salcedo, Tomas
Saldana, Manuel
Saldana, Nicolas
Sale, Antonio
Salgado, Alexando
Salgado, Juan
Salgado, Lorenzo
Salla, Cayetano

Salles, Luis de
Samaniego, Jose
Samano, Antonio
Samitier, Cayetano
Samoratey, Antonio
Sampini, Luis
San Fransua, Antonio
San Martin, Francisco
San Martin, Pedro
San Pedro, Antonio
San Pedro, Manuel de
San Suey, Antonio
Sanches, Domingo
Sanches, Jose
Sanches, Juan
Sanches, Mariano
Sanchez Ramirez, Josef
Sanchez, Andres
Sanchez, Antonio
Sanchez, Calixto
Sanchez, Diego
Sanchez, Erminio
Modesto, Antonio
Sanchez, Francisco
Sanchez, Gaspar
Sanchez, Jose Antonio
Sanchez, Jose Rafael
Sanchez, Juan Antonio
Sanchez, Lorenzo
Sanchez, Mariane
Sanchez, Nicolas
Sanchez, Ram Joseph
Sanchez, Ramon
Sanchez, Salvador
Sanchez, Ysidoro
Sancho, Pedro
Saneile, Jacinto
Sanglois, Pedro
Sanguinete, Carlos
Sanselier, Joseph
Sanselier, Luis
Sansolie, Luis
Sanson, Francois
Sans-soucy, Carlos
Santa Ana, Antonio
Santa Ana, Lucas

Santa Ana, Pedro
Santa Maria, Lucas
Santiago, Pedro
Santiago, Sorel
Santin, Jujan
Santos, Manuel
Santos, Domingo
Santos, Manuel
Sanz, Manuel
Sanz, Pedro
Saonero, Manuel
Sapiain, Miguel
Sardet
Sarpy, Del oro
Sartal, Miguel
Saso, Jose
Sastre, Jose
Saubadon (saubavon),
Francisco
Saucier, Juan
Saulais, Joseph
Saunier, Jean
Saunier, Silvin
Savan, Pedro
Savedra, Josef Eussevio
Savignac, Guillaume
Savignon, Francisco
Savoie, Jean
Savoir (Savoy), Jean
Savoy, Francois
Savoye, Pierre
Sazo, Jose
Schuit, Juan
Schweitzer, Francisco
Seasoie, Pierre
Seausier, Baptiste
Seda, Gaspar
Sedillo, Jose
Segobia, Ceronimo
Segobia, Juan
Segovia, Alonzo
Segovia, Geronimo
Segovia, Pedro
Segschneider, Ambrosio
Segschneider, Jorge
Segui, Juachin
Segura, Francisco

Semer, Baptiste
Senac, Bernard
Senel, Jacobo
Senette, Juan Bautista
Sentmenat, Ramon
Senzano, Juan
Serra, Matheo
Serran, Pascual
Serrano, Juan
Serrat, Jaime
Serrato, Jose
Serre, Baptista
Sevada, Juan
Sibillot, Miguel
Sierra, Benito
Sierra, Francisco
Sierra, Francisco Antonio
Sierra, Joaquin
Sierra, Mariano
Sigue, Lorenzo
Sigur, Lorenzo Sr.
Sigur, Pedro
Silba, Antonio de
Silva, Eugenio
Silva, Francisco
Silva, Gregorio
Silva, Jose Manuel
Silva, Manuel de
Silvestre, Anthoine
Silvestre, Joseph
Simans, Francisco
Simars de Belislle, Francisco
Simerre, Jean Baptiste
Simoene, Antonio
Simon, Cristobal
Simon, Francisco
Simone, Pedro
Soelo, Noel
Soigne, Silvano
Soileau, Auguste
Soileau, Juan Bautista
Soileau, Noel
Solano, Jose
Soldevilla, Antonio
Soler, JoseSolera, Ceferino
Solet Laine
Solet, Joseph

Solet, Renaldo
Solet, Rene
Solet, Thomas
Solet, Valentin
Solis, Jose
Solis, Josef Antonio
Solis, Juan
Solivellas, Miguel
Soliz, Jose Antonio
Solorzano, Jose
Sonne, Jean
Sonnieu, Joseph
Sopena, Blas
Sorel, Jacque
Sorel, Joseph
Soria, Pedro
Sorrel, Joseph Jaque
(Santiago)
Sorrilla, Mariano
Sosa, Jose de
Soto Mayor, Jose Joaquin
Soto Mayor, Josef
Soto, Anton
Soto, Jose de
Soto, Joseph
Soto, Juan
Soudric, Francois
Soudric, Louis
Soudric, Martin
Soules, Bernard
Soumande, Joseph
Sounier, Olivier
Souquet, Jean
Sousa, Francisco
Sousa, Manuel
Soylo, (Soileau) Manuel
Spinola, Marcelo
St. Amant, Alexandre
St. Amant, Antonio
St. Amant, Francois
St. Germain,
St. Marck Darvy, Juan
St. Maxent, Francisco
Maximiliano
St. Maxent, Gilberto Antonio
de
St. Romain

Ste. Anne, Antoine
Ste. Claire, J.B, Benito de
Ste. Claire, Juan Bautista
Benito de
Stelby, George
Sterling, Alexandro
Stery, Joseph
Stilly, Jean Baptiste
Strasheim, Juan Pedro
Striquert, Guillermo
Suarez, Bartholome
Suarez, Benito Francisco
Suarez, Carlos
Suarez, Josef
Suarez, Miguel
Suarez, Ramon
Suelo, Manuel
Sugranes, Ventura
Sugre, Laurant
Sullevan, Benito
Sumande, Joseph
Suprande, Esteban
Suriray, Juan
Surriret, Jean
Sweetman, Terencio
T
Tabo, Jacobo
Tacon, Andres
Tailar, Jacobo Rober
Tala, Juan
Tallan, Santiago
Tamaque, Renard
Tapia, Cayetano
Tarascon, Charles
Tardieu, Juan
Tardif, Jacques
Tardif, Juan Baptista
Tarielle, Carlos
Taso, Jose
Tayan, Carlos
Tayon, JosephTear, Agustin
Tecie, Joseph
Terga, Juan de la
Terraza, Luis
Terrian, Joseph
Terriere,
Terry y Palao, Antonio
Terry y Palao, Martin
Terry y Palao, Ygnacio

Terson, Jean
Tescira, Francisco
Tetreval, Simon
Texada, Manuel
Texier, Joseph
Texxier, Nicolas
Therior, (Teriau), Thomas
Therior, Paul
Theriot, Ambroise
Theriot, Joseph
Thery, Joseph
Thes, Juan
Thian, Pedro
Thibodeau, Charles
Tho, Jacobo
Thomas, Jose
Thomas, Meredit
Tibaudau, Baptiste
Tibaudau, Olivier
Tibeaudot, Pierre
Tibo, Carlos
Tibo, Joseph
Tibodau, Anselme
Tibodu, Paul
Tierre, Luiz
Tigre, Juan
Tirola, Bentura
Tison, Jean
Tisserand, Baltazar
Tisserand, Francois
Tisserand, Pierre
Tlax, Andres
Tobaudau, Amand
Tobidau, Pedro
Toiton, Simon
Toledano, Manuel
Toledo, Antonio
Toledo, Pedro
Tomas, Francisco
Tomas, Pedro
Tomasco, Juan
Toral, Martin
Toro, Jose
Toro, Joseph
Toro, Salvador
Torralba, Pedro
Torralva, Miguel

Torre, Jose Maria
Torreente, Antonio
Torres, Jose de
Torres, Miguel
Torres, Miguel Ramon
Toulon, Jean
Toulon, Pedro
Toupart, Antoine
Toups, Gaspar
Toups, Juan Luis
Toups, Luis
Toups, Pablo
Tourangin, Francisco
Tournier (Ternier), Nicolas
Toussain, Jean
Toussaint, Joseph
Toussaint, Benoist
Toussans,
Toutan Beaurregard, Elias
Toutchec, Jorge
Tovis, Diego
Toysa, Antonio
Trahan, Atanase
Trahan, Germain
Trahan, Honore
Trahan, Jean
Trahan, Olivier
Trahan, Paul
Trahan, Pierre
Trahan, Rene
Trapani, Jose
Trepagnier, Estevan
Trepanier (Tropagnie), Pedro
Tresfalacios, Mariano
Tresmayer, Federico
Trevino, Felipe
Triche, Juan Bautiste
Tronard, Achiles
Tronosso, Bernardo
Trouard, Aquiles
Trovar, Aquiles Maria
Troxel, Cristobal
Trudeau Lavaux
Trudeau, Felix
Trudeau, Zenon
Trujillo, Baltazar
Trujillo, Gregorio
Tuesca, Angel

Tuqui, Pablo
Tur, Antonio
U
Ubaldy, Tomas
Uberty, Francisco
Uchoinca, Dionisio
Ucles, Juan
Ugarte, Martin
Ugarte, Pedro
Ugarte, Thomas
Ulain, Luis
Unguera, Baltasar
Unquera, Bartolome
Urbina, Juan
Urgel, Jaime
Uriarte y Borja, Jose
Urraca, Jose
Urreuela, Juan
Urtado Mendoza, Joseph
Ussos, Martin
Ustillo, Diego
V
Vaible, Joseph
Valcarcel, Fernando
Valderas, Ygnacio
Valdes, Cayetano
Valencia, Juan
Valere, Josef
Valier, Antonio
Valier, Jose
Valiere Dauterive
Valiere, Antonio
Valle, Antonio
Valle, Antonio Ramon
Valle, Carlos
Valle, Eugenio
Valle, Francisco II
Valle, Francois
Valle, Juan Baptista
Valle, Juan
Vallee, Francisco
Vallee, Juan Bautista
Valleo, Carlos
Vamonde, Josef, Vazquez
Vanderbussche, Pedro
Var, Joseph

Varela, Jose
Varella, Nicolas
Vasor, Joseph
Vasques, Tomas
Vasquez, Benito
Vasquez, Tomas
Vaugine, Estevan de
Vaugine, Francisco
Vazquez, Benito
Vazquez, Juan
Veber, Nicolas
Vega, Andres
Vega, Andres de
Vega, Marinel
Vegas, Diego de
Veigle, Joseph
Veillon, Francois
Veillon, Luis
Velez, Angel
Velleestre, Francisco
Vellon, Francisco
Vellont, Francisco
Venzan, Antonio
Verbois, Nicolas
Verdino, Julian
Verdon, Joseph
Verdun, Juan Adam
Veret, Francois
Vergell, Jaime
Verosin, Alexandre
Verret, Agustin
Verret, Juan Bautista
Verret, Luis
Verret, Michel
Verret, Nicolas
Verret, Nicolas II
Verret, Santiago (Jacque)
Versaille
Vessaille Laine
Vessier, Juan
Vetanzos, Santiago
Vevet, Juan
Via, Joseph
Via, Philippe
Viana, Martin
Vibaren, Juan Baptista
Vicente
Vidal, Jose

Vidrine
Viela, Juan Francisco
Vien, Juan Bautista
Vienne, Julian
Vienvenu, Juan
Vieux, Pedro
Vigee, Charle
Viger,
Vigne, Lorenzo
Vigo, Francisco
Vigra, Joseph
Vilars, Julian
Villa Baroso, Tomas de
Villa Santa, Juan
Villa, Juan de la
Villabaso, Josef
Villafana, Cristoual
Villalobos, Cayetano
Villalva, Francisco Xavier
Villamayor, Josef
Villanueba (Villanueva), Jose
Villanueba Barroso, Thomas
Villanueva y Varroso, Thomas
Villanueva, Baltasar
Villar, Francisco
Villars dubreuil, Luis de
Villasenor, Jose
Villasenor, Juan
Villaverde, Manuel
Villavicencio, Agustin
Villavicencio, Antonio
Villavicencio, Miguel
Ville de Goutin, Carlos de
Ville de Goutin, Francisco de
Ville de Goutin, Jose de
Ville, Carlos de
Ville, Jose
Villegas, Juan
Villegas, Luis
Villegoutin, Carlos
Villela, Juan Francisco
Villemont, Carlos de
Villera, Carlos de
Villers, Balthazar de
Villers, Carlos
Villers, Marcos de

Villet, Baltazar de
Villet, Marcos de
Villiers, Fontenette
Vilse, Philipe
Vimecarty, Jose
Vincent, Joseph
Vincent, Pierre
Vinuela, Manuel
Vior, Luis
Virole, Juan (Jean)
Viron, Joseph
Vision, Aunoree
Visonet, Andres
Viten, Bartholome
Viulla Real, Thomas des
Vivare, Francisco
Vivare, Francois
Vivas, Joaquin
Vives, Juan
Vizcon, Manuel
Vizonet, Baptista
Vizonet, Francisco
Vlien, Luis
Vmete, Batista
Voisin, Pedro
Volui, Josef
Vorman, Pedro
W
Walker, Pedro
Wallsh, Juan
Whitaker, Daniel
White, Enrigue
Wilse, Joseph
Wiltz Laine
Wiltz, Bautista
Wiltz, Juan Bautista
Wiltz, Lorenzo

Wiltz, Lorenzo (Laurent) II
Wingins, Ichabod
Wirte, Phillippe
Wiste, Joseph
X
Ximenes, Juan
Ximenez, Alfonso
Ximenez, Antonio
Ximenez, Esteban
Ximenez, Francisco
Ximenez, Jose
Ximenez, Juan
Ximenez, Manuel
Ximeno, Francisco
Xorje, Augustin
Y
Yanes, Diego
Ybanez, Fernando
Ybanez, Jose
Ybarola, Antonio
Ydalgo, Matias
Ydalgo, Xptobal
Year, Thomas
Yebenes, Geronimo
Yevenes, Geronimo
Ygnacio, Jose
Ymelle, Carlos
Ymelle, David
Ymelle, Pedro
Ymeszo, Jose
Ynchaurraga, Antonio
Ynesta, Gregorio
Yngles, Belu
Yoberto, Pierre
Yoclec,
Ysquierdo, Jose

Yung, Antonio
Yuste, Manuel
Yvon, Thomas
Yxart, Francisco
Z
Zabala, Jose
Zaitord, Ricardo de
Zamorates, Antonio
Zamoratey, Antonio
Zaragozano, Manuel
Zavala, Francisco
Zavala, Jose
Zedillo, Josef
Zensano, Juan
Zequeira, Manuel
Zerezo, Jose Ygnacio
Zeringue, Jean
Zeringue, Jean Luis
Zeringue, Joseph
Zeringue, Pierre
Zerrat, Xaime
Zespedes, Rafael
Zorrilla, Joseph
Zumague, Antonio
Zunet, Felix

Spanish Louisiana Military and Militia 1776-1783

Author Jack D. L. Holmes researched Service Records of the Louisiana Military Units.

110

Louisiana Collection Series of documents on colonial Louisiana. Title of book is *"Honor and Fidelity."* The words indicate honor and loyalty added to the military banner. The Louisiana Infantry Regiment and the Louisiana Militia Companies, 1766-1821.

Service records of the Louisiana Military Units indicate the name, age at the time the sheet was filled out, his native land, his quality (noble or commoner), and his health. I will only use 1776-1783 of this information for my purposes. More information can be accessed through Jack D. L. Holmes book.

Most of Jack D. L. Holmes book sources came from *relaciones*, muster rolls, inspection reports, and lists of both veteran and militia units. He used over fifty-five lists from Spanish archives. Most sources came from AGI, PC, in *legajos* 13,14,30,41,131-a,159-a,160a-b,161a187a-b,193a-b,198,201,206,215-a,and 2368.

Names can be seen in Jack D. L. Holmes book.

Names in the Service Sheets of the Louisiana Infantry Regiment are as follows:

Acosta, Ignacio de
Acosta, Thomas de
Aguado, Antonio,
Agustino, Julian
Aleu, Magin
Andres, Pedro
Auteman, Federico
Balderas, Ignacio
Baloyra, Doming
Barea, Gabriel
Bassot, Juan Antonio de
Bearegard, Elias
Bellestre, Francisco
Bermudez, Francisco
Bertucat, Luis
Blanco, Juan
Blanco, Pedro
Borras, Francisco
Bouligney, Francisco
Castyell, Eudaldo
Caxigas, Francisco, Manuel de
Cayado, Josef
Cervera, Matias
Chalmette, Delino, Ignacio
Clarisen, Antonio
Colbert, Manuel
Collell, Francisco
Coudaugnan, Antonio

Cros, Baldirio del
Cruz, Juan Bauptista de la
Cruzat, Jose
deClouet, Luis
de la Pena, Josef Lopez
de la Ronde, Pedro
de Lassize, Juan
de la Villebeuvre, Juan
de Soto, Antonio (Antonio de Soto y Vaillant
de Salles, Lluis
de Verges de St. Sauveur, Francisco Xavier
de Ville de Goutin, Carlos
de Ville de Goutin, Francisco
de Ville de Goutin Bellechasse, Joseph
de Villiers, Carlos
de Villiers, Marcos
Dominguez, Josef
Dominguez, Juan
Duarte, Jose
Dubreuil, Jacobo
Estevan, Tomas
Fasiny, Josef
Favrot, Pedro
Fernandez, Diego
Fernandez de Ruiloba, Vicente
Folch y Juan, Vicente
Fortier, Miguel

111

Foucher, Pedro
Garcia, Julian
Garrell, Francisco
Gracia, Tomas
Grand-Pre, Carlos de
Guest (Ghessy), Francisco Xavier
Guillemard, Gilberto
Gutierrez, Manuel
Haverchy, Guillermo
Hernandez, Matias
Hidalgo, Cristoval
Lalanda, Luis
Lanzos, Manuel de
LeBlanc, Alexandro
LeBlanc, Joseph
LeBlanc, Valentin
Lisoro, Fernando
Lopez, Barolome
Macarty, Agustin
Maldonado, Antoni
Martinez, Francisco II
Martinez, Manuel
Martinez Rubio, Josef (also called Jose
Rubio)
Minor, Stephen (Estevan)
Monroy, Josef
Montreuil, Francisco
Noriega, Jose
Olcoz, Andres
Olivier, Pedro (Derneville)
O'Neill, Arturo
Ordonez, Manuel
Osorno, Joaquin Maria Angel Sebastian de

Palao y Pratz, Antonio
Palao y Pratz, Martin
Pastor, Alexo
Peralta, Juan
Perez, Luis, Caballero de Bellegarde
Perez, Manuel
Petely, Jose
Pierrnas, Joseph
Piernas, Luis
Piernas, Pedro
Pontalba, Josef de
Porell, Thomas
Postigo, Fernando del
Rivas, Francisco
Rousseau, Pedro
Saez, Juan
St. Maxent, Francisco Maximiliano
St. Maxent, Gilberto Antonio de
Solivellas, Miguel
Soto, Joseph
Trevino, Felipe
Trudeau, Felix
Trudeau, Zenon
Vamonde, Josef, Vazquez
Valiere, Antonio
Valere, Josef
Vaugine, Estevan de
Vazquez, Benito
Vegas, Diego de
Villanueba Barroso, Thomas
Villemont, Carlos de
White, Enrigue
Yebenes, Geronimo

Name	Service Sheet	Archive	Country	Age	Campaigns

Acosta, Ignacio de
Service Sheet (SH): Dec. 31, 1793, AGI, PC, Leg. 161-a
Country: Havana   Age: 36
Campaigns: Mobile (1780), Pensacola (1781)
Acosta, Thomas de
SH: June 30, 1795, AGI, PC, leg. 161-a
Country: Havana   Age: 47
Campaigns: Ft. Bute of Manchak and Baton Rouge, and Natchez, 1779
Aguado, Antonio,
SH: June 30, 1793, AGI, PC, leg. 161-b

Country: Castille, Spain   Age: 46
Campaigns: Pensacola (1781)
Agustino, Julian
SH: Dec. 31, 1792, AGS, GM, leg. 7291, VIII, 106
Country: Castille, Spain   Age: 46
Campaigns: Mobile (1781), Pensacola (1781)
Aleu, Magin
SH: June 30, 1793, AGI, PC, leg. 161-b
Country: Cataluna   Age: 34
Campaigns: 1780 sailed from Gibraltar blockade for Havana, Pensacola (1781)
Andres, Pedro
SH: Dec. 31, 1791, AGS, GM, leg. 7291, VII, 94
Country: Castilla la Nueva, Spain   Age: 43
Soldier 1767 and promoted to Sgt. first-class on 1787
Campaigns: none listed
Auteman, Federico
SH: June 30, 1793, AGI, PC, leg. 1501-b
Country: Germany   Age: 39 in 1793
Campaigns: Louisiana Regiment and member of convoy sent to upper Louisiana (Missouri) that
attacked and repulsed the English and Chickasaws.
Balderas, Ignacio
SH: June 30, 1805, AGI, PC, leg. 161-b
Country: Salamanca   Age: 58
Campaigns: As sergeant, he led sixteen men against eighteen enemy troops near Galvez-Town,
and succeeded in 1779
Baloyra, Domingo
SH: Dec. 31, 1787, AGS, GM, leg, 7291, I, 110
Country: Galicia, Spain   Age: 36
Campaigns: not given but in Louisiana Infantry before and during the American Revolution
Barea, Gabriel
SH: Dec. 31, 17, AGS, GM, leg. 7291, I, 85
Country: Castilla la Nueva, Spain   Age: 44
Campaigns: Europe and came to Louisiana with O'Reilly expedition during 1769. He remained
in the Louisiana Regiment before, during, and after the American Revolution.
Bassot, Juan Antonio de
SH: June 30, 1793, AGI, PC, leg. 161-a
Country: Lorraine, Germany   Age: 46
Campaigns: Manchak, Baton Rouge, Natchez (1779); Mobile (1780); Pensacola (1781); Isthmus
of Panama (1778)
Bearegard, Elias
SH: June 30, 1793, AGI, PC, leg. 161-a
Country: New Orleans   Age: 33
Campaigns: Mobile, Alabama
Bellestre, Francisco
SH: June 30, 1815, AGI, PC, leg. 161-b

113

Country: New Orleans   Age: 51
Campaigns: Manchak, Baton Rouge (1779); Mobile (1780); Pensacola (1781)
Bermudez, Francisco
SH: Dec. 31, 1792, AGS, GM, leg. 7291, VIII, 102
Country: Mexico   Age: 30
Campaigns: soldier (July 17, 1779) and last promotion was on (July 9, 1789) in the Louisiana
Regiment. No campaigns listed.
Bertucat, Luis
SH: June 30, 1793 AGI, PC, leg. 161-a
Country: France   Age: 54
Commander and training: Scientific corps; inventor and manufacturer of armor for Internal
Provincias; Engineer for the American Army operations; fortified Balize and Natchez;
Apalachee; Louisiana Infantry for 12 years and 11 months.
Blanco, Juan,
SH: Dec. 31, 1809, AGI, PC, leg. 161-a
Country: Galicia, Spain   Age: 36
Campaigns: Baton Rouge (1779), Pensacola (1781)
Blanco, Pedro
SH: June 30, 1793, AGI, PC, leg. 161-a
Country: Andalucía, Spain   Age: 50
Campaigns: Manchak and Baton Rouge (1779)
Borras, Francisco
SH: June 30, 1797, AGS, GM, leg. 7292, X, 65
Country: Cataluna, Spain   Age: 38
Campaigns: Gibraltar none other listed
Bouligney, Francisco
SH: June30, 1793, AGI, PC, leg. 161-a
Country: Alicante, Spain   Age: 56
Campaigns: Cadet 1758 and Colonel 1791, Manchak and Baton Rouge (1779), Grenadiers
commander at Mobile (1780), Pensacola (1781) captured enemy flag while under fire.
Castell, Eudaldo
SH: June 30, 1793, AGI, PC, leg. 161-b
Country: Cataluna   Age: 36
Campaigns: To Havana on 1780 and then Louisiana. None listed
Caxigas, Francisco Manuel de
SH: June 30, 1793, AGI, PC leg. 161-a
Country: Laredo, Santander, Spain   Age: 44
Campaigns: none given
Cayado, Josef
SH: Dec.31, 1787, AGS, GM, leg. 7291,I, 95
Country: Castilla la Nueva, Spain   Age36
Campaigns: expediton for Pensacola broken up by hurricane (1780), Prisoner in Jamaica
Cervera, Matias
SH: June 30, 1793, AGI, PC,, leg.161o-b
Country: Valencia, Spain   Age: 33

Campaigns: Uncertain if in Louisiana
Chalmettr Delino, Ignacio
SH: June 30, 1793, AGI, PC, leg. 161-a
Country: New Orleans   Age: 37
Campaigns: Mobile (1780)
Clarisen, Antonio
SH: June 30, 1793, AGI, PC, leg. 161-b
Country: Germany   Age: 40
Campaigns: Mobile (1779)
Colbert, Manuel
SH: Dec.31, 1792, AGS, GM, leg. 7291, VIII, 107
Country: Andalucía   Age: 31
Campaigns: Not given
Collell, Francisco
SH: June 30, 1795, AGI, PC, leg. 161-a
Country: Cataluna   Age: 48
Campaigns: Commandant of Galveztown post in 1779, he organized expedition against the English settlements on the Amit River and Captured them with seven ships, and 125 men captured. He trained 1200 men.
Coudaugnan, Antonio
SH: Dec. 31, 1793, AGI, PC, leg.161-a
Country: France   Age: 50 (1793)
Campaigns: Mobile (1779)
Cros, Baldirio del
SH: Dec. 31, 1787, AGS, GM, leg. 7291, I, 90
Rosellon, France   Age: 42
Campaigns: Baton Rouge (1779)
Cruz, Juan Bauptista de la
SH: June 30, 1793, AGI, PC, leg. 161-b
Country: Bragania, Portugal   Age: 42
Campaigns: Manchak and Baton Rouge (1779), Mobile (1780), Pensacola (1781)
Cruzat, Jose
SH: Dec 31, 1793, AGI, PC, leg.161-a
Country: Havana   Age; 24
Campaigns: none given, but in the Louisiana Infantry
deClouet, Luis
SH: June 30, 1793, AGI, PC, leg. 161-a
Country: New Orleans   Age: 24
Campaigns: Soldier since 1777, but no listed campaigns during the Am. Rev.
de la Pena, Josef Lopez
SH: June 30, 1793, AGI, PC, leg. 161-a
Country: Galicia   Age: 52
Campaigns: Commander of instruction for the cadets in Louisiana Infantry, Fort Bute and Manchek, and Baton Rouge (1779), expedition to defeat the Chickasaws led by the Colberts (1780)

de la Ronde, Pedro
SH: Dec. 31, 1800, AGI, PC, leg. 161-a
Country: New Orleans   Age: 36
Campaigns: Ft. Bute of Manchak and Baton Rouge (1779), Mobile (1780), Pensacola (1781)
de Lassize, Juan
SH: June 30, 1793, AGI, PC, leg.161-a; Dec. 31, 1797, AGS, GM, leg. 7292, X, 54
Country: New Orleans   Age: 27 (1793)
Campaigns: none given. Notes: demonstrated valor
de la Villebeuvre, Juan
SH: June30, 1793, AGI, PC, leg.161-a
Country: Britany, France   Age: 55
Campaigns: none given during the Am. Rev., however, promoted to Captain (Apr. 29, 1778) and
known valor
de Soto, Antonio (Antonio de Soto y Vaillant)
SH: Dec. 31, 1793, AGI, PC, leg.161-a
Country: Cadiz, Spain   Age: 31
Campaigns: Captured by the English in 1780 on way from Cadiz to join his regiment and left on
the beach of Venezuela. He demonstrated valor. Later he served in Havana and Louisiana.
de Salles, Luis
SH: June30, 1793, AGI, PC, leg. 161-a
Country: New Orleans   Age: 29
Campaigns: Ft. Bute of Manchak and Baton Rouge (1779), Mobile (1780).
de Verges de St. Sauveur, Francisco Xavier
SH: Dec.31, 1808, AGI, PC, leg. 161-a
Country: New Orleans   Age: 58
Campaigns: Mobile (1780), working with French Army for General Galvez
de Ville de Goutin, Carlos
SH: Dec.31, 1808, AGI, PC, leg. 161-a
Country: New Orleans   Age: 49
Campaigns: Ft. Bute of Manchak and Baton Rouge (1779), Mobile (1780), Pensacola (1781)
de Ville de Goutin, Francisco
SH: Dec. 31, 1793, AGI, PC, leg. 161-a
Country: new Orleans   Age: 27
Campaigns: none given
de Ville de Goutin Bellechasse, Joseph
SH: June 30, 1793, AGI, PC, leg. 161-a
Country: New Orleans   Age: 31
Campaigns: Ft. Bute of Manchak and Baton Rouge (1779), Mobile (1780), Pensacola (1781)
de Villiers, Carlos
SH: June 30, 1793, AGI, PC, leg. 161-a
Country: NewOrleans   Age: 27
Campaiggns: Ft. Bute of Manchak and Baton Rouge (1779), Mobile (1780), Pensacola (1781),
de Villiers, Marcos
SH: Dec. 31, 1812, AGI, PC, leg. 179-b
Country: New Orleans   Age: 51

Campaigns: Ft. Bute of Manchak and Baton Rouge (1779), Mobile (1780)
Dominguez, Josef
SH: June 30, 1793, AGI, PC, leg. 161-b
Country: Galicia   Age: 41
Campaigns: not given
Dominguez, Juan
SH: June 30, 1793, AGI, PC, leg. 161-a
Country: Andalucia   Age: 50
Campaigns: garrison on the warship of the Royal Armada San Juan Nepomuceno which suffered its mast being destroyed in the siege and capture of Pensacola (May 1781)
Duarte, Jose
SH: Dec. 31, 1792, AGI, PC, leg. 161-a
Country: Havana   Age: 29
Campaigns: none given
Dubreuil, Jacobo
SH: June 30, 1795, AGI, PC, leg. 161-a
Country: New Orleans   Age: 51
Campaigns: Engineer, Baton Rouge (1779), commandant to reinforce upper Louisiana (St. Louis), commandant of post in Arkansas.
Estevan, Tomas
SH: Dec. 31, 1815, AGI, PC, leg. 161-b
Country: Castilla la Vieja   Age: 54
Campaigns: none given
Fasiny, Josef
SH: Affiliation record, AGI, PC, leg. 159-b
Country: Piamonte, Italy   Age: 22 at enlistment
Campaigns: none given
Favrot, Pedro
SH: June 30, 1795, AGI, PC, leg. 161-a
Country: New Orleans   Age: 45
Campaigns: Ft. Bute de Manchak and Baton Rouge (1779), eventually became the commander.
Fernandez, Diego
SH: Dec. 31,, 1792, AGS, GM, leg. 7291, VIII, 93
Country: Estremadura   Age: 53
Campaigns: Ft. Bute and Baton Rouge (1779), Mobile (1780), Pensacola (1781)
Fernandez de Ruiloba, Vicente
SH: June 30, 1792, AGS, GM, leg. 7291, VIII, 51
Country: Ceuta, Spain   Age: 31
Campaigns: instructor of cadets
Fortier, Miguel
SH: Dec. 31, 1788, AGI, PC, leg. 161-a
Country: New Orleans   Age: 33
Campaigns: none given
Foucher, Pedro
SH: June 30, 1793, AGI, PC, leg. 161-a

117

Country: New Orleans   Age: 36 or 37
Campaigns: Ft. Bute and Baton Rouge (1779), Mobile (1780)
Garcia, Julian
SH: Affiliation record, Feb. 19, 1774, AGI, PC, leg. 159-b
Country: Pinila Ambruz, Segovia   Age: 19 in 1754
Campaigns: died July 30, 1778 while in the Louisiana Infantry
Garrell, Francisco
SH: June 30, 1793, AGI, PC, leg. 161-b
Country: Cataluna   Age: 35
Campaigns: Blockade of Gibraltar and expedition to America (1780)
Gracia, Tomas
SH: Dec. 31, 1797, AGI, GM, leg. 7292, X, 95
Country: Andalucía   Age: 36
Campaigns: Ft. Bute and Baton Rouge (1779), Pensacola (1781)
Grand-Pre, Carlos de
SH: June 30, 1793, AGI, PC, leg. 161-a
Country: New Orleans   Age: 47
Campaigns: Baton Rouge (1779), quelled uprising at Natchez (1781) as commander`
Guest (Ghessy), Francisco Xavier
SH: June 30, 1793, AGI, PC, leg. 161-a
Country: Alicante   Age: 46
Campaigns: Blockade of Gibraltar (1779), expedition to Havana (1780), siege and capture of the
British Island of Providence (1782), along with an American merchant ship. It had a large
British fortress.
Guillemard, Gilberto
SH: June 30, 1795, AGI, PC, leg. 1443-b
Country: Longwy, France   Age: 48
Campaigns: Ft. Bute of Manchak, in which he was first to enter the defenses, and Baton Rouge
(1779), Mobile (1780), crippled at Pensacola (1781) yet stayed on to serve.
Gutierrez, Manuel
Sh: Dec. 31, 1787, AGS, GM, leg. 7291, I, 91
Country: Palencia, Castilla la Vieja, Spain   Age: 46
Campaigns: reinforcements for Havana (Feb. 1776), expedition to New Orleans (1778), Ft. Bute
of Manchak and Baton Rouge (1779). Gutierrez previously served in Portuguese war and in the
Africa presidios.
Haverchy, Guillermo
SH: Dec. 31, 1795, AGS, GM, leg. 7292, II, 107
Country: Germany   Age: 35
Campaigns: none given
Hernandez, Matias
SH: June 30, 1793, AGI, PC, leg. 161-a
Country: Aragon, Spain   Age: 42
Campaigns: Reinforcement detachment for New Orleans (1778), Ft. Bute of Manchak and Baton
Rouge (1779), Mobile (1780, Pensacola (1781)
Hidalgo, Cristoval

118

SH: ....
Country: Andalucia, Spain   Age: 53
Campaigns: Baton Rouge (1779), Mobile (1780)
Lalanda, Luis
SH: Dec. 31, 1792, AGS, GM, leg. 7291, VIII, 59
Country: New Orleans   Age: 28
Campaign s: Ft. Bute of Manchak and Baton Rouge (1779), Pensacola (1781)
Lanzos, Manuel de
SH: June 30, 1793, AGI, PC, leg. 161-a
Country: Galicia (Padron)   Age: 52
Campaigns: Mobile (1780)
LeBlanc, Alexandro
SH: Dec. 31, 1787, AGS, GM, leg. 7291, I, 87
Country: New Orleans   Age: 21
Campaigns: none given
LeBlanc, Joseph
SH: June 30, 1797, AGS, GM, leg. 7292, X, 5
Country: New Orleans   Age: 36
Campaigns: Ft. Bute of Manchak and Baton Rouge (1779), Mobile (1780)
LeBlanc, Valentin
SH: June 30, 1793, AGI, PC, leg. 161-a
Country: New Orleans   Age: 29
Campaigns: Ft. Bute and Baton Rouge (1779), Mobile (1780)
Lisoro, Fernando
SH: Dec. 31, 1793, AGI, PC, leg. 161-a
Country: Andalucia   Age: 57
Campaigns: Ft. Bute of Manchak and Baton Rouge (1779)
Lopez, Bartolome
SH: June 30, 1793, AGI, PC, leg. 161-b
Country: Canary Islands   Age: 32 (1794)
Campaigns: none given
Macarty, Agustin
SH: Dec. 31, 1793, AGI, PC, leg. 161-a
Country: New Orleans   Age: 20
Campaigns: none given
Maldonado, Antoni
SH: June 3, 1793, AGI, PC, leg. 161-b
Country: Castilla la Vieja, Spain   Age: 34
Campaigns: Pensacola (1781)
Martinez, Francisco II
SH: June 30, 1815, AGI, PC, leg. 161-b
Country: Castilla la Vieja, Spain   Age: 58
Campaigns: Pensacola (1781)
Martinez, Manuel
SH: June 30, 1793, AGI, PC, leg. 161-a

Country: Castilla la Vieja   Age: 51
Campaigns: Baton Rouge (1779), and Mobile (1780)
Martinez Rubio, Josef (also called Jose Rubio)
SH: Dec. 31, 1793, AGI, PC, leg. 161-a
Country: Andalucia   Age: 48
Campaigns: none given
Minor, Stephen (Estevan)
SH: June 30, 1794, AGI, PC, leg. 161-a
Country: Jersey, U.S. (Pennsylvania)   Age: 33
Campaigns: Note: Minor was an American Company Volunteer from (1779-1781)
At Lake Pontchartrain under Captain Pickles. Captain Pickles obtained a ship and some Spanish
soldiers from New Orleans when on a naval battle on England's Florida Lake (1779). Minor was
involved with Ft. Bute of Manchak and Baton Rouge (1779), Mobile (1780), Pensacola (1781).
During 1781 he joined the Spanish Louisiana Infantry for 13 years.
Monrroy, Josef
SH: Dec. 31, 1787, AGS, GM, leg. 7291, I, 28
Country: Castilla   Age: 45
Campaigns: expedition to Havana (Feb. 1776), Pensacola (Oct. 17, 1780) and (May, 1781),
Providence (Bahamas) (1782)
Montreuil, Francisco
SH: June 30, 1793, AGI, PC, leg. 161-a
Country: New Orleans   Age: 29
Campaigns: Ft.l Bute of Manchak and Baton Rouge (1779), Mobile (1780)
Noriega, Jose
SH: Dec. 31, 1795, AGI, PC, leg. 32
Country: Asturias   Age: 38
Campaigns: Royal Academy of Madrid for courses in mathematics, Baton Rouge (1779), Mobile
(1780), Pensacola (1781)
Olcoz, Andres
SH: June 30, 1797), AGS, GM, leg. 7292, X, 107
Country: Castilla la Vieja   Age: 38
Campaigns: none given
Olivier, Pedro (Derneville)
SH: ...30, 1793,   Age: 39
Campaigns: Ft. Bute of Manchak and Baton Rouge (1779), Battle of Fort San Carlos (1780)
O'Neill, Arturo
SH: May 26, 1791, AGI, SD, leg. 2556
Country: Ireland   Age: 56
Campaigns: From one of famous Irish regiments for Spain expedition of Santa Catalina and other
Rio de la Plata Campaigns (1777), Pensacola aiding Bernardo de Galvez (1780-1781) likely
assigned in Cuba.
Osorno, Joaquin (Maria Angel Sebastian de)
SH: June 30, 1793, AGI, PC, leg. 161-a: Dec. 31, 1808, AGI, PC, leg. 161-b Age: 43 during
1808
Country: Ceuta, Africa (Spanish Presidio)

Campaigns: Pensacola (1781)
Palao y Pratz, Antonio
SH: June 30, 1793, AGI, PC, leg. 161-a
Country: Cataluna   Age: 32
Campaigns: Mobile (1780), Pensacola (1781)
Palao y Pratz, Martin
SH: June 30, 1793, AGI, pc, LEG. 161-A
Country: Barcelona   Age 46 in 1815
Campaigns: none given for period of the Am. Rev.
Pastor, Alexo
SH: June 30, 1793, AGI, PC, leg. 161-a
Country: Andalucia   Age: 48
Campaigns: defense of Ft Carlos III of Arkansas when attacked by British Colbert's with the
British ally Chickasaws (1783)
Peralta, Juan
SH: June 30, 1793, AGI, PC, leg. 161-a
Country: Catalonia   Age: 44
Campaigns: none given in Gulf area
Perez, Luis, Caballero de Bellegarde
  SH: Dec. 31, 1787, AGS, GM, leg. 7291, I, 36
Country: France   Age: 48
Campaigns: Ft. Bute of Manchak and Baton Rouge (1779)
Perez, Manuel
SH: June 30, 1793, AGI, PC, leg. 161-a
Country: Zamora   Age: 58
Campaigns: Ft. Bute of Manchak and Baton Rouge (1779), Mobile (1780), Pensacola (1781)
Petely, Jose
SH: Dec. 31, 1787, AGS, GM, leg. 7291, I, 51
Country: Alicante   Age: 44
Campaigns: Ft. Bute of Manchak and Baton Rouge (1779), Mobile (1780), Pensacola (1781)
Army of operations in Havana and Guarico under Bernardo de Galvez (1781-1783)
Pierrnas, Joseph
SH: June 30, 1795, AGI, PC, leg. 1443-b
Country: Barcelona   Age: 40
Campaigns: Battle of St. Louis (1780)
Piernas, Luis
SH: June 30, 1815, AGI, PC, leg 161-b
Country: New Orleans   Age: 35
Campaigns: not given
Piernas, Pedro
SH: Dec. 31, 1787, AGS, GM, leg. 7291, I, 1
Country: Vizcaya (San Sebastian)   Age: 58
Campaigns: Lt. Gov. of upper Louisiana (St. Louis) (1770-1776) interim-governor of Louisiana
(1779-1781)
Pontalba, Josef de

121

SH: Dc. 31, 1800, AGI, PC, leg. 161-a
Country: New Orleans   Age: 46
Campaigns: Served in France as lieutenant, sub-lieutenant, and adjutant-major and captain; member of the expedition of the Comte d'Estaing against Savannah (1779-1780)
Porell, Thomas
SH: June 30, 1795, AGI, PC, leg. 161-a
Country Catalonia   Age: 52
Campaigns: blockade of Gibraltar (1779), expedition to Havana with Army of Operations (1780)
Postigo, Fernando del
SH: Dec. 31, 1787, AGS, GM, leg. 7291, I, 34
Country: La Rambla (Andalucia)   Age: 45
Army of Operations to America (Aril 1780), member of the crew of the warship Guerrero,
Rivas, Francisco
SH: June 30, 1793, AGI, PC, leg. 161-a
Country: Catalonia   Age: 49
Campaigns: Baton Rouge (1779) as Lt.
Rousseau, Pedro
SH: June 30, 1795, AGI, PC, leg. 1443-b
Country: France   Age: 44
Campaigns: under Captain William Pickles, helped capture British warship West Florida, during which he received two serious wounds (1779), Mobile (1780), Pensacola (1780) as commander of brigantine Galvez-Town which led squadron past British batteries.
Note: Spanish military were combined with American forces under Captain Pickles in Florida
Saez, Juan
SH: June 30, 1793, AGI, PC, leg. 161-a
Country: Castilla de Vieja   Age: 47
Campaigns: 6 campaigns in the lesser presidios of Africa, expedition to America (1777), New Orleans (1779, Mobile (1780), expedition from Havana to Pensacola destroyed by hurricane (1780)
St. Maxent, Francisco Maximiliano
SH: Dec 31, 1815, AGI, PC, leg. 161-a
Coiuntry: New Orleans   Age: 53
Campaigns: prisoner of war when carrying dispatches to Europe as a Lt. (1780), Pensacola (1781)
St. Maxent, Gilberto Antonio de
SH: Dec. 31, 1788, AGI, PC, leg. 161-a
Country: Lorraine, France   Age: 67
Campaigns: Ft. Bute of Manchak and Baton Rouge (1779), Mobile 1780, Pensacola (1781)
Solivellas, Miguel
SH: June 30, 1793, AGI, PC, leg. 161-b
Country: Mallorca   Age: 40
Campaigns: Blockade of Gibraltar (1779), Army of Operations (1780), Providence, Nassau (1782)
Soto, Joseph
SH: not available; affiliation record, AGI, SD, leg 2543

Country: Sedeiro (Ferrol)   Age: 17 when enlisted
Campaigns: none available
Trevino, Felipe
SH: June 30, 1793, AGI, PC, leg. 1610a
Country: Barcelona   Age: AGI, PC, leg. 161-a
Campaigns: on royal armed ship San Juan Neponuceno during patrol duty outside of Havana
(1780), Pensacola ruined by hurricane (1780), Pensacola as commander of ranger forces (1781)
Trudeau, Felix
SH: June 30, 1793, AGI, PC, leg. 161-a
Country: New Orleans   Age: 29
Campaigns: Ft. Bute of Manchak and Baton Rouge (1779), Mobile (1780)
Trudeau, Zenon
SH: June 30, 1795, AGI PC, leg. 161-a
Country: New Orleans   Age: 46
Campaigns: Baton Rouge (1779), Pensacola (1781)
Vaamonde, Josef, Vazquez
SH: June 30, 1793, AGI, PC, PC, leg. 161-a
Campaigns: Baton Rouge (1779), Mobile (1780), Pensacola (1781), reinforcement's commander
for the brigantine Galvez-Town
Valiere, Antonio
SH: June 30, 1793, AGI, PC, leg. 161-a
Country: New Orleans   Age: 28
Campaigns: Ft. Bute and Baton Rouge (1779
Valere, Josef
Country: El Delfinado, France   Age: 52
Campaigns: none listed, except he was a Captain in Illinois and part of the Louisiana Infantry
Vaugine, Estevan de
SH: June 30, 1795, AGI, PC, leg. 1443-b
Country: France   Age: 67
Campaigns: Baton Rouge (1779), Mobile (1780), Military and civil commandant of Natchitoches
(July 15, 1780-Mar. 20, 1786)
Vazquez, Benito
SH: Dec. 31, 1787, AGI, PC, leg. 161-a
Country: Santiago de Compostela   Age: 50
Campaigns: defense of St. Louis (May26, 1780) as Captain, attack of Spanish boat led by British
James Colbert with aid of Chickasaws (1782), defended on convoy against James Colbert with
aid of Chickasaws on way to St. Louis (1783)
Vegas, Diego de
SH: June 30, 1793, AGI, PC, leg. 161-a
Country: Andalucia   Age: 47
Campaigns: expedition to Pensacola (likely from Havana) which was broken up by the hurricane
(1780), Pensacola (1781)
Villanueba Barroso, Thomas
SH: Dec 31, 1793, AGI, PC, leg. 161-a
Country: Canary Islands   Age: 33

Campaigns: Mobile (1780), Pensacola (1781)
Villemont, Carlos de
SH: June 30, 1797, AGS, GM, leg. 7292, X, 22
Country: France   Age: 35 in 1797
Campaigns: Ft. Bute of Manchak and Baton Rouge (1779), Mobile (1780)
White, Enrigue
Country: Ireland   Age: 51
Campaigns: after 1776, Buenos Aires and capture of Santa Catalina (1777), Army of Operations
to America (April 1780 to end of war 1783), sea duty in contemplated attack on Jamaica and
patrol duty from Havana to Vera Cruz and to Honduras, in pursuit of English convoy, two
expeditions to Guarico, and one against the English blockade of Havana
Yebenes, Geronimo
SH: Dec. 31, 1793, AGI, PC, leg. 161-a
Country: Toledo   Age: 45
Campaigns: reinforcements for Havana (1776), reinforcements for New Orleans (May 1778), Ft.
Bute of Manchak and Baton Rouge (1779)

The following is a List of officers and non-commissioned officers of the Louisiana Infantry Regiment without known service sheets. Only those with sufficient information of 1776-1783 are included in the following:

Andry, Luis
Bolling, M
Cartabona, Francisco
Coussot, Alexandro
Devilliers, Baltasar
Gutierrez, Manuel
Leybba, Fernando de
Martinez, Antonio
Onoro, Martin de

Service Sheets of the Louisiana Militia Units

Ailhaud, Ste. Anne, Juan Bautista
Alard, Luis
Allain, Agustin
Allain, Jun Francisco
Allain, Pedro
Andry, Gilberto
Argote, Antonio
Armas, (Y Arcila), Christoval de
Avart, Valentin Robert
Barat, Juan Bautisa
Barbin, Prosper Casimiro
Beltremieux, Luis
Bienvenu, Antonio

Blanchard, Anselmo
Boisdore, Luis
Boniquet, Antoni
Bossier, Pedro
Bouniquet, Josef Antonio
Cantrelle, MiguelCantrelle, Santiago
Castillo, Manuel del
Cavelier, Antonio
Champini, Luis
Croizet, Simon
Cuellar, Manuel Vincente
Dartigaux, Juan Bautista
deBlanc y St. Denis, Luis Carlos

124

deClouet, Alexandro, Caballero de Clouet
deClouet, Alejandro JR.
Decuir, Josef de la Chaise, Carlos
de la Chaise, Honorato
de la Morandier, Estevan Roberto
Delery, Francisco I
Desbordes, Santiago
Deslandes, Jorge
de Villiers, Luis
Dominguez, Juan
d'Ortolant, Bernardo
Dragon, Miguel
Dreax, Guido
Ducrest, (Louis) Armand
Durel, Francisco
Durel, Juan Bautista
Durel, Ursino
Duroche, Simon
Fago (Fagot), Andres
Federico, Josef
Fernandez, Josef
firsps (Firps?), Pablo
Flaidel, Jorge
Foltz, Antonio
Fointenu (Fontenot), Luis
Forsel, Carlos Olivier
Forstall, Nicolas
Fortier, Miguel
Fortier, Santiago
Galatus, Vizente
Garcia, Mariano
Garidel, Ambrosio
Grevenbert, Francois
Grezar, Santiago
Griffon, Antonio
Gruy, Juan Bautista de
Haidel, Jorge
Hazur Delarme, Luis Xavier
Herbert, Amand
Herbert, Josef Nicolas
Hollier, Santiago
Jones, Evan
Judice, Luis Sr.
Judice, Luis Jr.
Judice, Miguel

La Barre, Francisco Renato de
La Barre, Pedro Volan (Bolant)
La Branche, Alexandro
Landreaux, Francisco
Landry, Josef
Landry, Marin
Langlois, Francisco
Larcheveque, Santiago
Laysard (Layssard), Estevan (Eteinne Macaffries)
LeBlanc, Esteban
LeBlanc, Isac
Leblanc de Villenueve, Pablo Luis
LeBoourgeois, Pedro
LeBreton, Bartholome
LeDoux, Francisco
LeDoux, Juan Pedro
LeMelle, Francisco
Lessassier, Jose
Lessassier, Julian
Lessassier, Vizente Joseph
Lomme, Alejandro de
Lugar, Juan Antonio
Macarty, Juan Bautista
Macarty, Luis
Marchand, Simon
Marcollay, Pablo
Marigny, Pedro de
Marmilloon, Pedro
Martinez, Santiago
Martiny, Juan
Masicot, Santiago (Jacques)
Melancon, Josef
Mentzinger, Enrique
Mentzinger, Juan Bautista
Miranda, Josef de la
Molere, Josef
Morant, Carlos de Sr.
Motardy, Pedro
Mouy, Mauricio de
Norman, Martin
Olivier, Juan Bautista
Olivier de Forselle, Carlos
Pain, Francisco
Parisigny, Domingo

Pauly, Joseph
Pelletier de la Houssaye, Luis
Perez, Francisco
Perret, Alphonse
Perret, Manuel
Perret, Pedro Pujol
Reggio, Luis
Reine, Pedro
Reynaud, Juan
Riano, Francisco de (Francisco Reano
Guemes)
Rillieux, Loui9s
Roche, Simon de
Rodriguez, Manuel
Roig y Girona, Miguel
Roubieu, Gaspar
Rousseau, Nicolas
Rousseve, Juan Bautista
Ruby, Salvador
Rucerbe, Bautista
Rucher, Simon de
Ste. Claire, Juan Bautista Benito de
Sampini, Luis
Sanchez, Ramon
Sigur, Lorenzo Sr.
Sigur, Pedro
Soileau, Noel
Sorrel, Joseph Jaque (Santiago)
Tayon, Carlos

Terga, Juan de la
Toups, Pablo
Trepanier, Pedro
Trouard, Aquiles
Tur, Antonio
Uberty, Francisco
Valdes, Cayetano
Valle, Francisco II
Valle, Juan Baptista
Vega, Andres
Verbois, Nicolas de
Verret, Agustin
Verret, Juan Bautista
Verret, Luis
Verret, Nicolas II
Verret, Santiago
Vidal, Jose
Vienne, Julien
Vienvenu, Juan
Villanueba (Villanueva), Jose
Villanueba Barroso, Tomas de
Vivez, Juan
Voisin, Pedro
Wiltz, Juan Bautista
Wiltz, Lorenzo (Laurent) II
Ximenes, Juan
Ynesta, Gregorio
Zequeira, Manuel
Zorrilla, Joseph

Louisiana Militia Units with Service Sheets, 1776-1783

Ailhaud, Ste. Anne, Juan Bautista
SH: Dec. 31, 1792, AGI, PC, leg. 161-a
Country: Dauphine, France   Age: 39
Campaigns: From Natchitoches Infantry Militia Baton Rouge and Ft. Mute of Manchak (1779)
Alard, Luis
SH: Dec. 31, 1796, AGS, GM, leg. 7292, V, 3, Dec. 31, 1800, AGI, PC, leg. 160-a
Country: Delfinado, France   Age: 54 during 1800
Campaigns: Carbineer Company of New Orleans at Mobile (1780)
Allain, Agustin
SH: Dec. 31, 1797, AGS, GM leg, 7292, XIII, 7
Country: Louisiana   Age: 56
Campaigns: Ft. Bute of Manchak and Baton Rouge (1779), Natchez (1781)
Allain, Juan Francisco

126

SH: Dec. 31, 1797, AGS, GM, leg. 7292, XIII, 3
Country: Louisiana   Age: 58
Campaigns: Ft. Bute of Manchak and Baton Rouge (1779), Natchez (1781)
Allain, Pedro
SH: Dec. 31, 1797, AGS, GM, leg. 7292, XIII, 17
Country: Louisiana   Age: 35
Campains: T. Bute of Manchak and Baton Rouge (1779), Natchez (1781)
Andry, Gilberto
SH: Dec. 31, 1802, AGI, PC, leg. 161-a   Age: 38
Campaigns: Ft. Bute of Manchak and Baton Rouge (1779), Mobile (1780)
Argote, Antonio
SH: Dec. 31, 1768, AGI, PC, leg. 161-a
Country: Malaga   Age: 57 in 1802
Campaigns: Ft. Bute of Manchak and Baton Rouge (1779)
Armas, (Y Arcila), Christoval de
SH: Dec. 31, 1802, AGI, PC, leg. 161-b
Country: Santa Cruz de Tenerife   ,   Age: 47
Campaigns: none given
Avart, Valentin Robert
SH: Dec. 31, 1802, AGI, PC, leg. 161-b
Country: New Orleans   Age: 62
Campaigns: none given
Barat, Juan Bautista
SH: Dec. 31, 1797, AGGGS, GM, leg. 7292, XIII, 53   Age: 40
Campaigns: Baton Rouge (1779), Mobile (1780), Natchez (1781)
Barbin, Prosper Casimiro
SH: Dec. 31, 1802, AGI, PC, leg. 161-a   Age: 39 (43 in 1800)
Campaigns: Ft. Bute of Manchak and Baton Rouge (1779)
Bienvenu, Antonio
SH: Dec. 31, 1800, AGI, PC, leg. 160-a
Country: New Orleans   Age: 41
Campaigns: Ft. Bute of Manchak and Baton Rouge (1779)
Blanchard, Anselmo
SH: June 30, 1792, AGI, PC, leg. 161-a
Country: Acadia   Age: 51
Campaigns: Ft. Bute of Manchak and Baton Rouge (1779), Mobile (1780)
Boisdore, Luis
SH: Dec. 31, 1802, AGI, PC, leg. 161-b
Country: New Orleans   Age: 40
Campaigns: none given
Boniquet, Antonio
SH: Dec. 31, 1802, AGI, PC, leg. 161-b
Country: Barcelona   Age: 53
Campaigns: Pensacola (1781), action of Oct. 20, 1782 (unk. where)
Bossier, Pedro

127

SH: Dec. 31, 1800, AGI, PC, leg. 161-a
Country: St. Hohn the Baptist, German Coast   Age: 39
Campaigns: Ft. Bute of Manchak and Baton Rouge (1779), Mobile (1780)
Bouniquet, Josef Antonio
SH: Dec. 31, 1800, AGI, PC, leg. 161-a
Country: Barcelona   Age: 51
Campaigns: Pensacola (1781)
Cantrelle, Miguel
SH: Dec. 31, 1800, AGI, PC, leg. 161-a
Country: New Orleans   Age: 50
Campaigns: Ft. Bute of Manchak and Baton Rouge (1779), Mobile (1780)
Cantrelle, Santiago
SH: Dec. 31, 1800, AGI, PC, leg. 161-a
Country: New Orleans   Age: 49
Campaigns: none given
Castillo, Manuel del
SH: Dec. 31, 1789, AGI, PC, leg. 161-a
Country: Florida   Age: 46
Campaigns: Pensacola frustrated by hurricane (1780, Pensacola (1781)
Cavelier, Antonio
SH: Dec. 31, 1802, AGI, PC, leg. 161-b
Country: Rouan, France   Age: 53
Campaigns: none given
Champini, Luis
SH: Dec. 31, 1802, AGI, PC, leg. 161-b
Country: Potie (Poitiers?), France   Age: 38
Campaigns: none given
Croizet, Simon
SH: Dec. 31, 1797, AGS, GM, leg. 7292, XIII, 25
Country: Louisiana   Age: 42
Campaigns: Baton Rouge (1779), Natchez (1781)
Cuellar, Manuel Vincente
SH: June 30, 1793, AGI, PC, leg. 161-a
Country: Toledo   Age: 53
Campaigns: none given
Dartigaux, Juan Bautista
SH: Dec. 31, 1792, AGI, PC, leg. 161-a
Country: Bayonne, France   Age: 26
Campaigns: Ft. Bute of Manchak and Baton Rouge (1779)
deBlanc y St. Denis, Luis Carlos
SH: Dec. 31, 1792, AGI, PC, leg. 161-a
Country: Natchitoches, La.   Age: 40
Campaigns: Ft. Bute of Manchak and Baton Rouge (1779)
deClouet, Alexandro, Caballero de Clouet
SH: Aug. 31, 1788, AGI, PC, leg. 161-a

Country: Picardy, France   Age: 72
Campaigns: Ft. Bute of Manchak and Baton Rouge (1779)
deClouet, Alejandro JR.
SH: Dec. 31, 1797, AGS, kGM, leg. 7292, kXIII, 11
Country: Louisiana   Age: 36
Campaigns: Ft. Bute of Manchak and Baton Rouge (1779)
Decuir, Josef
SH: Louisiana   Age: 45
Campaigns: Baton Rouge (1779), Mobile (1780)
de la Chaise, Carlos
SH: Dec. 31, 1800, AGI, PC, leg. 160-a
Country: Louisiana   Age: 59
Campaigns: Ft. Bute of Manchak and Baton Rouge (1779), Mobile (1780), Pensacola (1781)
de la Chaise, Honorato
SH: Dec. 31, 1797, AGS, GM, leg. 7292, XIII, 15
Country: Louisiana   Age: 48
Campaigns: Ft. Bute of Manchak and Baton Rouge (1779), Mobile (1780)
de la Morandier, Estevan Roberto
SH: Aug. 31, 1788, AGI, PC, leg. 161-a
Country: Montreal, Canada   Age: 52
Campaigns: Mobile (1780), Natchez on July 23, 1781
Delery, Francisco I
SH: June 30, 1792, AGI, PC, leg. 161-a
Country: New Orleans   Age: 36
Campaigns: Ft. Bute of Manchak and Baton Rouge (1779), Mobile (1780)
Desbordes, Santiago
SH: Dec. 31, 1797, AGS, GM, leg. 7292, XIII, 18
Country: Louisiana   Age: 34
Campaigns: Ft. Bute of Manchak and Baton Rouge (1779)
Deslandes, Jorge
SH: Dec. 31, 1797, AGS, GM, leg. 7292, XII, 43
Country: New Orleans   Age: 43
Campaigns: none given
de Villiers, Luis
SH: Dec. 31, 1797, AGS, GM, leg. 7292, XIII, 20
Country: Louisiana   Age: 48
Campaigns: Mobile (1780), Pensacola (1781)
Dominguez, Juan
SH: Dec. 31, 1802, AGI, PC, leg. 161-b
Country: Cordoba, Andalucia   Age: 43
Campaigns: combat against English Squadron (Oct. 20, 1782)
d'Ortolant, Bernardo
SH: Dec. 31, 1797, AGI, PC, leg. 161-a
Country: Bordeaux, France   Age: 44
Campaigns: Ft. Manchak and Baton Rouge (1779)

Dragon, Miguel
SH: Dec. 31, 1802, AGI, PC, leg. 161-b
Country: Athens, Greece   Age: 56
Campaigns: none listed
Dreax, Guido
SH: Dec. 31, 1802, AGI, PC, leg. 161-b
Campaigns: Ft. Bute of Manchak and Baton Rouge (1779)
Ducrest, (Louis) Armand
SH: June 30, 1792, AGI, PC, leg. 161-a
Country: Adjutant major of the Attakapas Post, Ft. Bute of Manchak and Baton Rouge (1779)
                                                 Age: 68
Durel, Francisco
SH: Dec. 31, 1796, AGS, GM, leg. 7292, IV, 4
Country: New Orleans   Age: 38
Campaigns: two years aboard the Galveztown and various convoy and corsair expeditions
thereon
Durel, Juan Bautista
SH: Dec. 31, 1796, AGS, GM, leg. 7292, IV, 4
Country: New Orleans   Age: 42
Campaigns: Mobile (1780)
Durel, Ursino
SH: Dec. 31, 1802, AGI, PC, leg. 161-b   Age: 37
Campaigns: none given
Duroche, Simon
SH: June 30, 1793, AGI, PC, leg. 161-a   Age: 45
Campaigns: none given
Fago (Fagot), Andres
SH: Dec. 31, 1792, AGI, PC, leg. 161-a   Age: 34
Campaigns: Baton Rouge (1779), Mobile (1780), part of the St. Louis Milicia
Federico, Josef
SH: Dec. 31, 1797, AGS, GM, leg. 7292, XIII, 39
Country: Louisiana   Age: 52
Campaigns: Ft. Bute of Manchak and Baton Rouge (1779)
Fernandez, Josef
SH: June 30, 1792, AGI, PC, leg. 159-b   Age: 42
Campaigns: Baton Rouge (1779), Mobile (1780), Pensacola (1781)
Firsps (Firps?), Pablo
SH: Dec. 31, 1800, AGI, PC, leg. 161-a
Country: St. Charles, German Coast   Age: 49
Campaigns: none given
Flaidel, Jorge
SH: Dec. 31, 1797, AGS, GM, leg. 7292, XII, 48
Country: St. John the Baptist, German Coast   Age: 45
Campaigns: Ft. Bute of Manchak and Baton Rouge (1779), Mobile (1780)
Foltz, Antonio

SH: Dec. 31, 1800, AGI, PC, leg. 161-a
Country: St. John the Baptist, German Coast   Age: 45
Campaigns: Ft. Bute of Manchak and Baton Rouge (1779), Mobile (1780)
Fontenu (Fontenot), Luis
SH: Dec. 1, 1797, AGS, GM, leg. 7292, XIII, 63
Country: Louisiana   Age: 39
Campaigns: Mobile (1780), Natchez (1781)
Forsel, Carlos Olivier
SH: Dec. 31, 1800, AGI, PC, leg. 160-a
Country: New Orleans   Age: 48
Campaigns: Ft. Bute and Baton Rouge (1779), Mobile (1780)
Forstall, Nicolas
SH: Dec. 31, 1800, and Aug. 31, 1788, AGI, PC, leg. 161-a
Country: Martinique   Age: 74
Campaigns: Ft. Bute of Manchak and Baton Rouge (1779), former captain of Attakapas Militia, councilman of New Orleans Cabildo (1771-1803)
Fortier, Miguel
SH: June 30, 1792, AGI, PC, leg. 159-b   Age: 41
Campaigns: Ft. Bute of Manchak and Baton Rouge (1779)
Fortier, Santiago
SH: Dec. 31, 1800, AGI, PC, leg. 161-a
Country: New Orleans   Age: 29
Campaigns: Mobile (1780)
Galatus, Vizente
SH: June 30, 1793, AGI, PC, leg. 161-a
Country: Victoria, Spain   Age: 40
Campaigns: Mobile (1780), Pensacola (1781)
Garcia, Mariano
SH: March 31, 1790, AGI, PC, leg. 161-a
Country: Cuernavaca, Mexico   Age: 36
Campaigns: Pensacola (1781)
Garidel, Ambrosio
SH: Dec. 31, 1800, AGI, PC, leg. 161-a
Country: Louisbourg, Canada   Age: 35
Campaigns: none given
Grevenbert, Francois
SH: Aug. 31, 1788, AGI, PC, leg. 161-a; Dec. 31, 1797, AGS, GM, leg. 7292, XIII, 12
Country: Louisiana   Age: 40 during 1788
Campaigns: Ft. Bute of Manchak and Baton Rouge (1779)
Grezar, Santiago
SH: June 30, 1794, AGI, PC, leg. 161-a
Country: New Orleans   Age: 51
Campaigns: Mobile (1780)
Griffon, Antonio
SH: Dec. 31, 1802, AGI, PC, leg. 161-b

Country: New Orleans   Age: 44
Campaigns: Mobile (1780)
Gruy, Juan Bautista de
SH: Dec. 31, 1800, AGI, PC, leg. 161-a
Country: New Orleans   Age: 51
Campaigns: Ft. Bute of Manchak and Baton Rouge (1779), Mobile (1780)
Haidel, Jorge
SH: Dec. 31, 1800, kAGI, PC, leg. 161-a
Country: St. John the Baptist, German Coast   Age: 50
Campaigns: Ft. Bute of Manchak and Baton Rouge (1779), Mobile (1780)
Hazur Delarme, Luis Xavier
SH: Dec. 31, 1796, AGS, GM, leg. 7292 V, 5, Dec. 31, 1800, , AGI, PC, leg. 160-a
Country: New Orleans   Age: 52 during 1800
Campaigns: Mobile (1780), Pensacola (1781), *mariscal de logis* (Feb. 1, 1781
Herbert, Amand
SH: Dec. 31, 1800, AGI, PC, leg. 161-a
Country: Louisbourg, Canada   Age: 48
Campaigns: Ft. Bute of Manchak and Baton Rouge (1779)
Herbert, Josef Nicolas
SH: Dec. 31, 1800, AGI, PC, leg. 161-a
Country: Louisbourg, Canada   Age: 37
Campaigns: none given
Hollier, Santiago
SH: June 30, 1792, AGI, PC, leg. 161-a
Country: New Orleans   Age: 50
Campaigns: none given
Jones, Evan
SH: Dec. 1, 1800, AGI, PC, leg. 161-a
Country: New England (U.S.A.)   Age: 61
Campaigns: none given
Judice, Luis Sr.
SH: Dec. 31, 1800, AGI, PC, leg. 161-a
Country: New Orleans   Age: 66
Campaigns: Ft. Bute of Manchak and Baton Rouge (1779)
Judice, Luis Jr.
SH: Dec. 1, 1800, AGI, PC, leg. 161-a
Country: New Orleans   Age: 45
Campaigns: Ft. Bute of Manchak and Baton Rouge (1779), Mobile (1780)
Judice, Miguel
SH: Dec. 31, 1800, AGI, PC, leg. 161-a
Country: La Fourche, La.   Age: 41
Campaigns: Ft. Bute of Manchak and Baton Rouge (1779), Mobile (1780)
La Barre, Francisco Renato de
SH: Dec. 31, 1797, AGS, GM, leg. 7292,V, 6, Dec. 31, 1800, AGI, PC, leg. 160-a
Country: New Orleans   Age: 39 during 1800

Campaigns: Ft. Bute of Manchak and Baton Rouge (1779), Mobile (1780)
La Barre, Pedro Volan (Bolant)
SH: Dec. 31, 1797, AGS, GM, leg. 7292, V, 7: Dec. 31, 1800, AGI, PC, leg. 160-a
Country: New Orleans   Age: 38 during 1800
Campaigns: Baton Rouge (1779), Mobile (1780)
La Branche, Alexandro
SH: Dec. 31, 1800, AGI, PC, leg. 161-a
Campaigns: Ft. Bute of Manchak and Baton Rouge (1779), Mobile (1780)
Landreaux, Francisco
SH: Dec. 31, 1802, AGI, PC, leg. 161-a
Country: New Orleans   Age: 45
Campaigns: Ft. Bute of Manchak and Baton Rouge (1779), Mobile (1780), Pensacola (1781),
aided the shipwrecks off Mobile and saved many lives (1780)
Landry, Josef
SH: Dec. 31, 1800, AGI, PC, leg. 161-a
Country: Louisbourg, Canada   Age: 47
Campaigns: none given
Landry, Marin
SH: Dec. 31, 1800, AGI, PC, leg. 161-a
Country: Acadia, Canada   Age: 50
Campaigns: none given
Langlois, Francisco
SH: June 30, 1793, AGI, PC, leg. 161-a
Country: New Orleans   Age: 39 during 1793
Campaigns: Ft. Bute of Manchak and Baton Rouge (1779), Mobile (1780), Pensacola (1781)
Larcheveque, Santiago
SH: Dec. 31, 1801, AGI, PC, leg. 161-b
Country: New Orleans   Age: 72
Campaigns: none given
Laysard (Layssard), Estevan (Eteinne Macaffries)
SH: July 31, 1788, AGI, PC, leg. 161-a
Country: Rochefort, France   Age: 71
Campaigns: none given
LeBlanc, Esteban
SH: June 30, 1792, AGS, GM, leg. 7291
Country: Louisbourg, Canada   Age: 39
Campaigns: Ft. Bute of Manchak and Baton Rouge (1779), and Mobile (1780)
LeBlanc, Isac
SH: SH: June 30, 1792, AGS, GM, leg. 7291, II, 29
Country: Louisbourg, Canada   Age: 45
Campaigns: Ft. Bute of Manchak and Baton Rouge (1779), Mobile (1780), first attempt at
Pensacola (1780)
LeBlanc De VIllenuene, Pablo Luis
SH: June 30, 1795, AGI, PC, leg. 1441
Country: Delfinado, France   Age: 60 during 1795

Campaigns: expeditions of Bernardo de Galvez against the English to conduct troops to the Mississippi River (1779), Mobile (1780), Pensacola campaign (1781)
LeBourgeois, Pedro
SH: Dec. 31, 1800, AGI, PC, leg. 161-a
Country: Paris, France   Age: 48
Campaigns: none given
LeBreton, Bartholome
SH: June 30, 1792, AGI, PC, leg. 161-a
Country: New Orleans   Age: 26
Campaigns: American Revolution (1777), Captain with French Army
LeDoux, Francisco
SH: June 30, 1792, AGI, PC, leg. 161-a
Country: Louisiana   Age: 39 during 1792
Campaigns: none given
LeDoux, Juan Pedro
SH: June 30, 1792, AGS, GM, leg. 7291, V, 39
Country: Louisiana   Age: 39
Campaigns: Ft. Bute of Manchak and Baton Rouge (1779), Natchez (1781)
LeMelle, Francisco
SH: Aug. 31, 1788, AGI, PC, leg. 161-a
Country: New Orleans   Age: 50
Campaigns: Ft. Manchak and Baton Rouge (1779)
Lessassier, Jose
SH: Dec. 31, 1802, AGI, PC, leg. 161-a
Country: New Oreleans   Age: 53
Campaigns: none given
Lessassier, Julian
SH: Dec. 31, 1788, AGI, PC, leg. 161-a
Country: New Orleans   Age: 45
Campaigns: Baton Rouge (1779), Mobile (1780)
Lessassier, Vizente Joseph
SH: June 30, 1791, AGI, PC, leg. 161-a
Country: New Orleans   Age: 42
Campaigns: none given
Lomme, Alejandro de
SH: Dec. 31, 1797, AGS, GM, leg. 7292, XIII, 27
Country: Louisiana   Age: 39
Campaigns: Ft. Bute of Manchak and Baton Rouge (1779)
Lugar, Juan Antonio
SH: Dec. 31, 1797, AGS, GM, leg. 7292, XI, 36
Country: Alicante   Age: 41
Campaigns: campaign in the warship Santisima Trinidad (1778), Pensacola (1781), Shipwreck of the warship El Dragon (1782)
Macarty, Juan Bautista
SH: Dec. 31, 1800, AGI, PC, leg. 160-a

Country: New Orleans   Age: 49
Campaigns: Ft. Bute of Manchak and Baton Rouge (1779), Mobile (1780)
Macarty, Luis (the Chevalier Macarty)
SH: Dec. 31, 1800, AGI, PC, leg. 161-a
Country: New Orleans   Age: 49
Campaigns: Ft. Bute of Manchak and Baton Rouge (1779)
Marchand, Simon
SH: June 30, 1792, AGI, PC, leg. 159-b
Country: New Orleans   Age: 26
Campaigns: none given
Marcollay, Pablo
SH: Dec. 31, 1792, AGI, PC, leg. 161-a
Country: La Rochelle, France   Age: 47
Campaigns: Ft. Bute of Manchak and Baton Rouge (1779)
Marigny, Pedro de
SH: June 30, 1792, AGI, PC, leg. 161-a
Country: New Orleans   Age: 41
Campaigns: as a musqueteer in the French guard, and holder of the cross of the Royal Military
Order of St. Louis, in 1778, he was commissioned to establish the Canary Island families in
Louisiana, Ft. Bute of Manchak and Baton Rouge (1778), Mobile, where he commanded the
Negro and free Mulatto troops (1780), Pensacola, as adjutant or aide-de-camp of General
Bernardo de Galvez (1781),
Marmilloon, Pedro
SH: June 30, 1791, AGI, PC, leg. 161-a
Country: New Orleans   Age: 33
Campaigns: Baton Rouge (1779), Mobile (1780), Pensacola (1781)
Martinez, Santiago
SH: Dec. 31, 1802, AGI, PC, leg. 161-a
Country: Bercia, Germany   Age: 45
Campaigns: Baton Rouge (1779), Mobil (1780), Pensacola (1781)
Martiny, Juan
SH: Dec. 31, 1787, AGI, PC, leg. 161-a
Country: Montreal, Canada   Age: 76
Campaigns: English attack on St. Louis (1780), commanded detachment of 50 militiamen to
destroy fort on Missouri River (St. Joseph, Michigan) and return artillery (1780)
Masicot, Santiago (Jacques)
SH: June 30, 1792, AGI, PC, leg. 161-a
Country: New Orleans   Age: 55
Campaigns: Ft. Bute of Manchak and Baton Rouge (1779), Mobile (1780)
Melancon, Josef
SH: Dec. 31, 1800, AGI, PC, leg. 161-a
Country: Acadia   Age: 44
Campaigns: none given
Mentzinger, Enrique
SH: June 30, 1795, AGI, PC, leg. 1447

Country: New Orleans   Age: 49
Campaigns: Baton Rouge (1779), Mobil (1780), Pensacola (1781)
Mentzinger, Juan Bautista
SH: June 30, 1794, AGI, PC, leg. 161-a
Country: New Orleans   Age: 39 (41)
Campaigns: Baton Rouge (1779), Mobile (1780), Pensacola (1781), ambush at Amit River of two English ships with two companies of the Waldeck Regiment (1779)
Miranda, Josef de la
SH: Decx. 31, 1797, AGS, GM, leg. 7292, XIII, 64
Country: France   Age: 40
Campaigns: Baton Rouge (1779), Natchez (1781)
Molere, Josef
SH: Dec. 31, 1800, AGI, PC, leg. 161-a
Country: Acadian coast   Age: 37
Campaigns: Ft. Bute of Manchak and Baton Rouge (1779), Mobile (1780)
Morant, Carlos Sr.
SH: Dec. 31, 1798, AGI, PC, leg. 161-a
Country: New Orleans   Age: 48
Campaigns: none given
Motardy, Pedro
SH: Dec. 31, 1787, AGI, PC, leg. 161-a
Country: Languedoc, France   Age: 51
Campaigns: English attack on the Spanish fort in today's St. Louis (May 26, 1780)
Mouy, Mauricio de
SH: Dec. 31, 1792, AGI, PC, leg. 161-a
Country: Mobile   Age: 39
Campaigns: Ft. Bute of Manchak and Baton Rouge (1779), part of the Natchitoches Cavalry Militia
Norman, Martin (le)
SH: Dec. 31, 1797, AGS, GM, leg. 7292, XIII, 24
Country: Louisiana   Age: 41
Campaigns: Ft. Bute of Manchak and Baton Rouge (1779), Mobile (1780)
Olivier, Juan Bautista
SH: Dec. 31, 1802, AGI, PC, leg. 161-a
Country: Guarico Island, West Indies   Age: 42
Campaigns: Ft. Bute of Manchak and Baton Rouge (1779), Mobile (1780)
Olivier de Forselle, Carlos
SH: Dec. 31, 1796, AGS, GM, leg. 7292, V, 4
Country: New Orleans   Age: 44
Campaigns: Ft. Bute of Manchak and Baton Rouge (1779), Mobile (1780)
Pain, Francisco
SH: Dec. 31, 1800, AGI, PC, leg. 160-a
Country: New Orleans   Age: 52
Campaigns: Ft. Bute of Manchak and Baton Rouge (1779), Mobile (1780)
Parisigny, Domingo

SH: Dec. 31, 1802, AGI, PC, leg. 161-b
Country: Milan, Italy   Age: 46
Campaigns: Mobile (1780), Pensacola (1781)
Pauly, Joseph
SH: June 30, 1792, AGI, PC, leg. 161-a
Country: France   Age: 54
Campaigns: Capture of Post Green belonging to the English settlements of Louisiana, and
capture of two enemy craft on the lakes of the province and at Bayou Galvestown (1779)
Pelletier de la Houssaye, Luis
SH: June 30, 1792, AGI, PC, leg. 161-a
Country: Louisiana   Age: 32
Campaigns: Ft. Bute of Manchak and Baton Rouge (1779)
Perez, Francisco
SH: Dec. 31, 1802, AGI, PC, leg. 161-b
Country: Morillo, Andalucia, Spain   Age: 54
Campaigns: not given
Perret, Alphonse
SH: Dec. 31, 1800, AGI, PC, leg. 161-a
Country: St. John Baptist, German Coast   Age: 41
Campaigns: Ft. Bute of Manchak and Baton Rouge (1779), Mobile (1780)
Perret, Manuel
SH: Dec. 31, 1800, AGI, PC, 161-a
Country: St. John Baptist, German Coast   Age: 44
Campaigns: Ft. Bute of Manchak and Baton Rouge (1779), Mobile (1780)
Perret, Pedro Pujol
SH: Dec. 31, 1800, AGI, PC, leg. 161-a
Country: St. John Baptist, German Coast   Age: 39
Campaigns: Ft. Bute of Manchak and Baton Rouge (1779), Mobile (1780)
Reggio, Luis
SH: Dec. 31, 1800, AGI, PC, leg. 160-a
Country: New Orleans   Age: 38
Campaigns: Ft. Bute of Manchak and Baton Rouge (1779)
Reine, Pedro
SH: Dec 31, 1800, AGI, PC, leg. 161-a
Country: St. Charles, German Coast   Age: 48
Campaigns: none given
Reynaud, Juan
SH: June 30, 1793, and Dec. 31, 1802, AGI, PC, leg. 161-a and 161-b
Country: (Marseilles, France)   Age: 45
Campaigns: none given
Riano, Francisco de (Francisco Reano Guemes)
SH: Dec. 31, 1802, AGI, PC, leg. 161-b
Country: Mountains of Santander   Age: 53 (63)
Campaigns: Mobile (1780), Pensacola (1781)
Rillieux, Louis

SH: Dec. 31, 1802, AGI, PC, leg. 161-a
Country: New Orleans   Age: 40
Campaigns: Mobile (1780), Pensacola (1781)
Roche, Simon de
SH: Dec. 31, 1797, AGS, GM, leg. 7292, XI, 33
Country: New Orleans   Age: 50
Campaigns: none given
Rodriguez, Manuel
SH: Dec. 31, 1789, AGI, PC, leg. 161-a
Country: Mexico City, Mexico   Age: 30 plus
Campaigns: early expedition to Pensacola broken up by hurricane (1780), war duty in Mobile 3
mos. 15 days in 1780), capture of Pensacola (Mar. 16, 1781) stationed on Dauphin Island when
English attacked it and later defended the pass from the deserted beach (1781)
Roig y Girona, Miguel
SH: Dec. 31, 1802, AGI, PC, leg. 161-b
Country: Valtes, Catalonia, Spain   Age: 62
Campaigns: Ft. Bute of Manchak and Baton Rouge (1779), Mobile (1780)
Roubieu, Gaspar
SH: Dec. 31, 1787, AGI, PC, leg. 161-a
Country: Marseilles, France   Age: 41
Campaigns: none given
Rousseau, Nicolas
SH: June 30, 1792, AGI, PC, leg. 161-a
Country: France   Age: 40
Campaigns: none given
Rousseve, Juan Bautista
SH: June 30, 1793, AGI, PC, leg. 161-a
Country: New Orleans   Age: 37
Campaigns: Baton Rouge (1779), Mobile (1780)
Ruby, Salvador
SH: Dec. 31, 1812, AGI, PC, leg. 161-a
Country: New Orleans   Age: 47
Campaigns: Ft. Bute of Manchak and Baton Rouge (1779), Mobile (1780), Pensacola (1781)
Rucerbe, Bautista
SH: Dec. 31, 1796, AGI, PC, leg. 161-a
Country: New Orleans   Age: 41
Campaigns: Baton Rouge (1779), Mobile (1780)
Rucher, Simon de
SH: Dec. 31, 1796, AGS, GM, leg. 7292, VI, 33
Country: New Orleans   Age: 49
Campaigns: none given
Ste. Claire, Juan Bautista Benito de
SH: June 30, 1792, AGI, PC, leg. 161-a
Country: Louisiana   Age: 39
Campaigns: none given

Sampini, Luis
SH: Dec. 31, 1800, AGI, PC, leg. 161-a
Country: Diocese of Potie   Age: 36
Campaigns: none given
Sanchez, Ramon
SH: Dec. 31, 1792, AGI, PC, leg. 161-a
Country: Havana   Age: 26
Campaigns: none given
Sigur, Lorenzo Sr.
SH: Dec. 31, 1800, AGI, PC, leg. 161-a
Country: Metz (Lorraine), France   Age: 58
Campaigns: none given
Sigur, Pedro
SH: Dec. 31, 1800, AGI, PC, leg. 161-a
Country: Iberville   Age: 38
Campaigns: none given
Soileau, Noel
SH: Aug. 31, 1788, AGI, PC, leg. 161-a
Country: Natchez   Age: 44
Campaigns: Mobile (1780)
Sorrel, Joseph Jaque (Santiago)
SH: June 30, 1792, AGI, PC, leg. 161-a
Country: France (Delfinado)   Age: 50
Campaigns: Ft. Bute of Manchak and Baton Rouge (1779), Mobile (1780), Pensacola (1781)
Tayon, Carlos
SH: Dec. 31, 1787, AGI, PC, leg. 161-a
Country: Illinois (Missouri)   Age: 29
Campaigns: St. Joseph (Michigan) expedition against English (1780)
Note: This occurred just after the Spanish Fort Battle of St. Louis 1780 against the English attack
Terga, Juan de la
SH: not available; affiliation sheet: AGI, PC, leg. 159-b
Country: Cordoba, Spain   Age: 31 during 1784
Campaigns: Transferred to Artillery Militia of New Orleans (Oct. 31, 1777), and discharged
(Sept. 4, 1784)
Toups, Pablo
SH: June 30, 1792, AGI, PC, leg. 161-a
Country: German Coast, Louisiana   Age: 40
Campaigns: none given
Trepanier, Pedro
SH: June 30, 1792, AGI, PC, leg. 161-a
Country: St. Charles, German Coast   Age: 40
Campaigns: Ft. Bute of Manchak and Baton Rouge (1779), Mobile (1780)
Trouard, Aquiles
SH: Dec. 31, 1800, AGI, PC, leg. 161-a
Country: Paris, France   Age: 36

139

Campaigns: none given
Tur, Antonio
SH: Dec. 31, 1789, AGI, PC, leg. 161-a
Country: Ibiza (Balearies, Spain)   Age: 40 plus
Campaigns: none given
Uberty, Francisco
SH: Dec. 1, 1792, AGI, PC, leg. 161-a
Country: Morco, Piamonte, Italy   Age: 39
Campaigns: none given
Valdes, Cayetano
SH: Dec. 31, 1802, AGI, PC, leg. 161-a
Country: Puerto de Santa Maria, Spain   Age: 43
Campaigns: none given
Valle, Francisco II
SH: Dec. 31, 1787, AGI, PC, leg. 161-a
Country: Ste. Genevieve (Illinois Country)   Age: 31
Campaigns: English attack on Spanish fort in St. Louis (May 26, 1780)
Valle, Juan Baptista
SH: Dec. 31, 1787, AGI, PC, leg. 161-a
Country: Ste. Genevieve (Illinois country)   Age: 28
Campaigns: none given
Vega, Andres
SH: Dec. 31, 1800, AGI, PC, leg. 161-a
Country: Canary Islands   Age: 54
Campaigns: none given
Verbois, Nicolas de
SH: Dec. 31, 1800, AGI, PC, leg. 161-a
Country: New Orleans   Age: 44
Campaigns: Ft. Bute of Manchak and Baton Rouge (1779), serving as aide-de-camp to General
Bernardo de Galvez in the capture of Mobile (1780), attached to the ranger company of the
Flanders Regiment in the capture of Pensacola (1781)
Verret, Agustin
SH: Dec. 31, 1800, AGI, PC, leg. 161-a
Country: New Orleans   Age: 47
Campaigns: Ft. Bute of Manchak and Baton Rouge (1779), Mobile (1780)
Verret, Juan Bautista
SH: Dec. 31, 1800, AGI, PC, leg. 161-a
Country: New Orleans   Age: 49
Campaigns: Ft. Bute of Manchak and Baton Rouge (1779
Verret, Luis
SH: Dec. 31, 1800, AGI, PC, leg. 161-a
Country: New Orleans   Age: 39
Campaigns: none given
Verret, Nicolas II
SH: Dec. 31, 1800, June 30, 1790, AGI, PC, leg. 161-a

Country: New Orleans   Age: 49 during 1800
Campaigns: Ft. Bute of Manchak and Baton Rouge (1779)
Verret, Santiago
SH: Dec. 31, 1800, AGI, PC, leg. 161-a
Country: New Orleans   Age: 49
Campaigns: none given
Vidal, Jose
Sheet: June 30, 1794, AGI, PC, leg. 161-a
Country: Galicia, Spain   Age: 29
Campaigns: voyages in mail ships during war with England (Oct. 1779-1783)
Note: Subsequently part of San Marcos de Apalachee and Natchez
Vienne, Julien
SH: June 30, 1792, AGI, PC, leg. 159-b
Country: Normandy, France   Age: 48
Campaigns: Baton Rouge (1779)
Vienvenu, Juan
SH: Dec. 31, 1788, AGI, PC, leg. 161-a
Country: Bordeaux, France   Age: 47
Campaigns: none given
Villanueba (Villanueva), Jose
SH: Dec. 31, 1792, AGI, PC, leg. 161-a
Country: Havana   Age: 28
Campaigns: none given
Villanueba Barroso, Tomas de
SH: Dec. 31, 1800, AGI, PC, leg. 161-a
Country: Canary Islands   Age: 40
Campaigns: Mobile (1780), Pensacola and the assault on the "Half-moon" fort (1781)
Vivez, Juan
SH: Dec. 31, 1800, AGI, PC, leg. 161-a
Country: Denia, Valencia, Spain   Age: 45
Campaigns: none given
Voisin, Pedro
SH: Dec. 31, 1800, AGI, PC, leg. 161-a
Country: New Orleans   Age: 46
Campaigns: Ft. Bute of Manchak and Baton Rouge (1779)
Wiltz, Juan Bautista
SH: June 30, 1792, AGS, GM, leg. 7291, III, 31
Country: Germany   Age: 50
Campaigns: Mobile (1780)
Wiltz, Lorenzo (Laurent) II
SH: Dec. 31, 1800, AGI, PC, leg. 161-a
Country: New Orleans   Age: 62
Campaigns: none given
Ximenes, Juan
SH: Dec. 31, 1789, AGI, PC, leg. 161-a

Country: Sadaba (?)   Age: 3-(sic)
Campaigns: Capture of Providence, Nassau (1782), part of the Dragoons of America
Ynesta, Gregorio
SH: Dec. 31, 1802, AGI, PC, leg. 161-a
Country: Pedronera, Castilla, Spain   Age: 52
Campaigns: defense of Ft Carlos III from English Colbert and the Chickasaws (1783)
Zequeira, Manuel
SH: Dec. 31, 1789, AGI, PC, leg. 161-a
Country: Havana   Age: not given
Campaigns: none given
Zorrilla, Joseph
SH: June 30, 1793, AGI, PC, leg. 161-a
Country: Palencia, Spain   Age: 53 during 1793
Campaigns: none given

The following is a list of Officers and non-commissioned officers of the Louisiana militia. No service sheets were found

Allain, Francisco (Juan Francisco)
Armand, Louis
Bepeccher, Antonio
Beluche, Renaldo
Bergeron, George
Bertrand, Amable
Bibaren, Baptisa
Bivaren, Baptiste
Bofrer, Pedro
Bordelon, Antoine
Borman, Antonio
Borme, Louis
Boulard, Luis
Brasso (Brazau), Carlos
Broquedis, Pierre
Brunet, Agustin
Buyer, Juan Bautista
Campderos, Juan
Castillon, Pedro
Chanchelier, (Chancielleir), Louis
Chavert, Pedro
Coffigny, Claudio
Cote, Alexandro
Crooks, William
Cusot, Simon

Danelson, James
David, Etienne
David, Jean Jacques
De Alva, Narcisse
Decuir, Jean Paul
Defourd, Charles
De Lassized, Nicolas Lorant (Lorenzo)
Deloniers, Louis
Deluvigny, Andres
De Mezieres, Antonio Maria
Despres, Henrique's
Diaz, Antonio
Doze, Antoine
Duchessing, Diego
Duruy, Andres
Durant au, Pedro
Durocher, Pedro
Elias, Pedro
Emend, Charles
Estelle, George
Frenetic, Andres
Fontana, Baptiste
Fontana, Henry
Fontanel, Martin
Goon, Pedro

Grape, Francois
Gevembert, Agustin de
Guillory
Hollier, Luis
Honore, Francisco
Honore, Luis
Hot, Carlos
Huberdau, Simon
Hubert, Antonio
Imbaut, Juan Bautista
Jardelat, Pedro
Jaulin, Jean
Kelly, James
Labe, Jacobo
Labuciera (Labusciere), Joseph
La Casse........
Lapierre, Juan Baptista
LaVille, Pedro
Lazo, Pedro (Pedro Lazo de la Vega)
Le Brun, Guilleaume
Le Cour, Pierre
Lestage, Guillaume
Liebana y Pazuengos, Ambrosio de
Lopez, Andres

142

Macarty, Jacob	O'Hara, John	Ste. Anne, Antoine
MacNemorney, John	Otonere, Luis Sr.	St. Germain,.....
Marioneaux, Louis	Pavie, Joseph	Sanselier, Luis
Martinez (Martini), Juan Baptisa	Peyrin, Pedro	Sardet,....
	Plaisance, Mathieu	Simans, Francisco
Mauriac, Jean Baptiste	Porche, Simon	Suriray, Juan
Menard, Francisco	Porsley, Juan Pedro	Tournier (Ternier), Nicolas
Metoyer, Pierre	Pratte, Jean Baptiste	Triche, Juan Bautista
Mondion, Pedro	Purre (Pouree), Euginio	Ubaldy, Tomas
Mondon, ...	Quienel, Pedro	Valle, Carlos
Monget, Juan Luis	Rambiu, Antoine	Valle, Francois
Nicolas, Bertrand	Remedios, Juan de los	Venzan, Antonio
Nicolas, Juan	Robin, Roberto (Roberto	Vivare, Francisco
Nicolson, Henry	Robin de Laugni, Sr.),	Whitaker, Daniel
Nicolson, James	Robinet, Louis	Zumaque, Antonio
Oglesbey, Daniel	Roy, Nicolas	

Pensacola, 1781

Book "Yo Solo," Bernardo de Galvez y and the Volume of **Pensacola in 1781**, A Contribution of Spain to the independence of the United States by Carmen of Reparaz, published 1986.

This book does not give names of troops or sailors. However, this book is important because it provides insight into the organization and higher rank military personnel. In addition, this book lists regiments from soldiers of other places that participated in the capture of Pensacola, 1781.

Another reason this book is important is because this siege was preplanned along with George Washington and his *troops.* Benjamin Lincoln of the headquarters general wrote from Morris Town, on February 7, 1780, the following:

"Governor of Havana of the success of the Spaniards in the Florida's. If the remaining posts fall it will be a very important stroke and in all probability the operations there will have a favourable influence upon our affairs in your quarter. Though perhaps it may not be probable, it is not impossible, the British General if he has discretionary power on hearing of the progress of the Spaniards in the Florida's, may suspend his original plan and turn his attention that way, and endeavour to defend their own territories rather than attempt conquests. don Juan de Miralles, the Spanish agent, in a letter of th
"In addition to the advices you were obliging enough to communicate, I have just seen official accounts from the e 18th communicating the foregoing intelligence has the following paragraph:
By Royal Order, I am very strongly charged to influence your Excellency to make the greatest diversion with the troops of the United States against those of the enemy in Georgia, to the effect of attracting their attention and disabling them from sending succours to Pensacola and Mobile, which were prepared at Havanna with all the needful and ready to sail when the station would permit. This I transmit to you for your government satisfied that you will do every will do everything to effect the diversion desired, which the situation of your force and that of the enemy

combined with other circumstances will permit. If they act offensively against the Carolinas your whole attention will necessarily be engaged at home: But if they should direct their force elsewhere you may possibly have it in your power to pursue measures favourable to the operations of Spaniards and to the immediate interests of the United States."

In short, the Royal Order of Spain suggested a diversion from George Washington's troops in the south so that Spain, aided by French fleet, could overtake Mobile and Pensacola.

In a letter by General Washington to the Spanish Conde de Floridablanca, in part indicated, "It would not be surprising if the British General on hearing of the progress of the Spanish Arms in the Florida's should relinquish his primitive design and go the defense of their own territories."

Again in short, General Washington complied with the Spanish Kings' request. The British were caught off guard by United States faking an attack on the British south instead of sending reinforcements to the Florida's.

During 1780, there was an organized effort from the Spanish Navy Commander Solano and Captain General Bernardo Galvez ground troops to attack Pensacola. This attempt was intervened with a disastrous hurricane that cost lives and ships. The second attempt, approximately March 1781, with forces landing at the Island of Santa Rosa and into Pensacola was successful. The siege of Pensacola was an important position to control ships entering and leaving the Gulf Coast. This made it easier for aid to the United States from Spanish controlled south. This siege started on March 25, 1781 and ended on May 8, 1781. French Ships and troops were part of the siege under the command of Spanish Naval Commander Solano.

The Pensacola siege of 1781 included 7,677 persons. The numbers of deaths were 74 and the numbers of injuries were 198. Only higher level military names are listed.

Commanding General Bernardo Galvez

Aides to the camp of General
Baron de Kessel
Esteban Miro
Pedro Rodriguez
Arturo O'Neill

2nd Commander Juan Manuel de Cagigal

Aides de Camp 2nd. Commander
Francisco Miranda
Francisco Montalvo
Juan Cagigal

Major General Jose de Ezpeleta

Aids to the Major General

Benito Perez
Juan de Urbina
Veremundo Ramirez

Quarter Master General Francisco de Nava

Commander of Artillery Vicente Resel

Protection and trenches for fort or battle Jose Urraca

Military Army and Navy with armaments to attack Pensacola
1st Battalion

Commander and captain of ship Felipe Lopez Carrizosa
2nd. Commander and captain of frigate Miguel de Sousa
Sergeant Major and captain of troops from Toledo Francisco Equia
Aids to the commanders
Lt. of frigate Juan Mendoza y Argueda
Lt. of the Kings troops Manuel de San Pedro
Military Standard Bearer Francisco Gil

Grenadier, a foot soldier, formerly employed to throw grenades of Mallorca
Captain Juan Manglar
Lt. Antonio Jaramillo
2nd. Lt. Vicente Aragon
3 sergeants, 5 corporals, 1 drummer, 40 grenadiers for the ship guard for ship *San Luis*

1st. Co. of Fusiliers
Lt. of ship Josef Baleta
2nd. Lt. of ship Dionisio Ucho Inca
2nd. Lt. of frigate Fernando Murillo
3 sergeants, 5 corporals, 1 drummer, 40 soldiers on the ship *Paula*

2nd. Co.
Captain of the Kings Regiment Pedro Gutierrez
Lt. of the ship Antonio Chinchilla
Midshipman Officer Miguel Ribera
3 sergeants, 5 corporals, 1 drummer, 40 soldiers of the Kings Regiment on the ship *San Nicolas*

3rd. Co.
Lt. of the ship Enrique MacDonnell
2nd. Lt. of ship Gaspar Sanchez
2nd. Lt. of frigate Juan Arango
3 sergeants, 5 corporals, 1 drummer, 40 soldiers, on the ship *San Gabriel*

145

4th Co.
Captain of Soria Regiment Juan Vevet
Lt. Joaquin Blasco
2nd. Lt. Manuel de Dios
3 sergeants, 5 corporals, 1 drummer, and 40 soldiers of Soria Regiment on the ship Asis

5th. Co.
Lt. of ship Fernando Valcarcel
2nd. Lt. of ship Francisco Eliza
2nd. Lt. of frigate Jose Espinosa
3 sergeants, 5 corporals, 1 drummer, and 40 soldiers on the ship Gallardo

6th. Co.
Captain of the Guadalajara regiment Bruno Gonzalez
Lt. Joaquin Figueroja
2nd. Lt. Mauricio Catan
3 sergeants, 5 corporals, 1 drummer, 40 soldiers from the Guadalajara on the ship San Gabriel
7th. Co.
Lt. of the ship Fernando de Landa
2nd. Lt. of the ship Juan Guerrero
2nd. Lt. of the frigate Jose Olazabal
3 sergeants, 5 corporals, 1 drummer, 40 soldiers on the ship San Nicolas

8th Co.
Captain of the Spanish Regiment Jose de Hoz
Lt. Martin Arias
2nd. Lt. Gines de Oliva
3 sergeants, 5 corporals, 1 drummer, 40 soldiers of Spain's Regiment on the ship Magnanimo

9th Co.
Lt. of ship Teodico Argumosa
2nd. Lt. of ship Luis de Landa
2nd. Lt. of frigate Eugenio de Silva
3 sergeants, 5 corporals, 1 drummer, 40 soldiers on the ship of Magnanimo

Military Army and Navy with Armaments to Attack Pensacola
2nd. Battalion

Commander Captain of ship Jose Zabala
2nd. Commander Captain of frigate Andres Tacon
Sergeant Major and captain of regiment of Spain Juan Alcazar
Aid of the Camp Lt. of frigate Ciriaco Garcia de Prado

Aid of the Camp Lt. of regiment Mallorca Cayetano Samitier
Military Standard Bearer Manuel Gelaber

Grenadiers of navy

Lt. of ship Manuel Morales
2nd. Lt. of navy Felipe Cagigal
2nd. Lt. of frigate Pedro Pantoja
3 sergeants, 5 corporals, 1 drummer, 40 soldiers on the ship San Luis

1st. Co. of Fusiliers
Captain of regiment Mallorca Salvador Roquerol
Lt. of Toledo Manuel Aragon
2nd. Lt. Domingo Lorenzo
3 sergeants, 5 corporals, 1 drummer, 40 soldiers on the ships San Nicolas, Asis, Dragon, and Guerrero

2nd. Co.
Lt. of ship Joaquin Sierra
2nd. Lt. of ship Jose Roca y Juan
2nd. Lt. of frigate Francisco Mateus
3 sergeants, 5 corporals, 1 drummer, 40 soldiers on the ship dragon

3rd. Co.
Captain of regiment Aragon Antonio Pinillos
Lt. paymaster Pedro Santiago
2nd. Lt. midshipman Baltasar Unguera
3 sergeants, 5 corporals, 1 drummer, 40 soldiers of regiment Aragon on ship Paula

4th. Co.
Lt. of ship Jose Ramos
2nd. Lt. of ship Alonso Heredia
2nd. Lt. of frigate Jose Alcala
3 sergeants, 5 corporals, 1 drummer, 0 soldiers, on the ship Arrogante

5th. Co.
Captain of regiment Navarra Antonio Colas
Lt. Juan Urruela
2nd. Lt. Francisco Carredondo
3 sergeants, 5 corporals, 1 drummer, 40 soldiers of Navarra on the ship Asis

6th. Co.
Lt. of ship Juan Calbo

2nd. Lt. of ship Juan Ontanon
2nd. Lt. of frigate Angel Velez
3 sergeants, 5 corporals, 1 drummer, 40 soldiers on the ship Astuto

7th. Co.
Captain of regiment Hibernia Terencio Sweetman
Lt. Guillermo Delaney
2nd. Lt. Luis Russell
3 sergeants, 5 corporals, 1 drummer, 40 soldiers of Hibernia on the ship Dragon

8th. Co.
Lt. of ship Bruno Ayala
2nd. Lt. of ship Pedro Acebedo
2nd. Lt. of frigate Juan Osorno
3 sergeants, 5, corporals, 1 drummer, 40 soldiers on the ship Guerrero

9th. Co.
Captain of Volunteers Antonio Rabasa
Lt. Rafael Montagut
2nd. Lt. Jose Soler
3 Sergeants, 5 Corporals, 1 drummer, 40 soldiers of Volunteers of Cataluna on the ship Arrogante

Military Army and Navy with armaments to attack Pensacola
Corps of Reserves

Commander Captain of ship Jose Pereda
2nd. Commander Captain of frigate Pedro Obregon
Sergeant Major captain of regiment Principe Rafael de la Luz
Aid to the camp Lt. of frigate Luis Roca
Aid of the Camp, 2nd. Lt. of regiment of Spain Pedro Garcia
Military Standard Bearer Jose Labadores

1st. Co.
Lt. of regiment Navarra Manuel Arjona
2nd. Lt. of ship Joaquin Lamoneda
2nd. Lt. of frigate Luis Ibarra
3 sergeants, 5 corporals, 1 drummer, 40 soldiers of Navarra and Kings Regiments on the ship
San Nicolas, Paula and Arrogante

2nd. Co.

Lt. of ship Joaquin Sierra
2nd. Lt. of ship Jose Roca y Juan
2nd. Lt. of frigate Francisco Mateus
3 sergeants, 5 corporals, 1 drummer, 40 soldiers on the ship Dragon

3rd. Co.
Captain of the Kings regiment Domingo Molina
Lt. of regiment Soria Francisco Silva
2nd. Lt of frigate Silvio Conti
3sergeants, 5 corporals, 1 drummer, 40 soldiers of the Kings regiment, fixed navy and marines of Havana on the ship Paula, San Nicolas, and Magnanimo

4th Co.
Captain of Principe regiment Felipe Perez
Lt. of Mallorca regiment Juan de Soto
2nd. Lt. of regiment Soria Miguel Fernandez
3 sergeants, 5 corporals, 1 drummer, 40 soldiers of Soria, Principe and Mallorca on the ship San Gabriel, Guerrero, and Astuto

5th Co.
Captain of regiment Navarra Antonio Colas
Lt. Juan Urreuela
2nd. Lt. Francisco Carredondo
3 sergeants, 5 corporals, 1 drummer, 40 soldiers of Navarra on ship Asis

6th. Co.
Captain of Regiment Flanders Santiago Baurain
Lt. Carlos Montero
2nd. Lt. Felix Zunet
3 sergeants, 5 corporals, 1 drummer, 40 soldiers of Flanders (Netherlands) on the ship Arrogante and Galardo

7th. Co.
Lt. of ship Ignacio Iturriaga
2nd. Lt. of ship Jose Bochoni
2nd. Lt. of frigate Fernando Folganes
3 sergeants, 5 corporals, 1 drummer, 40 soldiers of Marines on the frigates Clara, Cecilia, chambequin Caiman and paquebotes pio and San Gil

Royal Corp of Artillery of Brigade
Commander Captain of frigate Fernando Quiros
In charge of Brigade Lt. of ship Manuel Herrera
Aid of Camp Lt. of Infantry Fernando Munoz of San Clemente

Paymaster and aid on the ship dragon Francisco Garcia
Artillery officer, 1 corporal, and 9 artillery soldiers on the ship San Luis
Artillery officer, 1 corporal, and 7 artillery soldiers on the ship San Nicolas
2nd. in charge of artillery, and 13 artillery soldiers on the ship Guerrero
46 artillery, bombardiers, and aids to the other ships of the squadron

"Yo Solo" Appendix

Promotional Military Personnel

Galvez, Bernardo de	Commander General of Pensacola Expedition
Cagigal, Manuel de	Brigadier and commander of Headquarters
Giron, Geronimo	Brigadier
Ezpeleta, Jose	Coronel of Regiment of Infantry Navarra
Pineda, Manuel	Coronel of Soria regiment
Kessel, Baron	Coronel of Cavalry

Recommended for Pensacola due to military actions in Mobile

Miro, Esteban	Lt. Coronel of Regiment of Louisiana
Pelaez, Miguel	Lt. Coronel of Regiment infantry Inmemorial del Rey
Salla, Cayetano	1st. Lt. Coronel
Rodriguez, Pedro	1st. Lt. Coronel
Urraca, Jose	Sgt. Major of Soria
Mayone, Joaquin	Lt. Coronel
Carondelet, Baron	Lt. Coronel
Chacon, Francisco	Sgt. Major of Principe Regiment
Corral, Carlos	Captain of Soria Regiment
Ogan, Juan	Captain of Grenadiers
Oneylli, Eugenio	Captain of Grenadiers and Fusiliers of Hibernia
Alvarez, Manuel Marques	Atayde of Aragon and Coronel
Llano, Antonio	Lt. Coronel and Captain of 2nd Infantry light troops of Catalonia
Bouligni, Francisco	Lt. Coronel and Captain of Louisiana Regiment
Bofarull, Casimiro	Sgt. Major of 2nd Battalion of Catalonian soldiers
Amoros, Vicente	Captain of Inmemorial del Rey regiment
Miralles, Antonio	Captain of Inmemorial del Rey Regiment
Sentmenat, Ramon	Captain of Inmemorial del Rey Regiment
Gutierrez, Manuel	Captain of 1st Battalion Grenadiers and Fusiliers of Principe Regiment
Alture, Miguel	Captain of 1st Battalion Grenadiers and Fusiliers of Principe Regiment

Luz, Rafael de la	Captain of 1st Battalion Grenadiers and Fusiliers of Principe Regiment
Lumbreros, Juan	Captain of Grenadiers of Soria, Spain, Regiment
Villalva, Francisco Xavier	Captain of Grenadiers and Fusiliers of Guadalajara
Mazorra, Agustin	Captain of Grenadiers and Fusiliers of Guadalajara
Ucles, Juan	Captain of Grenadiers
Cevallos, Sebastian	Fusiliers of Spain
Salcedo, Ignacio	Fusiliers of Spain
Escales, Miguel	Fusiliers of Spain
Alcazar, Juan Ignacio	Fusiliers of Spain
Eguia, Francisco	Captain of Toledo, Spain
Grimarest, Enrique	Captain
Trevino, Felipe	Captain
Perez, Gabriel	Captain
Flon, Manuel	Captain
Samaniego, Jose	Captain
Pardo, Benito	Ayudante Mayor promoted to Captain of the Navarra Regiment
O'Coner, Hugo	Captain of the Irish Hibernia Regiment
Arriola, Mateo	Captain of Grenadiers
Pinillos, Manuel Antonio	Fusiliers of Aragon, Spain, Regiment
Miranda, Francisco	Fusiliers of Aragon, Spain, Regiment
Demeaux, Felipe	Captain of Grenadiers
Fouquet, Jose	Fusiliers
Casas, Juan de las	Fusiliers
Bulliers, Alexandro	Lt. of Grenadiers promoted to Captain of Flanders (Flemish) Regiment
Jurado, Pablo	Captain of Habana military
Onoro, Francisco	Captain of Habana military
Cabello, Manuel	Captain of Habana military
Lelis, Federico	Captain of Infantry light troops of Aquella Plaza and promoted to Lt. Colonel
Urbina, Juan	Captain promoted to Lt. Coronel of Regiment of Navarra
Rios, Ramon de los	Lt. of Grenadiers
Mesias, Jose	Lt. of Fusiliers del Inmemorial del Rey (King)
Michavila, Jose	del Principe
Julia, Ignacio	Grenadiers
Figueroa	Lt. of Grenadiers and Fusiliers of Soria
Garcia-Borio, Jose	Lt. of Grenadiers

Castanoz, Francisco

Figuerola, Joauin

Calonge, Juan — Fusiliers of Guadalajara

Munoz, Fernando — Ayundante Mayor

Cervantes, Melcor — Lt. Grenadiers

Garcia, Roque — Fusilier of Spain

Otondo, Miguel — Fusilier of Spain

Arias, martin — Fusilier of Spain

Campos, Francisco — Fusilier of Spain

Vellon, Francisco — Fusilier of Spain

Samitier, Cayetano — Lt. of Mallorca Regiment

Perez, Benito — Ayudante Mayor

Sastre, Jose — Lt. of Navarra Regiment

Alonso, Francisco — Lt. of Navarra Regiment

Carbajal, Pedro — Lt. of Navarra Regiment

Nugent, Eduardo — Ayundante of Hibernia Regiment

Butler, Tomas — Lt. of Hibernia Irish Regiment

Molina, Jose — Lt. of 1st Grenadiers and 2nd Fusiliers of Aragon

Langele, Joaquin — Lt. of 1st Grenadiers and 2nd. Fusiliers of Aragon

Robira, , Diego — Lt. del 2nd Catalonia

Bekers, Jose — Lt. of Flanders Regiment

Cespedes, Fernando — 2nd. Lt. Regiment of Havana promoted to 1st. Lt.

Oro, Antonio — Lt. of Grenadiers

Baamonde, Jose — Fusiliers Regiment of Louisiana promoted to Captain

Fajardo, Juan — 2nd. Lt of Rigiment of Spain, Tenencia

Conget, Pascual — 2nd Lt. Inmemorial del Rey

Serrano, Juan — 2nd. Lt. Inmemorial del Rey

Castillo, Gregorio del — 2nd. Lt. Inmemorial del Rey

Calonge, Mariano — Principe

Martinez, Vicente — Granadiers

Gahinza, Gabino — Fusiliers of Soria

Bigodet, Juan — Fusiliers of Soria

Cabezas, Juan — Guadalajara

Catani, Mauricio — Guadalajara

Cagigal, Juan Francisco — Guadalajara

Garcini, Miguel — Guadalajara

Menchaca, Joaquin — Guadalajara

Herrera, Miguel — Grenadier

Lara, Jose — Fusiliers

Eguiarreta, Vicente	Fusiliers
Torralva, Miguel	Flag of Spain
Lorenzo, Domingo	Toledo
Aragon, Manuel	Toledo
Alonso, Pedro	Grenadiers
Ixart, Francisco	Fusiliers of Navarra
Revellon, Francisco	Fusiliers of Navarra
Ramiriez, Veremundo	Fusiliers of Navarra
O'Reilly, Felipe	Hibernia Regiment (Irish)
O'Conor, Dionisio	Hibernia Regiment
Santa Maria, Lucas	Hibernia Regiment
Trapani, Jose	Hibernia Regiment
Marin, Joaquin	Aragon Regiment
Santa Maria, Lucas	Aragon Regiment
Robiera, Mariano	2nd. Catalonians
Galvez, Jose	Flanders Regiment
Torre, Jose Maria de la	Regiment of Habana
Palomino, Antonio	Regiment of Habana
Noriega, Jose	Regiment of Louisiana promoted to Lt.
Martinez, Geronimo	Sgt. Inmemorial del Rey
Alcoceba, Antonio	Sgt. Principe Regiment
Aldana, Pedro	Cadet Principe Regiment
Ochagarria, Liberato	Cadet of Soria Regiment
Obregon, Jose	Distinguished Soldier of Spain
Munoz, Juan	Distinguished Soldier of Spain
Ocharan, Francisco	Sgt. of Navarra Regiment
Pastor, Manuel	Sgt. of Navarra Regiment
Beguinet, Jose	Sgt. Grenadier of Flanders
Conde, , Manuel	Sgt. Regiment of Habana
Onoro, Domingo	Regiment of Habana
Justiz, Santiago	Regiment of Habana
Pizarro, Ignacio	Cadet Regiment of Habana
Orrueta, Ventura	Sgt. Regiment of Louisiana promoted to 2nd Lt.
Petely, Jose	Sgt. Regiment of Louisiana promoted to 2nd Lt.
Godoy, Juan	Cadet of Louisiana Regiment promoted to 2nd Lt. at first vacancy
Villers, Carlos	Cadet of Louisiana Regiment promoted to 2nd Lt. at first vacancy

Villegoutin, Carlos	Cadet of Louisiana Regiment promoted to 2nd Lt. at first vacancy
Acosta, Jose	Cadet of Louisiana regiment promoted to 2nd Lt. at first vacancy
Ville, Jose	Cadet of Louisiana Regiment promoted to 2nd Lt. at first vacancy
Campana, Jose	Cadet of Louisiana Regiment promoted to 2nd Lt. at first vacancy
Fernandez, Antonio	Captain of Dragoons from Habana
Fides, Jose	Captain of Company of Dragoons of Louisiana promoted to Lt. Coronel
Vilars, Julian	Lt. of Dragoons from Habana
Crespo, Antonio y Nove	Lt. of Dragoons from Habana
Chabert, Pedro	Promoted to Captain 2nd Carabineers of Louisiana
Chaise, Carlos	Provincial Commander of Carabineers of Louisiana
Estrada, Ignacio	Lt. of Dragoons from Habana
Basarte, Jose	2nd Lt. of Louisiana and promoted to Lt.
Figueroa, Jose	Cadet of Dragoons from Habana and promoted to Lt.
Caballero, Juan	Cadet of Royal College of Caballeria de Ocana and served under the Commander General Bernardo Galvez and promoted to Lt.
Segovia, Geronimo	Cadet of Royal College of Caballeria de Ocana and served under the Commander General Bernardo Galvez and promoted to Lt.
Cabrera, Francisco	Cadet of Royal College of Caballeria de Ocana and served under the Commander General Bernardo Galvez and promoted to Lt.
Risel, Vicente	Captain promoted to Lt. Colonel of the Royal Corp of Artillery
Rey, Francisco Juan del	Captain of the Corp and promoted to Lt. Colonel
Toro, Salvador	Lt. promoted to Captain of Ejercito, Company of Artillery
Alvarez, Julian	Lt. promoted to Captain of Ejercito, Company of Artillery
Remedios, Juan de los	2nd Lt. promoted to 1st Lt.
Nova, Manuel de	2nd Lt. promoted to 1st. Lt.
Navas, Francisco	Engineer promoted to Coronel
Valle, Antonio Ramon	Engineer promoted to Coronel
Peramas, Joaquin	Engineer promoted to Coronel
Fernandez Trebejo, Antonio	Distinguished Engineer promoted to Lt. Colonel

154

Gelebert, Francisco	Engineer distinguished promoted to Captain of Ejercito
Larroque, Mariano	Commander Major of Regiment Infantry de Principe and Engineers
Maxent, Giberto	Lt. Coronel of Ejercito Commander of the Milicias of New Orleans promoted to Coronel regular military to Lt. Coronel of Ejercito
Guillemard, Gilberto	Lt. 2nd in Command of la Plaza of New Orleans promoted to Captain
Punzano, Jose	Commander of Pardos of Habana, Cuba, promoted to Captain
Ferrer, Ramon	Commander of Morenos of Aquella Plaza, Cuba, promoted to Captain
Marigni, Pedro	Lt. of Ejercito served as Commander of Headquarters for the General
Dezprez, Enrique	Captain of Militias of Louisiana promoted to Lt. of Ejercito
Verbois, Nicolas	Lt. of Ejercito
Brazo, Carlos	Captain of Militias of Louisiana
Fontenel, Martin	Captain of the Corp
Trujillo, Baltazar	Company Commander of Tiradores of Yucaton and promoted to Lt. of Ejercito
Sabadon, Juan	2nd Lt. Infantry and Captain of Militias of Louisiana
Calfa, Simon	Captain Commander of Pardos and Morenos of Louisiana
Calfa, Carlos	2nd. Lt. of Pardos of Louisiana
Tomas, Pedro	Lt. of Morenos of the Louisiana Milicias given Distinguished recognition for Valor

Note: The rest of Officials from the same Militias of color have the distinction of compensation for their families.

O'Reilly, Arturo	Captain of Regiment of Hibernia promoted to Lt. Colonel. The King named O'Reilly Governor Internal of the Plaza of Pensacola
Galvez, Bernardo	King Carlos III addresses his pleasure to concede that the Spanish Corp of the Royal Armada aided with the attack of Pensacola
Solano, Jose	Lt. General Chief of Squadron (Navy)
Carrizosa, Felipe Lopez	Brigadier Captain of Navy
Alderete, Miguel	Captain of Navy of "Frigate" war ship
Sousa, Miguel	Captain of Navy of "Frigate" war ship

155

Serrato, Jose	Captain of Navy of "Frigate" war ship
Goycochea, Miguel	Captain promotion in Navy
Penalver, Ignacio	Lt. of Navy promoted to Captain of Frigate
Morales, Manuel	Lt. of Navy promoted to Captain of Frigate
Iturriaga, Ignacio	Lt. of Navy promoted to Captain of a Frigate
Barreda, Hermenegildo	Lt. of Navy promoted to Captain of a Frigate
Macdonel, Enrique	Lt. of Navy promoted to Captain of a Frigate
Valcarcel, Fernando	Lt. of Navy promoted to Captain of a Frigate
Villavicencio, Agustin	Lt. of Navy promoted to Captain of a Frigate
Pineda, Pedro	Lt. of Navy promoted to Captain of a Frigate
Aguirre, Juan	Lt. of Navy promoted to Captain of a Frigate
Chacon, Jose	Lt. of Navy promoted to Captain of a Frigata
Rio, , Francisco	Lt. of Navy promoted to a Frigate
Sapiain, Miguel	Lt. of Navy promoted to a Frigate
Munoz de San Clemente, Fernando	Lt. of Navy promoted to a Frigate
Spinola, Marcelo	Lt. of Navy promoted to a Frigate
Garcia Prado, Ciriaco	Lt. of Navy promoted to a Frigate
Uriarte y Borja, Jose	Lt. of Navy promoted to a Frigate
Riano, Juan	Lt. of Navy promoted to a Frigate
Cagigal, Felip Jado	2nd. Lt. to 1st Lt. Navy to a Frigate
Bachoni, Jose	2nd. Lt. to 1st Lt. Navy to a Frigate
Heredia, Alonso	2nd. Lt. to 1st Lt. Navy to a Frigate
Elisa, Francisco	2nd. Lt. to 1st Lt. Navy to a Frigate
Uchoinca, Dionisio	2nd. Lt. 1st Lt. Navy to a Frigate
Guerra, Rafael	2nd. Lt. to 1st Lt. Navy to a Frigate
Butron, Rafael	2nd. Lt. to 1st. Lt. Navy to a Frigate
Concha, Juan de la	2nd. Lt Navy to a Frigate
Velez, Angel	2nd. Lt Navy to a Frigate
Silva, Gregorio	2nd. Lt Navy to a Frigate
Mateos, Francisco	2nd. Lt Navy to a Frigate
Ibarra, Luis	2nd. Lt Navy to a Frigate
Jolganes, Fernando	2nd. Lt Navy to a Frigate
Murillo, Fernando	2nd. Lt Navy to a Frigate
Osornoy, Juan	2nd. Lt Navy to a Frigate
Pantoja, Pedro	2nd. Lt Navy to a Frigate
Rivera, Miguel	2nd. Lt Coast Guard protecting the Frigate
Unquera, Bartolome	2nd. Lt Coast Guard protecting the Frigate
Morales, Fernando	2nd. Lt Coast Guard protecting the Frigate
Garcia, Francisco	2nd. Lt Coast Guard protecting the Frigate

Evia, Ramón	2nd Lt Pilot of Navy
Navarro, Francisco	Sgt. of Battalion
Castillo, Pedro	Constable of Brigade
Gil, Francisco	Volunteer Officer
Gelabert, Manuel	Volunteer Officer
Labadores, Jose	Volunteer Officer
Tomasco, Juan	Chief of Squadron Encomienda of Ballaga and Algarga in the order of Calatrava
Quiros, Fernando	Captain of Frigate
Pereda, Jose	Captain
Zavala, Jose	Captain of Navy distinguished by order of King Carlos III of Spain
Tacon, Andres	Officer of Frigate
Obregon, Pedro	Officer of Frigate
Ruiz, Manuel	Sgt. of Battalion and of three squadrons
Mote, Jose	Sgt. of Battalion and of three squadrons

Sources:

Churchill, Charles Robert, Bernardo de Galvez, Services to the American Revolution, Louisiana Society Sons of the American Revolution, March 4, 1925, Self Published.

Holmes, Jack D. L. Holmes, Jonor and Fidelity, The Louisiana Infantry Regiment and the Louisiana Militia Companies, 1766-1821, Birmingham, 1965.

Reparaz, Carmen de, Yo Solo, Bernardo de Galvez y la toma de Panzacola en 1781, Una contribucion espanola a la indedpendencia de los Estados Unidos, Ediciones del Serbal, 1986, Spanish Version. (I Alone, Bernardo de Galvez and the Battle of Pensacola, Florida, and the Spanish Contribution to the Independence of the United States)

Salamanca Archive: Florida and Louisiana; LEG, 6912-yrs. 1779-1785. Expedientes, emleos relativos a la conquista de Movila y puestos del Rio Mississippi; Leg, 6913, exp.1-12-Battle of Pensacola, Toma de Pensacola.

Papeles Procedentes de Cuba,General Archive of the Indies (AGI), Seville, Spain. Florida Occidental. Corresponencia y documentos oficiales de los Governadores. Anos 1776 a 1779

Regiment Inmemorial del Rey in the Seize of Panzacola (Pensacola)

May 11, 1781 to May 19, 1781, Military Archives in Madrid, Javier Romero, Rear Admiral, Spanish Navy, Defense Attaché. *Spaniards Participating in the American Revolutionary War.*

Regiment Inmemorial del Rey was transcribed by the Military Archive of Madrid.

Regiment Inmemorial Del Rey No 1

Names from the Military Archive of Madrid

Name	Rank		
Illegible, Jorge	Aznar, Antonio	Campos, Blas
Illegible, Senaris	Balaguer, Alberto	Campos, Juan Jose Ramon
	Ballesteros, Francisco	Canadas, Ramón
Adeva, Ramon	Ballesteros, Rafael	Candado, Francisco
Aguado, Jose	Balmacedo	Cano, Vicente
Aguilar, Agustin	Balza, Baltazar	Capilla, Sebastian
Aguilera, Gavino	Barea, Antonio	Carnes (?), Antonio
Aguillera, Agustin	Barraves, Jose	Carnicer, Francisco
Aguirre, Miguel	Bazquez, Nicolas	Carnicer, Manuel
Alarcon, Manuel	Beltran, Manuel	Caro, Juan
Albanil, Lazar	Benito, Jose	Carrasco, Manuel
Albuquelquel, Francisco	Betes, Jose	Carrasco, Rugino
Alcan (illegible), Sebastian	Blanco, Bonifacio	Casa, Jose
Alcantara, Fernando	Blanco, Vicente	Castillo, Felipe
Alcantara, Pedro	Bona, Antonio	Castro, Gabriel
Alcazar, Felipe	Bonet, Antonio	Castro, Juan de
Alcolado, Juan	Bonilla, Manuel	Castro, Ramon
Alfos, Mariano	Borne, Sebastian	Cerro, Francisco del
Alonso, Isidro	Brabo, Francisco	Cerro, Ramon
Alonso, Pedro	Brigida, Manuel	Chacon, Francisco
Alvarez, Baltasar	Bruella, Pedro	Charmar, Agustin
Monte (Monfe illegible), Jacinto	Bueno, Vicente	Chaves, Pedro Lopez Jose
	Bustamante, Antonio	Cheval, Vicente
Alvarez, Felix	Caballero, Antonio Sgt.	Chico, Gregorio
Alvarez, Jose Luis	Caballerro, Angel	Chozas, Domingo
Alvarez, Jose	Calderon, Marcos	Ciriel, Luis
Ambros, Domingo	Caldona, Lucas	Clos, Francisco
Ana, Manuel	Callejas, Juan	Collado, Simon
Aragon, Manuel	Calvo, Juan	Conde, Jose
Arriola, Jose	Camino, Manuel	Conti, Manuel
Arroyo, Jose	Campo, Manuel del	Copado, Agustin
Aveliano, Joaquin	Campos, Andres Dos	Corbato, Cosme

158

Cordoves, Juan
Corro, Francisco
Cortes, Jose
Cortes, Nicolas
Crespo, Sebastian
Croquer, Vicente
Cuerda, Francisco
Cuesta, Rafael
Cueto, Pascual
Cuetos, Diego
Cura, Antonio
Delgado, Antonio
Delgado, Juan Jose
Diez, Francisco
Diez, Tomas
Domingo, Santiago
Dominguez, Antonio
Dominguez, Pablo
Eras, Francisco
Escudero, Jose
Esteban, Dionisio
Esten, Agustin
Estevan, Manuel
Estun, Luis
Eugeni, Angel
Felipe, Matias
Fernandez, Andres
Fernandez, Antonio
Fernandez, Carlos
Fernandez, Francisco
Fernandez, Ignaio
Fernandez, Javier
Francisco
Fernandez, Juan
Fernandez, Manuel
Fernandez, Nicolas
Fernandez, Santiago
Ferran, Martin
Ferrer, Jaime

Ferrerio, illegible
Ferrero, Juan
Figuer, Isidro
Flores, Celestino
Florez, Agustin de
   Capitan
Frayle, Sebastian
Fuente, Melchor de la
Fustes, Lucas
Galiciano, Manuel
Galisteo, Francisco
Gallus, Francisco
Garcia, illegible
Garcia, Alfonso
Garcia, Andres
Garcia, Antonio
Garcia, Bonifacio
Garcia, Elias
Garcia, Enrique
Garcia, Francisco
Garcia, Joaquin
Garcia, Jose
Garcia, Jose
Garcia, Juan
Garcia, Lorenzo
Garcia, Manuel
Garcia, Mateo
Garcia, Matias
Garcia, Pedro
Garcia, Ylario
Gascon, Francisco
Genocien, Jose
Gigante, Gabriel
Gil, Felix
Gil, Jose
Gil, Julio
Gil, Ramon
Gomales, Alonso
Gomales, Florencio

Gomez, Agustin
Gomez, Eugenio
Gomez, Francisco
Blanco, Benito
Gomez, Gabriel
Gomez, Jose
Gomez, Manuel
Gomez, Nicolas
Gomez, Pedro
Gomez, Salvador
Gomez, Torivio
Gonzales, Gregorio
Gonzalez, Baltasar
Gonzalez, Domingo
Gonzalez, Francisco
Gonzalez, Jose
Gonzalez, Juan
Gonzalez, Luis
Gordo, Manuel
Gudiel, Ysisdro
Guerencio, Jose
Guerrero, Agustin
Gutierrez, German
Gutierrez, Pablo
Gutierrez, Pedro
Hermoso, Juan
Hernandez, Antonio
Hernandez, Francisco
Hernandez, Juan
Hernandez, Manuel
Hernandez, Vicente
Herrando, Domingo
Herrera, Francisco
Herrera, Juan
Herrero, Manuel
Herrero, Matio
Hurracca, Sebastian
Hurtado, Lorenzo
Ibanez, Juan

Iglesias, Pedro
Iglesias, Ramon
Izquierdo, Manuel
Jamudo, Jose
Juarez, Calixto
Junquera, Pedro
La Torre, Francisco
La Vega, Francisco
Labro, Juan
Lafuente, Jose
Latre, Francisco
Leal, Jose
Leon, Jose
Leon, Juan
Litago, Sebastian
Loeches, Manuel
Loise, Tomas
Lopez, Antonio
Lopez, Bernabe
Lopez, Blas
Lopez, Casimiro
Lopez, Francisco
Lopez, Jacinto
Lopez, Javier Miguel
Lopez, Jose
Lopez, Jose
Lopez, Juan
Lopez, Manuel
Lopez, Romualdo
Lopez, Tomas
Lopez, Vicente
Losa, Francisco
Lucas, Pedro
Luque, Felipe
Madrid, Benito
Madrid, Gil de la
Madrid, Mariano
Maicanague, Jose
Maicas, Antonio

Maldonado, Antonio
Manrrique, Martin
Mansebo, Jose
Manzanilla, Dionisio
Manzano, Crispulo
Marco, Manuel
Maroto, Manuel
Marquez, Juan
Martelo, Jose
Martin, Andres
Martin, Bernardo
Martin, Bruno
Martin, Francisco
Martin, Juan
Martin, Juan
Martin, Nicolas
Martinez, Cirilo
Martinez, Francisco
Martinez, Jose Diaz
Martinez, Juan Manuel
Martinez, Juan
Martinez, Manuel
Martinez, Matias
Masa, Jose
Mataranz, Jose
Mateo, Jose
Mayordomo, Pedro
Medinero, Antonio
Medranda, Andres
Mena, Francisco
Mena, Jose
Mena, Xavier de
Mendez, Cayetano
Menendez, Antonio
Menudo, Juan
Mier, Leonardo de
Miguel, Manuel
Millan, Jose

Millan, Manuel
Martinez, Manuel
Millan, Mateo
Millanes, Joaquin
Miramon, Pedro
Montal …, Gabriel
Montoliu, Cristoval
Morales, Domingo
Moreno, Gabriel
Moreno, Juan
Moreno, Lucas
Moreno, Manuel
Moreno, Narciso
Moreno, Nicolas
Munoz, Agustin
Munoz, Alfonso
Munoz, Francisco
Munoz, Mariano
Muro, Jose
Navarro, Julian
Navas, Jose Manuel de
Captain
Navas, Rafael
Navasques, Facundo
Navasques, Jazinto
Nicolas, Francisco
Notario, Bartolome
Obero, Manuel
Olaya, Francisco
Olmo, Juan del
Olmo, Manuel del
Ontanaya, Francisco
Orrego, Francisco
Ortega, Vicente
Ortiz, Francisco
Ortiz, Pedro
Ortiz, Vicente
Otero, Pascual
Otin, Ramon

Pablo, Francisco
Paez, Cristoval
Pajarero, Manuel
Pajes, Manuel
Palomino, Antonio
Panadero, Santiago
Pardo, Cristoval
Parra, Calixto
Parra, Cayetano
Parrilla, Francisco
Pasqual, Joaquin
Pastor, Antonio
Patino, Francisco
Pedrosa, Juan Jose
Pelaez, Miguel
Pena, Francisco de la
Pena, Ysidro
Penaranda, Gabriel
Peralta, Antonio
Perez, Domingo
Perez, Francisco
Perez, Juan
Perez, Manuel
Perez, Mariano
Perez, Miguel
Perez, Santiago
Perez, Vicente
Pertierra, Santos
Pico, Tomas
Piconfreras, Jose
Pielgan, Francisco
Piris, Geronimo
Pita, Pedro
Plaza, Juan
Porcel, Juan
Porrero, Gabriel
Postigo, Fernando del
Prado, Antonio
Puches, Blas

Puello, Simon
Puerta, Nicolas
Pulgar, Francisco
Rafaeles, Felix
Ramires, Antonio
Ramirez, Gregorio
Ramirez, Juan
Ramos, Francisco
Ramos, Simon de
Rebollono, Antonio
Recio, Rafael
Redondo, Francisco
Revidiego, Gregorio
Rey, Roque
Reyes, Antonio
Rio, Domingo
Rios, Ramon de los
Rivas, Bernardo
Rivera, Hermenegildo
Rivera, Jaime
Riveras, Marcos
Robles, Nicolas
Rodriguez ...
Rodriguez, Agustin Garcia
Rodriguez, Antonio
Rodriguez, Bernardo
Rodriguez, Esteban
Rodriguez, Francisco
Rodriguez, Juan
Rodriguez, Manuel
Rodriguez, Tomas
Rodriguez, Victor
Rodriguez, Pedro
Rojas, Manuel
Roman, Manuel
Romero, Bernabe
Romero, Francisco
Romero, Joaquin
Romero, Juan

Romero, Manuel
Rota, Ysidro
Rubio, Antonio
Rui, Antonio
Rui, Domingo
Rui, Vicente
Ruiz, Calixto
Runi, Francisco
Ruvio, Juan
Ruvio, Leon
Saavedra, Manuel
Saavedra, Mauel
Sael, Gregorio
Saes, Pedro
Castro, Salvador de
Saez, Pedro
Salas, Joaquin
Salazar, Manuel
Salcedo, Juan
Salcedo, Leon
Salcedo, Tomas
Salgado, Juan
San Pedro, Antonio
Sanchez, Andres
Sanchez, Antonio
Sanchez, Calixto
Sanchez, Diego
Sanchez, Erminio
Modesto, Antonio
Sanchez, Francisco
Sanchez, Juan Antonio
Sanchez, Lorenzo
Sancho, Pedro
Santiago
Santos, Domingo
Santos, Manuel
Sanz, Manuel
Sanz, Pedro
Saonero, Manuel

Seda, Gaspar de	Toro, Jose	Villegas, Juan
Segovia, Pedro	Ugarte, Pedro	Villegas, Luis
Serran, Pascual	Ustillo, Diego	Vinuela, Manuel
Sierra, Benito	Valencia, Juan	Vivas, Joaquin
Soler, Jose	Valle, Antonio del	Vizcon, Manuel
Solorzano, Jose	Valle, Eugenio del	Ximenez, Esteban
Sopena, Blas	Valle, Juan del	Ximenez, Francisco
Soria, Pedro	Vasques, Tomas	Ximenez, Juan
Soto, Anton	Vazquez, Juan	Ydalgo, Matias
Sugranes, Ventura	Vega, Marinel	Ymeszo, Jose
Toledano, Manuel	Vicente	Ysquierdo, Jose
Toledo, Antonio	Villa, Juan de la	Yuste, Manuel
Toledo, Pedro	Villanueva, Baltasar	Zaragozano, Manuel
Tomas, Francisco	Villaverde, Manuel	

Source:
Spain's regiment Immemorial del Rey of soldier's roster can be located at the National Sons of the American Revolution Society Library, Louisville, Kentucky.

1st Battalion, 1a Company, Grenadiers

Name	Rank		
Pelaez, Miguel	Captain	Bonilla, Manuel	
Rebollono, Antonio	Sgt.	Madrid, Mariano	
Bustamante, Antonio		Salcedo, Leon	Grenadier
Ortega, Vicente	Drummer	Escudero, Jose	
Eugeni, Angel	Corporal	Martin, Francisco	
Salazar, Manuel		Miguel, Manuel	
Alfos, Mariano			

1st Battalion, 1a Company, Grenadiers

Name	Rank		
Aragon, Manuel		Betes, Jose	Sael, Gregorio
Ontanaya, Francisco		Garcia, Matias	Ramires, Antonio
Ortiz, Pedro		Hernandez, Juan	Perez, Juan
Segovia, Pedro		Montoliu, Cristoval	Caro, Juan
Aguilera, Gavino		Garcia, Bonifacio	Ymeszo, Jose
Caballerro, Angel		Esten, Agustin	Mansebo, Jose
Brabo, Francisco		Cerro, Francisco del	Cuerda, Francisco

Rui, Domingo
Solorzano, Jose
Herrero, Matio
Castro, Gabriel
Madrid, Benito

Albanil, Lazaro
Rodriguez, Manuel
Revidiego, Gregorio
Iglesias, Pedro
Cano, Vicente

Sanchez, Antonio
Gomez, Manuel
Lopez, Romualdo
Genocien, Jose

1st Battalion, 1a Company, Grenadiers

Name	Rank
Garcia, illegible	
Muro, Jose	

1st Battalion, 1a Company, Fusiliers

Name	Rank
Rios, Ramon de los	Lt
Ugarte, Pedro	Sgt.
Carrasco, Rugino	Corporal
Guerrero, Agustin	
Castro, Ramon	
Lopez, Jose	
Aguillera, Agustin	
Hernandez, Vicente	
Ruvio, Leon	
Pita, Pedro	

Campos, Juan Jose Ramon
Martin, Francisco
Garcia, Francisco
Campos, Andres Dos
Gonzalez, Baltasar
Puches, Blas
Peralta, Antonio
Moreno, Lucas
Garcia, Pedro
Yuste, Manuel

1st Battalion, 2a Company, Fusiliers

Name	Rank
Croquer, Vicente	Lt.
Corbato, Cosme	Drummer
Hermoso, Cabo Juan	Corporal
Marco, Manuel	
Ana, Manuel	
Borne, Sebastian	
Sanchez, Lorenzo	

1st Battalion, 2a Company, Fusiliers

Name	Rank
Carnes (?), Antonio	

1st Battalion, 3a Company, Fusiliers

Name	Rank
Gutierrez, Pedro	Capitan

Litago, Sebastian

Villaverde, Manuel   Sgt.
Prado, Antonio
Salcedo, Tomas
Bueno, Vicente
Mateo, Jose
Martinez, Manuel
Navarro, Julian
Bruella, Pedro
Marquez, Juan
Menudo, Juan
Saonero, Manuel
Fernandez, Juan
Lopez, Jacinto
Calderon, Marcos
Gomez, Pedro

Ortiz, Francisco
Pena, Francisco de la
Garcia, Lorenzo
Vazquez, Juan
Diez, Francisco
Pertierra, Santos
Villegas, Juan
Rivera, Jaime
Recio, Rafael
Lopez, Blas
Vizcon, Manuel
Ximenez, Esteban
Sanz, Manuel
Gomez, Agustin

1st Battalion, 3a Company, Fusiliers

Name	Rank
Fernandez, Juan	
Moreno, Manuel	

1st Battalion, 4a Company, Fusiliers

Name	Rank
Balza, Baltazar	Sgt.
Porcel, Juan	
Villa, Juan de la	Drummer
Parrilla, Francisco	Corporal
Gomez, Gabriel	
Menendez, Antonio	
Rodriguez, Esteban	
Perez, Vicente	
Ruiz, Calixto	
Ramirez, Gregorio	
Garcia, Andres	
Rodriguez, Manuel	

Hurtado, Lorenzo
Esteban, Dionisio
Lopez, Tomas
Rui, Vicente
Rodriguez ...
Garcia, Mateo
Navasques, Facundo
Valle, Antonio del
Paez, Cristoval
Chaves, Pedro Lopez Jose
Cortes, Jose

1st Battalion, 5a Company, Fusiliers

Name	Rank
Florez, Agustin de	Capitan
Postigo, Fernando del	Lt.

Martin, Nicolas
Manzano, Crispulo

Name	Rank		
Herrero, Manuel	Sgt.	Parra, Cayetano	
La Vega, Francisco	Drummer	Rodriguez, Juan	
Ibanez, Juan		Olmo, Juan del	
Maroto, Manuel		Blanco, Bonifacio	
Gil, Ramon		Gil, Julio	
Perez, Manuel		Izquierdo, Manuel	
Iglesias, Ramon		Mena, Francisco	
Lopez, Bernabe		Ramos, Simon de	
Campos, Blas		Martinez, Cirilo	
Arroyo, Jose		Fernandez, Juan	
Olmo, Manuel del		Alvarez, Felix	
Sanz, Pedro		Perez, Francisco	
Patino, Francisco		Cortes, Nicolas	
Lopez, Manuel			
Mayordomo, Pedro			

1st Battalion, 6a Company, Fusiliers

Name	Rank		
Mier, Leonardo de	Lt	Redondo, Francisco	
Alonso, Isidro	Sgt.	Loeches, Manuel	
Lopez, Jose	Drummer	Sugranes, Ventura	Corporal
Romero, Joaquin	Corporal	Gomez, Francisco	
Fernandez, Nicolas		Blanco, Benito	
Gonzalez, Jose		Otin, Ramon	
Munoz, Alfonso		Alvarez, Baltasar	
Sanchez, Diego		Monte (Monfe), Jacinto	
Toledo, Antonio		Ferran, Martin	2nd. Lt.

1st Battalion, 7a Company, Fusiliers

Name	Rank	
Alcazar, Felipe	Captain	Perez, Santiago
Salcedo, Juan	Lt.	Roman, Manuel
Delgado, Antonio	Sgt.	Alcan (illegible), Sebastian
Balaguer, Alberto	Drummer	Gomez, Nicolas
Garcia, Jose	Corporal	Alcantara, Pedro
Lopez, Antonio		Gonzalez, Juan
Balmacedo		Ydalgo, Matias
Vicente		Soto, Anton
Santiago		Ximenez, Juan
Garcia, Alfonso		Castro, Juan de

165

Labro, Juan
Ferrerio, illegible
Hernandez, Francisco
Masa, Jose

1st Battalion, 8a Company, Fusiliers

Name	Rank
Miramon, Pedro	Sgt.
Ambros, Domingo	Corporal
La Torre, Francisco	
Collado, Simon	
Dominguez, Pablo	
Romero, Manuel	
San Pedro, Antonio	
Lopez, Casimiro	
Rodriguez, Miguel	
Alonso, Pedro	
Sanchez, Erminio	
Modesto, Antonio	

2nd Battalion, 2a Company, Grenadiers

Name	Rank
Chacon, Francisco	Captain
Mena, Jose	2nd. Lt
Villegas, Luis	Sgt.
Callejas, Juan	Corporal
Aznar, Antonio	
Sopena, Blas	
Pablo, Francisco	
Orrego, Francisco	
Gil, Felix	Granadero
Chozas, Domingo	
Toledo, Pedro	
Morales, Domingo	
Sanchez, Calixto	
Reyes, Antonio	
Fernandez, Ignaio	
Rodriguez, Tomas	
Bazquez, Nicolas	
Gonzalez, Domingo	
Flores, Celestino	

Perez, Vicente
Herrera, Juan

Benito, Jose
Palomino, Antonio
Martinez, Juan Manuel
Gonzales, Gregorio
Lopez, Tomas
Rodriguez, Francisco
Martin, Juan
Saavedra, Mauel
Pajes, Manuel
Rui, Antonio
Castro, Juan de
Pastor, Antonio

Manzanilla, Dionisio
Figuer, Isidro
Seda, Gaspar de
Lopez, Tomas
Rodriguez, Victor
Estevan, Manuel
Hernandez, Antonio
Maicanague, Jose
Martinez, Francisco
Moreno, Nicolas
Campo, Manuel del
Valle, Eugenio del
Garcia, Enrique
Cueto, Pascual
Parra, Calixto
Puello, Simon
Hurracca, Sebastian
Lafuente, Jose
Sierra, Benito

Saavedra, Manuel
Sancho, Pedro
Millanes, Joaquin
Millan, Mateo
Rodriguez, Agustin Garcia
Garcia, Juan
Junquera, Pedro

Salgado, Juan
Dominguez, Antonio
Soria, Pedro
Garcia, Elias
Aguirre, Miguel
Gigante, Gabriel
Soler, Jose

2nd Battalion, 1a Company, Fusiliers

Name	Rank
Pico, Tomas	2nd. Lt
Lucas, Pedro	Corporal
Ramos, Francisco	
Martin, Bruno	
Gonzalez, Francisco	
Eras, Francisco	
Carnicer, Francisco	
Cheval, Vicente	
Gutierrez, German	
Aguado, Jose	
Gomez, Francisco	
Pajarero, Manuel	
Lopez, Javier Miguel	
Palomino, Antonio	
Estun, Luis	

Gordo, Manuel
Maicas, Antonio
Notario, Bartolome
Millan, Jose
Adeva, Ramon
Carrasco, Manuel
Hernandez, Francisco
Fernandez, Antonio
Capilla, Sebastian
Garcia, Ylario
Ferrer, Jaime
Fernandez, Javier Francisco
Sanchez, Francisco

2nd Battalion, 3a Company, Fusiliers

Name	Rank
Arriola, Jose	Captain
Rafaeles, Felix	2nd Lt.
Aguilar, Agustin	Drummer
Herrando, Domingo	Corporal
Leon, Jose	
Villanueva, Baltasar	
Loise, Tomas	
Munoz, Francisco	
Rodriguez, Pedro	
Martin, Bernardo	

Alvarez, Jose
Otero, Pascual
Losa, Francisco
Romero, Juan
Albuquelquel, Francisco
Frayle, Sebastian
Barraves, Jose
Vasques, Tomas
Ysquierdo, Jose

2nd Battalion, 3a Company, Fusiliers

Name	Rank

Charmar, Agustin
Ferrero, Juan
Martinez, Francisco
Mena, Xavier de
Rodriguez, Bernardo
Serran, Pascual
Ximenez, Francisco
Toro, Jose

Munoz, Mariano
Latre, Francisco
Piconfreras, Jose
Saes, Pedro
Castro, Salvador de
Plaza, Juan
Rio, Domingo

2nd Battalion, 4a Company, Fusiliers

Name	Rank
Fernandez, Carlos	Sgt.
Rey, Roque	Corporal
Fernandez, Juan	
Cuetos, Diego	
Luque, Felipe	
Moreno, Narciso	
Galisteo, Francisco	
Bonet, Antonio	
Ciriel, Luis	
Mendez, Cayetano	
Ortiz, Vicente	
Santos, Domingo	
Calvo, Juan	
Copado, Agustin	

Rodriguez, Manuel
Millan, Manuel
Martinez, Manuel
Gascon, Francisco
Cura, Antonio
Pena, Ysidro
Cordoves, Juan
Martin, Juan
Gomales, Alonso
Martinez, Juan
Perez, Miguel
Perez, Mariano
Vega, Marinel

2nd Battalion, 5a Company, Fusiliers

Name	Rank
Castillo, Felipe	Corporal
Penaranda, Gabriel	
Gudiel, Ysisdro	
Vivas, Joaquin	
Caldona, Lucas	
Obero, Manuel	
Valencia, Juan	
Conti, Manuel	
Medranda, Andres	
Navas, Rafael	
Jamudo, Jose	

Martelo, Jose
Leal, Jose
Santos, Manuel
Ballesteros, Rafael
Martinez, Jose Diaz
Carnicer, Manuel
Ruvio, Juan
Gomales, Florencio
Fernandez, Andres
Rivas, Bernardo
Vinuela, Manuel

2nd Battalion, 6a Company, Fusiliers

Name	Rank
Pedrosa, Juan Jose	2nd. Lt.
Canadas, Ramón	Corporal
Saez, Pedro	
Casa, Jose	Drummer
Lopez, Juan	
Medinero, Antonio	
Felipe, Matias	
Guerencio, Jose	
Gutierrez, Pablo	
Chico, Gregorio	
Camino, Manuel	

Gomez, Eugenio
Puerta, Nicolas
Martinez, Juan
Rivera, Hermenegildo
Panadero, Santiago
Salas, Joaquin
Zaragozano, Manuel
Clos, Francisco
Runi, Francisco
Maldonado, Antonio

2nd Battalion, 7a Company, Fusiliers

Name	Rank
Gil, Jose	Corporal
Conde, Jose	
Perez, Santiago	
Munoz, Agustin	
Mataranz, Jose	
Romero, Francisco	
Illegible, Jorge	
Sanchez, Antonio	
Rojas, Manuel	
Herrera, Francisco	

Martinez, Matias
Garcia, Antonio
Diez, Tomas
Lopez, Vicente
Moreno, Juan
Alarcon, Manuel
Blanco, Vicente
Nicolas, Francisco
Cuesta, Rafael

2nd Battalion, 8a Company, Fusiliers

Name	Rank
Robles, Nicolas	Lt
Caballero, Antonio	Sgt
Martin, Juan	Corporal
Piris, Geronimo	Drummer
Rodriguez, Antonio	
Pasqual, Joaquin	
Fustes, Lucas	
Riveras, Marcos	

Pardo, Cristoval
Illegible, Senaris
Porrero, Gabriel
Gomez, Salvador
Bona, Antonio
Hernandez, Manuel
Leon, Juan
Lopez, Juan

Plana Mayor

Name	Rank
Navas, Jose Manuel de	Captain

Warship "Luis" Crew

Name	Rank
Madrid, Gil de la	Sgt
Aveliano, Joaquin	
Galiciano, Manuel	
Moreno, Gabriel	
Tomas, Francisco	
Delgado, Juan Jose	
Gonzalez, Luis	
Alcolado, Juan	
Sanchez, Andres	
Crespo, Sebastian	
Perez, Domingo	
Gomez, Torivio	
Garcia, Joaquin	
Valle, Juan del	
Navasques, Jazinto	
Martin, Andres	
Corro, Francisco	
Domingo, Santiago	
Pielgan, Francisco	Corporal
Fuente, Melchor de la	
Candado, Francisco	
Lopez, Francisco	
Fernandez, Santiago	

Frigate "Santa Clara" Crew

Name	Rank
Gallus, Francisco	Sgt.
Alvarez, Jose Luis	Corporal
Sanchez, Juan Antonio	
Beltran, Manuel	
Ustillo, Diego	
Barea, Antonio	
Montal (illegible), Gabriel	
Toledano, Manuel	
Garcia, Alfonso	

Frigate "Santa Clara" Crew

Name	Rank
Sanchez, Antonio	
Juarez, Calixto	
Lopez, Jose	
Fernandez, Francisco	
Cerro, Ramon	
Perez, Juan	
Gomez, Jose	
Garcia, Jose	
Garcia, Manuel	
Olaya, Francisco	
Pulgar, Francisco	Corporal
Brigida, Manuel	
Martinez, Manuel	
Ramirez, Juan	
Rota, Ysidro	
Alcantara, Fernando	
Romero, Bernabe	
Rubio, Antonio	
Manrrique, Martin	
Ballesteros, Francisco	
Fernandez, Manuel	
Mendez, Cayetano	

Summary of the Spanish Invasion of Pensacola, 1781

A first Spanish attack against the British at Fort George, Pensacola, Florida, failed due to a hurricane storm on February 28, 1781.

Subsequently, a second attack, on March 18, 1781, against Fort George, Pensacola, Florida, was attempted by Bernardo Galvez applying both naval and army coordination. Bernardo Galvez initiated the attack on small boats under cannon fire. The British prepared for large ships entering the Pensacola Bay and used most of the cannon balls.Thereafter the large ships entered the bay with no damage from the reefs or cannons. By May 10, 1781, the Spanish siege ended with the surrender of Pensacola against the British.

Circumstances leading up to the Pensacola attack began from the Havana Cuban Bay. The plan was to land on the Island of Santa Rosa, which was at the entrance of the Pensacola Bay. Galvez reached Santa Rosa Island on March 9, 1781, where soldiers landed. The next day some British sailors came to feed the Island cattle and were captured. Two days later Galvez entered the bay with small boats. March 16, 1781, 900 soldiers arrived from Mobile to Pensacola for reinforcement. The New Orleans army was in on its way; however, a storm threatened the Galvez attack and he chose to attack before the New Orleans army arrived. The larger vessels did not move into the bay until March 19, 1781, which had no difficulty due tothe less shallow water way. One vessel did not enter the bay because the commander thought it was unwise to enter his ship in reef waters.

On March 23, 1781, the New Orleans army of 550 Spanish soldiers arrived. Sailors and infantry military fought side by side. On April 19, 1781, Admiral Jose Solano's fleet arrived with 1600 seasoned infantry and 750 of the Irish regiment which arrived on French ships. The French sailors also engaged in the land battle. The Spanish siege continued until May 8, 1781. On this date a Spanish grenade landed on the British gunpowder causing an explosion. The British General John Campbell sought to surrender under certain terms. The surrender terms were negotiated and finished on May 10, 1781. Pensacola was now under the Spanish flag.

The conflict with the British was not over. The Caribbean (Nassau and Bahamas) and Florida were still part of the strategy for protection against the British navy.

Source: Florida Historical Society, *The Americas,* Vol. 45, No. 1, July 1988, page 79-95, published by: Academy of American Franciscan History. Author Eric Beerman

Espana y la Independencia de Estados Unido (Spain and the Independence of the United States), Spanish collection of the United States, Spanish edition only, by Eric Beerman, 1992

Bernardo de Galvez, Services to the American Revolution, was authored by Charles Robert Churchill, March 4, 1925. This book is located at the National Sons of the American Revolution Library. It can be viewed on the Louisiana State Society of the Sons of the American Revolution website.

Source: General Archive of the Indies, Seville, Spain. Papeles procedentes de Cuba, Legajo 159 - 161 (Papers of proceedings relating to Cuba Archives).

Military Archive from Madrid, Spain

Gulf of Mexico Map

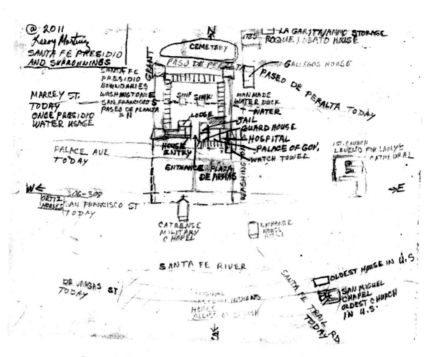

Santa Fe Presidio, New Mexico, and surrounding area

Chapter X

New Mexico

Santa Fe Presidio Records, 1776 –1783

Santa Fe Presidio roster, New Mexico, November, 1779

Santa Fe Presidio Rosters, 1779 - 1783

Early Spanish explorer expeditions went into New Mexico. During 1598 the Onate expedition was for the settlement of this province. The Spanish first settled near the San Juan de los Caballeros Pueblo before moving to Santa Fe during 1610. Santa Fe became the capital of the New Mexico province. It is the oldest capital in the United States today.

Unlike California, Arizona, Texas and Louisiana, there are record names of the 1780 King Carlos III request for the voluntary donation for the war effort against the British. Henrietta as author of "The Santa Fe Presidio Soldiers: Their Donation to the American Revolution. Henrietta's book was published by New Mexico Geneology Society, 2006.

The X under the Daughters of the American Revolution (DAR) indicates which soldiers contributed to the voluntary donation of the war effort against the British from the Santa Fe.

175

Soldiers' Names	DAR	SAR
Abeyta, Juan de Jesus	X	X
Abeyta, Antonio Jose	X	X
Abrego, Juan	X	X
Aguilar, Jose Rafael	X	X
Alarid, Jose Antonio	X	X
Alarid, Jose Ygnacio	X	X
Alarid, Juan Antonio	X	X
Alarid, Manuel Isidro	X	X
Alire, Jose Miguel	X	X
Alire, Tomas		X
Anaya, Francisco Domingo		X
Anaya, Juan Antonio	X	X
Anza, Juan Bautista de	X	X
Arce, Jose Antonio	X	X
Armenta, Antonio		X
Armijo, Antonio	X	X
Armijo, Jose Antonio	X	X
Azuela, Manuel	X	X
Baca, Diego Manuel Pedro	X	X
Baca, Jose Antonio	X	X
Baca, Jose Manuel	X	X
Baca, Jose Maria		X
Baca, Luis Maria Cabeza de Baca		X
Benavides, Bartolo	X	X
Benavides, Juan	X	X
Bermejo, Fray (Nunez)	X	X
Bustamante, Bernardo	X	X
Campo Redondo, Jose		X
Casados, Antonio	X	X
Cordero, Jose Maria		X
Delgado, Manuel	X	X
Dominguez, Juan		X
Duran, Salvador	X	X
Duran, Ygnacio	X	X
Duan, Ygnacio	X	X
Escudero, Tomas		X
Esquibel, Antonio de la Cruz Alexandro	X	X
Esquibel, Buenaventura	X	X
Esquibel, Ramon	X	X
Fernandez, Bartolome Antonio Roberto	X	X
Fernandez, Carlos	X	X
Fernandez, Manuel Yldefonso		X
Fragoso, Jose Manuel		X
Gallegos, Anselmo	X	X
Gallegos, Diego	X	X
Gallegos, Jose Antonio	X	X

Gallegos Baca, Juan	X	X
Gallegos, Manuel Antonio	X	X
Gallegos, Miguel	X	X
Garcia (de Noriega), Francisco	X	X
Garcia de Noriega, Vicente	X	X
Gonzales, Baltazar		X
Gonzales, Geronimo	X	X
Gonzales, Juan Antonio	X	X
Griego, Jose Antonio	X	X
Griego, Bartolome Bernardo Antonio		X
Griego, Hernando "Fernando"	X	X
Griego, Jose Miguel	X	X
Guerrero, Antonio	X	X
Gutierrez, Antonio	X	X
Gutierrez, Bartoleme		X
Gutierrez, Jose Miguel	X	X
Herrera, Juan Luis	X	X
Lain, Joaquin		X
Lobato, Bartolome		X
Lobato, Luis	X	X
Lobato, Roque	X	X
Lopez, Jose Antonio	X	X
Lopez, Tomas Antonio	X	X
Luera, Felipe Santiago	X	X
Lujan, Antonio		X
Luna, Tomas		X
Madrid, Antonio Xavier	X	X
Madrid, Tomas		X
Madrid, Ygnacio	X	X
Maes, Bartolome	X	X
Maes, Jose Antonio		X
Maes, Jose Francisco	X	X
Maes, Jose Miguel	X	X
Maes, Ysidro Antonio	X	X
Maldonado, Gaspar	X	X
Maldonado, Jose	X	X
Maldonado, Jose Miguel		X
Morquecho, Vicente	X	X
Mares, Jose Julian		X
Mares, Manuel	X	X
Martin, Bartolo	X	X
Martin, Francisco	X	X
Martin, Luis	X	X
Martin, Manuel	X	X
Mestas, Pedro Antonio		X
Miera, Anacleto	X	X
Miera, Bernardo	X	X

Name	DAR	SAR
Miera, Manuel	X	X
Ortega, Alejandro	X	X
Ortega, Antonio		X
Ortega, Francisco		X
Ortiz, Antonio de Jesus		X
Ortiz, Francisco Xavier	X	X
Ortiz, Gaspar		X
Ortiz, Joaquin Alexandro	X	X
Ortiz, Jose Antonio		X
Ortiz, Jose Miguel		X
Ortiz, Tomas	X	X
Ortiz, Vicente		X
Pacheco, Jose	X	X
Pacheco, Jose Antonio		X
Padilla, Antonio		X
Padilla, Tomas		X
Pena, Diego Antonio	X	X
Pena, Juan de Dios	X	X
Prada, Jose Bernardo		X
Rael, Jose Antonio Rael	X	X
Rael Aguilar, Jose Pablo		X
Real Aguilar, Manuel Paulin		X
Rivera, Gerbasio Alfonso	X	X
Rivera, Antonio		X
Rivera, Baltasar Antonio	X	X
Rivera, Jose Viterbo	X	X
Rivera, Luis Felipe		X
Rivera, Matias de San Juan	X	X
Rivera, Salvador	X	X
Rodriguez, Felipe	X	X
Rodriguez, Ysidro Antonio	X	X
Romero, Antonio Jose	X	X
Romero, Manuel Cristobal	X	X
Romero, Pedro Antonio	X	X
Romo, Jose Manuel		X
Roybal, Tomas		X
Sans Garvisu, Juan Manuel	X	X
Sanchez, Antonio Roman	X	X
Sanchez, Juan Antonio	X	X
Sanchez de Tagle, Manuel Banares	X	X
Sandoval, Andres	X	X
Sandoval, Antonio Jose	X	X
Sandoval, Francisco Cayetano	X	X
Sandoval, Francisco Matias	X	X
Sandoval, Jose	X	X
Sandoval, Juan	X	X
Sandoval, Manuel	X	X
Sandoval, Pablo	X	X
Sandoval, Salvador Antonio		X
Sandoval, Vicente Ferrer	X	X
Santistevan, Domingo Anselmo	X	X
Sena, Jose Miguel	X	X
Sena, Matias	X	X
Sena, Pablo Antonio	X	X
Serrano, Francisco Perez		X
Tafoya, Jose Francisco	X	X
Tafoya, Jose Miguel	X	X
Tafoya, Juan Andres	X	X
Tafoya, Juan Antonio	X	X
Tenorio, Joaquin	X	X
Tenorio, Jose Miguel	X	X
Tenorio de Alba, Miguel		X
Tenorio, Salvador de Orta	X	X
Torres, Francisco Antonio	X	X
Torres, Francisco Martin	X	X
Torres, Martin		X
Trebol, Francisco		X
Troncoso, Vicente	X	X
Trujillo, Juan Jose	X	X
Trujillo, Juan Miguel	X	X
Urioste, Jose Antonio	X	X
Urioste, Juan	X	X
Velarde, Jose Miguel/Manuel	X	X
Vigil, Antonio de los Reyes	X	X
Vigil, Cristobal Faustin	X	X
Vigil, Jose	X	X
Vigil, Juan Cristobal	X	X
Vigil, Salvador de Jesus	X	X
Villapando, Toribio		X

Note:

DAR: Daughters of the American Revolution
SAR: Sons of the American Revolution

Santa Fe Military list of November 1, 1779

Muster roll executed by the Leutenant, with the rank of Captain, Don Juan Baptista de Anza of the Royal Presidio of Santa Fe, of this company that is guarding, and is responsible this day 1st of November 1779

Rank:	Name:	Located at:
Governor and Captain	Don Juan Baptista de Anza	Present
Lt. in charge as Captain	Don Manuel de la Azuela	Present
Lt. in charge as Captain	Don Joseph Maria Cordero	Present
Sub-Lieutenant	Don Joseph Maldonado	Present
Sub-Lt. of Light Troops	Don Salvador Rivera	Present
Chaplain	Don Juan Bermejo	Present
Armorer	Roque Lovato	Present
Drummer	Jose Manuel Fragoso	Present

Tropa de cuera-Leather Jacket Troop

1st. Sgt.	Antonio Guerrero	Present
2nd Sgt.	Pablo Sandoval	with horse herd
Corporal	Barolo Gutierrez	Present
Corporal	Juan Luis de Herrera	with horse herd
2nd. Corporal	Cleto Miera	Present
2nd. Corporal	Juan de Jesus Beitia	with horse herd
Cadet	Don Francisco Perez Serrano	military detail

Soldiers

	Salvador Antonio Sandoval	Present
	Joseph Pacheco	Present
	Cayetano Sandoval	Present
	Ysidro Maese	Present
	Ysidro Rodriguez	Present
	Jose Rael Aguilar	Present
	Ygnacio Duran	Present
	Diego Pena	Present
	Juan Sandoval	Present
	Joseph Griego	with horse herd
	Jose Antonio Meese	with horse herd
	Francisco Xavier (Antonio) Madril	with horseherd
	Manuel Fernandez	with horse herd
	Joseph Tafolla	Ill

178

Gaspar Ortiz	with horse herd
Ventura Esquibel	with horse herd
Ygnacio Madrid	Ill
Geronimo Gonzales	Ill
Joseph Antonio Lopez	Present
Manuel Sandoval	Present
Diego Gallego	Present
Pedro Felipe Rodriguez	Present
Francisco de Ortega	Present
Tomas Ortiz	Present
Joseph Sandoval	Present
Juan Gonzales	Present
Juan Urioste	Present
Salvador Montes Vegil	Ill
Domingo Santistevan	with horse herd
Manuel Mares	Ill
Manuel Saenz Garvizo	with horse herd
Jose Francisco Maese	with horse herd
Bartolo Fernandes	Present
Jose Campo Redondo	with horse herd
Alonso Rivera	with horse herd
Jose Pablo Rael	with horse herd
Antonio Casaus	Present
Vizente Monguccho	Present
Antonio Armijo	Present
Bernardo Bustamante	with horse herd
Gaspar Maldonado	with horse herd
Baltasar Rivera	with horse herd
Antonio Roman Sanchez	with horse herd
Cristobal Vegil	with horse herd
Anselmo Gallego	Present
Miguel Gallego	with horse herd
Antonio Reyes Vexil	Present
Manuel Alari	Present
Thomas Luna	Ill
Jose Miguel Alari	with horse herd

Flying Troops

Rank:	Name:	Located at:
3rd. Sgt.	Juan de Abrego	Present

1st. Corporal	Antonio Sandoval	Present
1st. Corporal	Juan de Dios Pena	Present
2nd. Corporal	Juan Antonio Alary	Present
2nd. Corporal	Antonio Romero	Present
Soldiers:		

Don Carlos Fernandes	Present	
	Don Bernardo Miera	Present
	Manuel Gallego	Present
	Jose Antonio Baca	Present
	Manuel Baca	Present
	Ramon Esquivel	Present
	Joseph Miguel Maese	Present
	Salvador Thenorio	Ill
	Manuel Miera	Present
	Andres Sandoval	Present
	Tomas Lopes	Present
	Joseph Antonio Ortis	Present
	Joseph Antonio Sanches	Present
	Pefro Antonio Romero	Present
	Bartolo Martin	Present
	Jose Antonio Beitia	Present
	Vizente Garcia	Present
	Jose Antonio Rael	Present
	Jose Antonio Urioste	Present
	Bartolo Gutierres	Present
	Jose Antonio Armijo	Present
	Bernardo Griego	Present
	Diego Manuel Baca	Present
	Jose Antonio Gallego	Present
	Francisco Torres	Present
	Jose Francisco Martinez	Present
	Jose Miguel Tafolla	Present
	Antonio Padilla	Present
	Juan Benavides	Ill
	Antonio Esquivel	Present
	Tomas Escudero	Present
	Juan Jose Truxillo	Present
	Bartolo Maese	Present

Jose de Alari	Present
Jose Antonio Garcia	Ill
Manuel Sanches Tagle	Present
Luis Martin	Present
Antonio Gutierres	Present
Manuel Romero	Present
Francisco Torres	Present
Vicente Sandoval	Present
Joseph Vejil	Present
Matias Rivera	Present
Joseph Miguel Sena	Present
Pablo Sena	Present
Jose Rivera	Present
Matias Sena	Present
Luis Lovato	Present
Manuel Martin	Present
Juan Antonio Anaya	Present

Governor	1		
Lt. / Captains	2		
2nd. Lt.	2	Retired:	None
Chaplain	1		
Sgt.	3		
Corporals	8		
Cadet	1		
Armorer	1		
Drummer	1		
Cavalry	19		
Ill	9		
Present	72		
Total:	**120**		

Note: Invalid soldier Joachin Tenorio did not muster with this company of soldiers
Signed: Juan Baptista de Anza (rubric)
Refer to microfilm

Santa Fe Military List for September 1, 1780

Cavalry

Rank:	Name:	Located at:
Governor & Captain	Don Juan Baptista de Anza	Present
Lt. in charge as Captain	Don Manuel de la Azuela	Present
Lt. in Charge as Captain	Don Joseph Maria Cordero	Chihuahua
2nd. Lt of Light Troops	Don Joseph Maldonado	Present
2nd. Lt of Light Troops	Don Salvador Rivera	Paso del Norte
Chaplain	Don Juan Bermejo	Present
Armorer	Roque Lovato	Present
Drummer	Jose Manuel Fragoso	Present

Leather Jacket Troops

Rank:	Name:	Located at:
1st. Sgt.	Antonio Guerrero	with horse herd
2nd. Sgt.	Pablo Sandoval	Present
Corporal	Bartolo Gutierres	Present
Corporal	Juan Luis de Herrera	In el Paso
2nd. Corporal	Don Cleto Miera	with horse herd
2nd. Corporal	Juan de Jesus Beitia	Present
Cadet	Don Francisco Perez Serrano	Present
Soldiers:	Salvador Antonio Sandoval	with horse herd
	Joseph Pacheco	Present
	Cayetano Sandoval	Present
	Ysidro Maese	Ill
	Ysidro Rodriguez	with horse herd
	Jose Rael Aguilar	Present
	Ygnacio Duran	Present
	Diego Pena	with horse herd
	Juan Sandoval	with horse herd
	Joseph Griego	In El Paso del Norte
	Jose Antonio Maese	Present
	Francisco Xavier (Antonio) Madril	In El Paso del Norte
	Manuel Fernandez	In El Paso del Norte
	Jose Tafolla	In El Paso del Norte
	Gaspar Ortiz	with horse herd
	Ventura Esquibel	In El Paso del Norte
	Ygnacio Madrid	In El Paso del Norte
	Geronimo Gonzales	with horse herd
	Joseph Antonio Lopez	with horse herd

182

	Manuel Sandoval	with horse herd
	Diego Gallego	Present
	Pedro Felipe Rodriguez	Present
	Francisco de Ortega	Present
	Tomas Ortiz	Ill
	Jose Sandoval	Present
	Juan Gonzales	Present
	Juan Urioste	Present
	Francisco Montes Vegil	In El Paso del Norte
	Domingo Santistevan	In El Paso del Norte
	Manuel Mares	Present
	Manuel Saenz Garvizo	In El Paso del Norte
	Jose Francisco Maese	In El Paso del Norte
	Bartolo Fernandes	with horse herd
	Jose Campo Redondo	Ill
	Alonso Rivera	Detail to Galisteo
	Antonio Casaus	Ill
	Vizente Monguccho	Present
	Antonio Armijo	Present
	Bernardo Bustamante	Present
	Gaspar Maldonado	In El Paso del Norte
	Baltasar Rivera	In El Paso del Norte
	Antonio Roman Sanchez	In El Paso del Norte
	Cristobal Vejil	In El Paso del norte
	Anselmo Gallego	with horse herd
	Miguel Gallego	In El Paso del Norte
	Antonio Reyes Vejil	with horse herd
	Manuel Alari	Present
	Jose Ygnacio Alari	In El Paso del Norte
	Distinguished Manuel Miera	Present
	Manuel Gallegos	with horse herd
Flying Troops		
3rd. Sgt.	Juan de Abrego	Present
1st Corporal	Antonio Sandoval	with horse herd
1st Corporal	Juan de Dios Pena	Present
2nd Corporal	Juan Antonio Alary	Present
2nd Corporal	Antonio Romero	Present
Cadet	Don Jose Antonio Ortis	Present
Soldiers:	Distinguished Don Carlos Fernandes	Present

183

Distinguished Don Bernardo Miera	Present
José Antonio Baca	with horse herd
Manuel Baca	Present
Ramon Esquivel	Present
Joseph Miguel Maese	Ill
Salvador Tenorio	with horse herd
Andres Sandoval	with horseherd
Tomas Lopes	Present
Joseph Antonio Ortis	with horse herd
Joseph Antonio Sanches	Present
Pedro Antonio Romero	Present
Bartolo Martin	Present
Jose Antonio Beitia	with horse herd
Vizente Garcia	Detail to Galisteo
Jose Antonio Rael	Present
Jose Antonio Urioste	Present
Bartolo Gutierres	with horse herd
Jose Antonio Armijo	Present
Diego Manuel Baca	Present
Jose Antonio Gallego	Present
Francisco Torres	Present
Jose Francisco Martinez	Present
Jose Miguel Tafolla	with horse herd
Antonio Padilla	with horseherd
Juan Benavides	Present
Antonio Esquivel	Present
Tomas Escudero	Present
Juan Jose Trujillo	Present
Bartolo Maese	Detail to Galisteo
Jose de Alari	Present
Jose Antonio Garcia	Detail to Savinal
Manuel Sanches Tagle	Present
Luis Martin	Detail to Savinal
Antonio Gutierres	Detail to Savinal
Manuel Romero	Present
Francisco Torres	Present
Vicente Sandoval	with horse herd
Jose Vejil	with horse herd
Matias Rivera	with horse herd

Jose Miguel Sena	with horse herd
Pablo Sena	Present
Jose Rivera	with horse herd
Matias Sena	Present
Luis Lovato	Present
Manuel Martin	Present
Juan Antonio Anaya	Present
Pedro Antonio Maese	Present
Vizente Garzia	Present

Summary:

Governor	1
Lt/Captains	2
2nd. Lt	2
Chaplain	1
Sgt.	3
Corporals	8
Cadets	2
Armorer	1
Drummer	1
Cavalry	23
In El Paso	16
In Savinal	3
Ill	5
Present	49
Total:	**120**

Retired:

Lt. Don Thomas Madrid	Present
Joaquin Tenorio	Present
Antonio Ortega	Present
Jose Mares	Present
Salvador Duran	Present
Antonio Rivera	Present
Francisco Garzia	Present
Jose Antonio Griego	Present
Manuel Martin	Present
Juan Tafoya	Present
Bartolo Benavides	Present

In compliance with the muster roll, I the Governor and Captain, on the said day, month, and year certify

Signed: Juan Baptista de Anza (rubric)

185

Santa Fe Military List for November 1, 1781

Cavalry

Muster roll executed by me the Lt. Coronel Don Juan Baptista de Anza of the Royal Presidio of Santa Fe, of this company that is guarding, and is my responsibility this day 1st of November 1781.

Rank:	Name:	Located at:
Governor & Captain	Don Juan Baptista de Anza	Present
Lt. in charge as Captain	Don Manuel de la Azuela	Present
2nd Lt. in charge as Captain	Don Jose Maria Cordero	Chihuahua
2nd Lt of Light Troops	Don Jose Maldonado	Present
2nd Lt of Light Troops	Don Salvador Rivera	Present
Chaplain	Don Fray Juan Bermejo	Present
Armorer	Roque Lovato	Present
Drummer		Vacant
Leather Jacket Troops		
1st Sgt.	Antonio Guerrero	Present
2nd. Sgt	Pablo Sandoval	Horseherd
1st Corporal	Juan Luis de Herrera	Present
1st Corporal	Distinguished Juan Cleto Miera	Horseherd
2nd Corporal	Juan de Jesus Beytia	Present
2nd Corporal	Antonio Sandobal	Horseherd
Cadet	Don Francisco Perez Serrano	Present
Soldiers:	Distinuished Don Carlos Fernandes	Present
	Joseph Pacheco	Horseherd
	Cayetano Sandoval	Horseherd
	Ysidro Maese	Present
	Ysidro Rodriguez	Present
	Joseph Rael Aguilar	Horseherd
	Ygnacio Duran	Present
	Diego Pena	Present
	Juan Sandoval	Present
	Joseph Griego	Horseherd
	Antonio Madril	Present
	Jose Miguel Tafoya	Present
	Ventura Esquibel	Present
	Ygnacio Madrid	Horseherd
	Geronimo Gonzales	Present

	Antonio Lopez	Present
	Manuel Sandoval	Horseherd
	Diego Gallego	Horseherd
	Pedro Felipe Rodriguez	Horseherd
	Francisco de Ortega	Horseherd
	Jose Sandoval	Horseherd
	Juan Gonzales	Horseherd
	Juan de Urioste	Horseherd
	Francisco Salvador Vejil	Horseherd
	Domingo Santistevan	Present
	Manuel Mares	Present
	Manuel Saenz Garvizo	Ill
	Joseph Francisco Maese	Present
	Bartolo Fernandes	Present
	Alonso Rivera	Present
	Antonio Casaus	Present
	Vizente Monguccho	Ill
	Antonio Armijo	Ill
	Bernardo Bustamante	Present
	Gaspar Maldonado	Horseherd
	Baltasar Rivera	Horseherd
	Antonio Roman Sanchez	Horseherd
	Cristobal Faustin Vejil	Ill
	Anselmo Gallego	Horseherd
	Miguel Gallego	Horseherd
	Manuel Alari	Present
	Antonio Reyes Vejil	Horseherd
	Ygnacio Alari	Horseherd
	Distinguished Don Manuel Miera	Present
	Manuel Gallegos	Horseherd
Flying Troops		
3rd Sgt.	Juan de Abrego	Present
1st Corporal	Juan de Dios Pena	Present
1st Corporal	Juan Antonio Alari	Horseherd
2nd Corporal	Antonio Romero	Ill
2nd Corporal	Tomas Ortiz	Present
Cadet	Don Jose Antonio Ortiz	Present
Soldiers	Distinguished Don Bernardo Miera	Present
	Jose Antonio Baca	Present

187

Ramon Esquivel	Present
Salvador Tenorio	Present
Andres Sandoval	Present
Tomas Lopes	Present
Jose Antonio Ortis	Horseherd
Joseph Antonio Sanches	Present
Pedro Antonio Romero	Present
Bartolo Martin	Present
Joseph Antonio Beytia	Horseherd
Vizente Garcia	Present
Jose Antonio Rael	Present
Jose Antonio Urioste	Present
Miguel Gutierres	Present
Jose Antonio Armijo	Horseherd
Diego Manuel Baca	Horseherd
Jose Antonio Gallego	Present
Francisco Torres	Horseherd
Jose Francisco Martin	Horseherd
Juan Benavides	Present
Jose Antonio Esquibel	Horseherd
Juan Joseph Trujillo	Horseherd
Bartolo Maese	Horseherd
Jose Alari	Present
Jose Antonio Garcia	Horseherd
Manuel Sanches Tagle	Horseherd
Luis Martin	Present
Antonio Gutierres	Horseherd
Manuel Romero	Present
Francisco Martin Torres	Present
Vicente Sandobal	Ill
Jose Vexil	Present
Matias Rivera	Present
Joseph Miguel Sena	Horseherd
Pablo Sena	Present
Jose Rivera	Present
Matias Sena	Present
Luis Lovato	Present
Manuel Martin	Present
Juan Antonio Anaya	Horseherd

Pedro Mestas		Present
Vizente Garcia Noriega		Present
Miguel Trujillo		Present
Jose Miguel Tenorio		Present
Jose Maria Caveza de Baca		Present
Juan Gallegos Baca		Present
Juan Tafoya		Ill
Jose Antonio Alari		Present
Francisco Matias Sandobal		Present
Alexandro Ortiz		Present
Jose Manuel Belarde		Present
Juan Chistobal Vejil		Horseherd

Summary

Governor	1
Lt./Captain	2
2nd. Lt.	2
Chaplain	1
Armorer	1
Drummer	0
Sgt.	3
Corporals	8
Cadets	2
Soldier &Cavalry	36
Soldiers Ill	6
Soldiers Present	57
Total	**119**

Rank:	Name:	Located at:
Retired	Joaquin Tenorio	Present
"	Antonio Ortega	Present
"	Jose Mares	Present
"	Salvador Duran	Present
"	Antonio Rivera	Present
"	Francisco Garcia	Present
"	Jose Antonio Griego	Present
"	Manuel Martin	Present
"	Juan Tafoya	Present
"	Bartolo Benavides	Present
"	Tomas Roibal	Present

In compliance with the muster roll, I the Captain, on the said day, month and year that certify.
Signed: Juan Baptista de Anza (rubric)

Santa Fe Military List for December 1, 1785
Cavalry
Muster roll executed by me the Lt. Coronel don Juan Baptista de Anza of the Royal Presidio of
Santa Fe, of this company that is guarding, and is my responsibility this day 1st of December
1785.

Rank:	Name:	Located at:
Governor & Captain	Don Juan Baptista de Anza	Present
Lt. in charge as Captain		Vacant
2nd Lt. in charge as Captain	Jose Maldonado	Present
2nd Lt.	Salvador Rivera	Present
2nd Lt	Antonio Guerrero	Road to Chihuahua
Chaplain	Fray Juan Bermejo	Present
Armorer	Roque Lovato	Present
1st. Sgt.	Juan Abrego	Present
2nd. Sgt.	Pablo Sandobal	Road to Chihuahua
3rd. Sgt.	Distinguished Cleto Miera	With horse herd
Drummer	Jose Prada	Road to Chihuahua
Corporals	Juan Luis Herrera	Present
	Juan de Dios Pena	Road to Chihuahua
	Juan Antonio Alary	Present
	Manuel Jesus Beitia	With horse herd
	Antonio sandobal	Road to Chihuahua
	Antonio Romero	Present
Cadet	Jose Lain	Present
	Jose Trebol	Present
Carbineers	Tomas Ortis	Present
	Distinguished Jose Ortis	Road to Chihuahua
	Diego Pena	With horse herd
	Jose Miguel Tafoya	Present
	Ventura Esquibel	Road to Chihuahua
	Ygnacio Madrid	Present
	Jose Pacheco	With horse herd
	Cayetano Sandobal	Road to Chihuahua
	Ysidro Rodrigues	With horse herd
	Jose rael Aguilar	Road to Chihuahua
	Ygnacio Duran	Road to Chihuahua

Juan Sandobal	Ill
Jose Miguel Griego	With horse herd
Antonio Madrid	Present
Geronimo Gonsales	Ill
Antonio Lopes	With horse herd
Manuel Sandobal	Road to Chihuahua
Diego Gallego	Road to Chihuahua
Jose Sandobal	Ill
Juan de Urioste	With horse herd
Salvador Vegil	With horse herd
Domingo Santistevan	Present
Manuel Mares	Ill
Manuel Saenz Garvizo	Ill
Joseph Francisco Maese	Present
Bartolo Fernandes	With horse herd
Alonso Rivera	Ill
Antonio Casaus	With horse herd
Vizente monguccho	Present
Bernardo Bustamante	Present
Gaspar Maldonado	Present
Baltasar Rivera	Road to Chihuahua
Antonio Roman Sanchez	With horse herd
Cristobal Faustin Vegil	Road to Chihuahua
Anselmo Gallego	Road to Chihuahua
Antonio Reyes Vegil	Road to Chihuahua
Manuel Alary	Ill
Miguel Gallego	Road to Chihuahua
Distinguished Manuel Miera	Ill
Manuel Gallego	With horse herd
Jose Antonio Baca	With horse herd
Manuel Baca	With horse herd
Ramon Esquibel	Present
Salvador Tenorio	With horse herd
Andres Sandobal	Road to Chihuahua
Tomas Lopes	With horse herd
Pedro Antonio Romero	Present
Bartolo Martin	With horse herd
Jose Miguel Gutierres	With horse herd
Jose Antonio Beytia	Road to Chihuahua

Vizente Garcia	Present
Jose Antonio Rael	Road to Chihuahua
Jose Antonio Uriose	Road to Chihuahua
Jose Antonio Armijo	Road to Chihuahua
Joseph Antonio Gallego	With horse herd
Francisco Torres	Road to Chihuahua
Jose Francisco Martin	Road to Chihuahua
Diego Manuel Baca	Road to Chihuahua
Juan Benabides	Ill
Antonio Esquibel	Road to Chihuahua
Juan Joseph Truxillo	Present
Bartolo Maese	Present
Jose Alary	Ill
Jose Antonio Garcia	With horse herd
Manuel sanches	Ill
Luis Martin	Ill
Antonio Gutierres	Present
Manuel Romero	Road to Chihuahua
Francisco Torres	Road to Chihuahua
Vicente Sandobal	Ill
Jose Vegil	With horse herd
Jose Miguel Sena	Road to Chihuahua
Pablo Sena	Road to Chihuahua
Joseph Rivera	Present
Matias Sena	Present
Luis Lobato	Ill
Manuel Martin	Present
Juan Antonio Anaya	with horse herd
Pedro Mestas	Ill
Juan Miguel Truxillo	With horse herd
Jose Miguel Tenorio	Road to Chihuahua
Jose Maria Caveza de Baca	with horse herd
Juan Tafoya	Present
Jose Antonio Alary	Present
Juan Gallego Baca	Present
Matias Sandobal	Present
Jose Manuel Belarde	Present
Alexandro Ortis	Present
Juan Christoval Vegil	Road to Chihuahua

Jose Antonio Pacheco	Present
Jose Antonio Romo	Road to Chihuahua
Antonio Jesus Ortis	Road to Chihuahua
Jose Miguel Maldonado	Present
Toribio Villapando	Present
Distinguished Vicente Ortis	Road to Chihuahua
Francisco Xavier Baca	Road to Chihuahua
Pedro Ortiz	Road to Chihuahua
Manuel Rivera	Present
Miguel Antonio Maese	Present
Antonio Jose Baca	Road to Chihuahua
Juan Christoval Baca	Present
Distinguished Carlos Ferrnandes	Present

Summary

Governor	1
Lt/Captain	1
2nd. Lt	2
Chaplain	1
Armorer	1
Sgt.	3
Drummer	1
Corporal	6
Cadets	2
Carbineers	6
Soldiers	26
Total:	**120**

Rank:	Name:	Located at:
Retired	Lt. Joaquin Lain	Present
"	Joaquin Tenorio	Present
"	Salvador Duran	Present
"	Jose Mares	Present
"	Antonio Ribera	Present
"	Martin Torres	Present
"	Juan Tafoya	Present
"	Bartolo Benabides	Present
"	Tomas Roybal	Present
"	Baltasar Gonsales	Present
"	Joaquin Trujillo	Present

Notes for upper: (New Mexico, NM)

Notes for lower: (NM) The soldier, retired, Antonio Ortega, died the 2nd of last month. In compliance with the muster roll, I the Captain, on the said day, month and year that certify. Signed: Juan Baptista de Anza (rubric)

Sources:
New Mexico Library, Archives and Records Center Building, 1205 Camino Carlos Rey, Santa Fe, NM 87507, SANMII, Rolls 9-19
Christmas, Henrietta M., Military Records, Colonial New Mexico, Published by Hispanic Genealogical Research Center, Albuquerque, New Mexico, 2004
Salamanca Archive: LEG, 7279, EXP, 2

Grey Stone Santa Fe Presidio

194

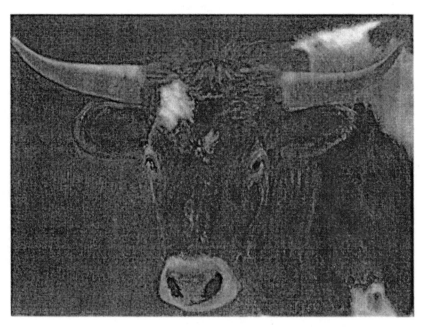

Criollo Cattle. Painting
With permission of New Mexico Mimbres Mountain Ranch owners Susie and Jon Eickhoff

Original Spanish cattle were introduced into the American Continent during the 1500 period by Spaniards. Texas had many cattle raised by Vaqueros (original cowboys). Governor Bernardo Galvez of Louisiana ordered that cattle and horses be sent to Louisiana from Texas for feeding the Spanish soldiers and *milicia*. Long distant cattle drives covered a four year period, during 1779-1783. Some soldiers who participated in the cattle drive remained and fought with Governor Bernardo Galvez. Defeated were the British forts in Baton Rouge, Nachez, Mobile, and Pensacola.

Chapter XI

Texas

San Antonio de Bexar

and La Bahia

Presidio's Records, 1776 –1783

La Bahia del Espiritu Santo Presidio partial archive copy for May 1, 1782

Two Texas Spanish Presidios (Forts) are discussed, although there was a detachment at garrison El Fuerte del Cibolo. The garrison El Fuerte del Cibolo was actually located on the San Bartolo Ranch, which was midway between the Presidios. Owners of the Ranch San Bartolo were Juana de Ollos and her sons.

Soldiers and people of this area of Texas have a colorful history regarding cattle aid and military assistance to the American Revolution. The cattle drives and other animals sent to feed the troops are included in the guidelines for membership to the Society of the Sons of the American

Revolution and the Society of the Daughters of the American Revolution. However, only being in the military is sufficient for membership for the Sons of the American Revolution.

The following format of soldier's names, rank, and source should be given credit to Jesse O. Villarreal, Sr., *Tejano Patriots of the American Revolution 1776-1783*. This author has copies of the soldiers list from the Archives at the Austin Library, University of Texas.

Name	Rank	Source	Station
A			
Abila or Avila, Juan Jose	Private	Bat Dec. 1, 1780	La Bahia
Abrego, Jose Ramon Flores	Private	Bat Jan. 2, 1782	Bexar
Acosta, Domingo Diego	Private	Bat Dec. 1, 1788	Bexar
Aguilar, Jose	Sgt.	Bat Aug. 6, 1778	La Bahia
Aldape, Damasio	Private	Bat Apr. 6, 1778	La Bahia
Aldape, Juan Nepomuccno	Private	Bat May 1, 1782	La Bahia
Alvarado or Albarado, Antonio	Private	Bat Nov. 1, 1778	La Bahia
Amangual, Don Francisco	2nd. Lt.	Bat Jan. 2, 1782	Bexar
Arocha, Jose de	Private	Bat Dec. 2, 1782	Bexar
Avila, Francisco Theodoro	Private	Bat Sept. 3, 1776	Bexar
B			
Baca, Antonio Rodriguez	Private	Bat Jan. 3, 1776	Bexar
Barron, Joseph Antonio	Private	Bat Nov. 2, 1778	Bexar
Baquera, Jose Antonio	Private	Bat Aug. 1, 1782	Bexar
Basquez, Antonio I	Private	Census Jan. 3,4,5, 1780	La Bahia
Basquez, Antonio II	Private	"	La Bahia
Basquez, Francisco Jabier	Private	Bat Dec. 1, 1780	La Bahia
Becerra, Jose Antonio	Private	Bat Nov. 2, 1782	Bexar
Bela, Jose Pantaleon	Private	Bat Dec. 1, 1780	La Bahia
Benites or Venites, Antonio	Private	Bat Dec. 1, 1780	La Bahia
Benites or Venites, Don Xavier	Lt.	Bat Jan. 1, 1782	La Bahia
Benites or Venites, Francisco	Private	Bat Dec. 1, 1780	La Bahia
Benites, Manuel Narisco	Private	Bat Dec. 1, 1780	La Bahia
Beran, Francisco Xabier	Private	Bat Aug. 1, 1782	Bexar
Berban, Manuel	Private	Bat Aug. 1, 1782	Bexar
Bezerra or Becerra, Pedro	Corporal	Bat Jan. 1, 1778	La Bahia
Bezerra or Becerra, Miguel	Private	Bat Jan. 1, 1778	La Bahia
Bocanegra, Francisco	Private	Bat Jan. 1, 1778	La Bahia
Borra, Francisco	Sgt.	Bat Dec. 1, 1780	La Bahia
Borrego, Marcelo	Private	Bat Jan. 2, 1782	Bexar
Bueno, Juan Francisco	Private	Bat Nov. 2, 1778	Bexar

Bueno, Juan Jose	Private	Bat Nov. 3, 1783	Bexar
Buentello, Francisco	Corporal	Bat Dec. 1, 1780	La Bahia
Buentello, Francisco Antonio	Private	Bat Sept. 4, 1778	La Bahia

C

Cabello, Don Domingo	Captain	Bat Dec. 2, 1782	Bexar
Cadena, Diego de los Santos	Private	Bat Aug. 1, 1782	La Bahia
Cadena, Juan	Private	Bat Aug. 1, 1782	Bexar
Cadena, Juan Jose	Private	Bat Aug. 1, 1782	Bexar
Calderon, Juan Jose	Drummer	Bat Nov. 3, 1783	Bexar
Camacho, Francisco`	1st Corporal	Bat Dec. 2, 1782	Bexar
Cano, Casimiro	Private	Bat Oct. 4, 1779	La Bahia
Cano, Juan Batista	Private	Bat Oct. 4, 1779	La Bahia
Cano, Marzelino	Private	Bat Dec 1, 1780	La Bahia
Carabajal, Joseph Francisco	Corporal	Bat Nov. 2, 1778	Bexar
Carabajal, Nicolas	Private	Bat Nov. 3, 1783	Bexar
Carmona, Diego	Private	Bat Nov. 3, 1783	Bexar
Carrion, Jose	Private	Bat Jan. 1, 1778	La Bahia
Casanova, Juan	Corporal	Bat Nov. 3, 1783	Bexar
Casanova, Juan Antonio	Private	Bat Nov. 3, 1783	Bexar
Casanova, Juan Feliciano	Corporal	Bat Dec. 2, 1782	Bexar
Castro, joseph Francisco de	Private	Bat Nov. 3, 1783	Bexar
Castro, Manuel de	Private	Bat Nov. 3, 1783	Bexar
Castro, Martin de	Carbineer	Bat Nov. 3, 1783	Bexar
Cazoria, Don Luis	Captain	Bat Dec. 1, 1780	La Bahia
Cepeda or Zepeda, Javier	Private	Bat Nov. 3, 1783	Bexar
Chirino or Chirinos, Diego	Private	Bat Nov. 1, 1782	La Bahia
Chirino, Jose	Private	Bat Dec. 1, 1782	La Bahia
Chirino, Juan	2nd Corporal	Bat May 1, 1782	La Bahia
Chirino, Pedro	Private	Bat Aug. 1, 1782	Bexar
Chirinos, Juan	Private	Bat Oct. 3, 1776	Bexar
Conejo, Jose Antonio	Private	Bat Nov. 1, 1778	La Bahia
Contreras, Jose	Private	Bat Dec. 1, 1780	La Bahia
Contreras, Juan Andres	Private	Bat Dec. 1, 1780	La Bahia
Cordoba, Juan Jose	Private	Bat Jan. 2, 1782	Bexar
Cordoba, Cristobal de	Lt.	Bat Jan. 3, 1792	Bexar
Cortes, Juan	Private	Bat Jan. 1, 1778	La Bahia
Courbiere, Andres	Private	Bat Dec. 2, 1782	Bexar
Coy, Francisco de los Santos	Private	Bat Nov. 2, 1778	Bexar

D

Delgado, Carlos	Private	Bat Nov. 1, 1782	La Bahia
Delgado, Santiago	Private	Bat Oct. 4, 1779	La Bahia
E			
Enrique, Diego	Private	Bat Feb. 28, 1781	Bexar
Enrique, Pedro José	Private	Bat Jan. 1, 1782	Bexar
F			
Farias, Joseph or Jose	Private	Bat Dec. 2, 1777	Bexar
Fernandez, Don Bernardo	2nd Lt.	Bat Nov. 2, 1778	Bexar
Fernandez, Don Eugenio	Lt.	Bat Dec. 1, 1780	La Bahia
Flores, Andres	Private	Bat Dec. 2, 1777	Bexar
Flores, Gerardo	Private	Bat Oct. 4, 1779	La Bahia
Flores, Jose	Private	Bat June 5, 1778	La Bahia
Flores, Juan	Private	Bat May 1, 1782	La Bahia
Flores, Joseph or Jose Antonio	2nd. Corp.	Bat Dec. 1, 1782	Bexar
Flores, Lorenzo	Private	Bat Dec. 2, 1777	Bexar
Flores, Manuel	Private	Bat Jan. 2, 1782	Bexar
Flores, Pedro	Private	Bat Jan. 2, 1782	Bexar
Flores, Ramon	Private	Bat Nov. 3, 1782	Bexar
Flores, Ygnacio	Private	Bat Jan. 2, 1782	Bexar
G			
Galan, Fernando	Private	Bat Jan. 1, 1778	La Bahia
Galan, Joaquin	Private	Bat Dec. 1, 1780	La Bahia
Galban, Jose Manuel	Private	Bat Aug. 1, 1782	Bexar
Gallardo, Antonio	Corporal	Bat Dec. 2, 1777	Bexar
Galvan or Galban, Manuel	Corporal	Bat Nov. 2, 1778	Bexar
Games, Jose Miguel	Private	Bat Jan. 2, 1782	Bexar
Gamez, Jose Mariano	Private	Bat Nov 3, 1783	Bexar
Gamez, Juan Jose	Private	Bat Dec. 1, 1780	La Bahia
Garcia, Ignacio	Private	Bat Oct. 4, 1779	La Bahia
Garza, Antonio de la	Private	Bat Oct. 4, 1779	La Bahia
Garza, Eugenio de la	Private	Bat Oct. 4, 1779	La Bahia
Garza, Eusebio de la	Private	Bat Jan. 2, 1782	Bexar
Garza, Francisco de la	Private	Bat Oct. 1, 1782	La Bahia
Garza, Jose Alexandro de la	Private	Bat Jan. 2, 1782	La Bahia
Garza, Jose Antonio de la	Private	Bat Jan. 2, 1782	La Bahia
Garza, Jose Bernardo de la	2nd. Corp.	Bat Jan. 1, 1778	La Bahia
Garza, Jose Manuel de la	Private	Bat Dec. 1, 1780	La Bahia
Garza, Juan Agustin de la	Private	Bat June 1, 1779	La Bahia

Garza, Mariano de la	Private	Bat Jan. 1, 1782	Bexar
Garza, Mathias de la	Private	Bat Jan. 2, 1782	Bexar
Garza, Pablo de la	Private	Bat Jan. 2, 1782	Bexar
Garza, Tomas de la	Private	Bat Jan. 1, 1778	Bexar
Gil, Jose	Private	Bat Dec. 1, 1780	La Bahia
Gil, Jose de Leyba	Private	Bat Jan. 2, 1782	Bexar
Gomes, Antonio	Private	Bat June 1, 1782	La Bahia
Gomes, Bernardino	Corporal	Bat April 3, 1779	La Bahia
Gomes or Gamez, Hermenegildo	Private	Bat Jan. 1, 1778	La Bahia
Gomes, Jose Antonio	Private	Bat Jan. 2 1782	Bexar
Gomez, Francico Sales	Private	Bat July 4, 1776	Bexar
Gomez, or Gamez, Ildefonso	Private	Bat Feb. 4, 1777	Bexar
Gomez, Jose Miguel	Private	Bat Jan. 3, 1777	Bexar
Gomez, Manuel Leal	Private	Bat May 2, 1776	Bexar
Gonzales, Jose	Private	Bat Jan. 1, 1778	Bexar
Gonzalez, Antonio	Private	Bat Jan. 3, 1777	Bexar
Gonzalez, Pedro	Private	Bat Jan. 3, 1777	Bexar
Granados, Francisco	Private	Bat Aug. 1, 1782	Bexar
Granados, Josef Manuel	Private	Bat Dec. 2, 1777	Bexar
Granados, Pedro	Sgt.	Bat Nov. 2, 1778	Bexar
Grande, Pedro Josef	Private	Bat June 1, 1779	La Bahia
Guerra, Miguel	Private	Bat Nov. 2, 1778	Bexar
Guerra, Xptobal or Cristobal	Private	Bat Jan. 2, 1782	Bexar
Guerra y Bela, Jose Pantalcon	Private	Bat Dec. 1, 1780	La Bahia
Guizar or Huizar, Juan	Private	Bat June 1, 1779	La Bahia
Gutierrez, Joseph Antonio	Private	Bat Nov. 2, 1778	Bexar
Gutiierrez, Miguel	Private	Bat Nov. 2, 1778	Bexar
Guzman, Eusebio	Private	Bat Nov. 2, 1778	Bexar

H

Hernandez, Bonifacio	Private	Bat Aug. 1, 1782	Bexar
Hernandez, Carlos	Private	Bat Aug. 1, 1782	Bexar
Hernandez, Cayetano	Private	Bat Feb. 28, 1781	Bexar
Hernandez, Francisco	Private	Bat Oct. 4, 1779	La Bahia
Hernandez, Jose Agustin	Private	Bat Jan. 2, 1782	Bexar
Hernandez, Joseph Maria	Private	Bat Oct. 1, 1777	Bexar
Hernandez, Pedro	Private	Bat Jan. 2, 1782	Bexar
Hidalgo, or Ydalgo, Alejandro	Private	Bat Oct. 3, 1777	Bexar
Hidalgo, or Ydalgo, Don Joseph	2nd Lt	Bat Oct. 3, 1777	Bexar
Higuera, Ambrosio	Private	Bat Oct. 4, 1779	La Bahia

J

Jimenez or Ximenez, Toribio	Private	Bat July 4, 1776	Bexar

L

Lara, Raphel	Private	Bat Sept. 1, 1782	La Bahia
Leal, Francisco	Private	Bat Jan. 2, 1782	Bexar
Leal, Vicente	Private	Bat Jan. 3, 1777	Bexar
Leme, Don Nicolas	Private	Bat Jan. 2, 1782	Bexar
Leon, Alexo de	Private	Bat Feb. 14, 1778	La Bahia
Leon, Juan Jose	Private	Bat May 1, 1782	La Bahia
Leon, Julian	Private	Bat Dec. 1, 1780	La Bahia
Liendro, Jose Dionisio	Private	Bat Dec. 1, 1780	La Bahia
Lopez or Lopes, Justo	Private	Bat Dec. 1, 1780	La Bahia
Losoya, Francisco	Private	Bat Dec. 2, 1777	Bexar
Losoya, Jose	Private	Bat Nov. 3, 1783	Bexar
Luna, Jose de	Private	Bat Nov. 3, 1783	Bexar
Luna, Pedro Antonio de	Private	Bat May 1, 1782	La Bahia
Luna, Tomas de	Private	Bat Jan. 2, 1782	Bexar

M

Macias, Thomas	Private	Bat May 1, 1782	La Bahia
Maldonado, Jose Hilario	2nd Corporal	Bat Dec. 1, 1780	La Bahia
Maldonado, Sebastian	Private	Bat May 1, 1782	La Bahia
Maldonado, Xavier	Private	Bat May 1, 1782	La Bahia
Mansolo, Facundo	Private	Bat Sept. 2, 1782	Bexar
Mansolo or Manzolo, Pedro	Private	Bat Sept. 2, 1782	Bexar
Manzolo, Jose	Private	Bat Sept. 2, 1782	Bexar
Martinez, Antonio	Private	Bat Jan. 2, 1782	Bexar
Martinez, Jacino	Private	Bat Nov. 1, 1782	La Bahia
Matinez, Juan Jose	Private	Bat Oct. 4, 1779	Bexar
Martinez, Manuel Leandro	Private	Bat Jan. 2, 1782	Bexar
Martinez, Miguel Antonio	Private	Bat Nov. 2, 1778	Bexar
Menchaca, Francisco Antonio	Private	Bat Aug. 1, 1782	Bexar
Menchaca, Jose Bruno	Private	Bat Aug. 1, 1782	Bexar
Menchaca, Don Joseph	1st Lt.	Bat Nov. 2, 1778	Bexar
Menchaca, Don Luis Antonio	Captain	Bat Nov. 3, 1783	Bexar
Mendez, Manuel	Private	Bat Jan. 1, 1778	La Bahia
Mescieres, Don Antonio	2nd Lt.	Bat Oct. 1, 1782	La Bahia
Minon, Pedro	Private	Bat Aug. 1, 1782	Bexar
Montalbo, Juan	Private	Bat Oct. 4, 1779	Bexar
Montalbo, Pedro	Private	Bat Aug. 1, 1782	Bexar

Monzon, Pedro de	Private	Bat Aug. 1, 1782	Bexar
Morin, Gil	Private	Bat Nov. 2, 1778	Bexar

O

Olibarri, Jose Maria	Private	Bat Aug. 1, 1782	Bexar
Oliva, Tomas Antonio	Private	Bat Nov. 2, 1778	Bexar
Orandain, Francisco	Armorer	Bat Sept. 2, 1782	Bexar
Orandain, Don Juachin	Lt.	Bat Nov. 2, 1776	Bexar
Ortiz, Pedro Antonio	Private	Bat Jan. 2, 1782	Bexar
Ortiz, or Ortis, Tomas	Private	Bat June 5, 1778	La Bahia

P

Padilla, Jose Francisco	Private	Bat Jan. 2, 1782	Bexar
Peres, Don Balthazar	2nd Lt.	Bat Nov. 3, 1783	Bexar
Peres, Jose Joaquin	Private	Bat Jan. 2, 1782	Bexar
Peres or Perez, Jose Polinario	Private	Bat Dec. 1, 1780	La Bahia
Peres, Ygnacio	Private	Bat Jan 2, 1782	Bexar
Perez or Peres, Domingo	2nd Sgt.	Bat Jan. 2, 1782	Bexar
Perez, Juan	Private	Bat Nov. 3, 1777	Bexar
Perez or Peres, Pedro	1st Corporal	Bat Aug. 1, 1782	Bexar
Prada, Don Policarpo	1st Lt.	Bat Nov. 1, 1782	La Bahia

R

Ramon, Antonio	Private	Bat Dec. 1, 1780	La Bahia
Ramon, Felix	Private	Bat July 1, 1776	Bexar
Ramon, Francisco	1st Corporal	Bat May 1, 1782	La Bahia
Ramon, Don Jose Felix	Chaplain	Bat Jan. 1, 1778	La Bahia
Ramon, Jose Leonardo	Private	Bat May 1, 1782	La Bahia
Ramon, Jose Maria	Private	Bat May 1, 1782	La Bahia
Ramon, Manuel	Private	Bat July 1, 1776	Bexar
Rangel, Joseph Guadalupe	Private	Bat Nov. 2, 1778	Bexar
Rangel, Thomas Antonio	Private	Bat Feb. 3, 1774	Bexar
Ribas or Rivas, Jose Andres	Drummer	Bat Sept. 1, 1779	La Bahia
Rico, Bentura	Private	Bat Dec. 1, 1782	Bexar
Rio, Andres del	Private	Bat Oct. 1, 1782	La Bahia
Rio Antonio del	Private	Bat Oct. 1, 1782	La Bahia
Rio Bernabe del	1st Corporal	Bat Oct. 1, 1782	La Bahia
Rio, Pablo	Private	Bat Jan. 2, 1782	Bexar
Rios, Anacleto	2nd Corporal	Bat May 1, 1782	La Bahia
Rios, Francisco	1st Corporal	Bat May 1, 1782	La Bahia
Pippenda, Juan Mario, Baron	Captain	Bat Dec. 2, 1777	Bexar
Rodriguez, Josef Maria	Private	Bat Dec. 2, 1777	Bexar

Rodriguez, Juan	Private	Bat Jan. 3, 1777	Bexar
Rodriguez, Mariano	3rd Sgt.	Bat Nov. 2, 1782	Bexar
Rodriguez, Patricio	Private	Bat Feb. 4, 1777	Bexar
Rodriguez, Prudencio	1st Corporal	Bat Oct. 1, 1782	Bexar
Rosales, Bartholome	Private	Bat Jan. 2, 1782	Bexar
Rosas, Joseph Sosa de	Private	Bat oct. 3, 1777	Bexar

S

Sais, Jose Xavier	Private	Bat Oct. 4, 1779	La Bahia
Salas, Esteban	Private	Bat June 1, 1779	La Bahia
Salas, Francisco	Private	Bat Dec. 1, 1780	La Bahia
Salinas, Manuel	Private	Bat Dec. 2, 1782	Bexar
Salinas, Pedro Javier	Private	Bat Nov. 2, 1778	Bexar
Sanchez, Francisco	Private	Bat Nov. 2, 1782	Bexar
Sanchez, Juan Joseph	2nd Corporal	Bat Jan. 2, 1782	Bexar
San Miguel, Prudencio de	Private	Bat Nov. 1, 1782	La Bahia
Santoja, Don Jose	Lt.	Bat Nov. 1, 1782	La Bahia
Santos, Cayetano de los	Private	Bat Oct. 4, 1779	La Bahia
Santos, Francisco de los	2nd Corporal	Bat Nov. 2, 1782	Bexar
Santos, Pedro de los	Private	Bat June 1, 1779	La Bahia
Sausedo, Joseph Antonio	Private	Bat Nov. 2, 1778	Bexar
Sena, or Zerna, Vicente	Private	Bat Dec. 1, 1780	La Bahia
Solis, Joseph Vicente	Private	Bat Dec. 2, 1777	Bexar
Sosa, Andres de	Corporal	Bat Dec. 2, 1777	Bexar
Sosa, Francisco Javier de	2nd Corporal	Bat Nov. 2, 1782	Bexar
Sosa, Jose Leandro	Private	Bat Nov. 3, 1783	Bexar
Sosa, Juan Joseph	Private	Bat Nov. 2, 1778	Bexar

T

Texeda or Tegeda, Mariano	Private	Bat Dec. 3, 1778	La Bahia
Texeda, Pedro Jose	Private	Bat May 1, 1782	La Bahia
Thorres, Joseph Bernardo	Private	Bat Feb. 3, 1774	Bexar
Torres, Juan Remigio	Private	Bat Nov. 2, 1778	Bexar
Torres, Lazaro de	Private	Bat Jan. 2, 1782	Bexar
Trebino or Trevino, Marciano	Private	Bat Dec. 1, 1780	La Bahia
Trevino, Antonio	2nd Sgt.	Bat Nov. 1, 1782	La Bahia
Trevino, Pedro	Private	Bat Nov. 1, 1782	La Bahia

U

Urrutia, Francisco Antonio	Private	Bat Aug. 4, 1777	Bexar
Urrutia or Vrrutia, Juan	Private	Bat Aug. 4, 1777	Bexar

Urrutia, Juan Antonio	Private	Bat Aug. 4, 1777	Bexar
Urrutia or Vrrutia, Manuel	Sgt.	Bat Aug. 4, 1777	Bexar
V			
Valdes, Don Marcelo	2nd Lt.	Bat Jan. 2, 1782	Bexar
Valle, Andres del	1st Corporal	Bat Jan.2, 1782	Bexar
Valle, Joseph del	Private	Bat Nov. 2, 1778	Bexar
Vargas, Jose Maria	Private	Bat Jan. 2, 1782	Bexar
Vasquez or Basquez, Antonio	Private	Bat Sept. 1, 1779	La Bahia
Villafranca, Jose Francisco de	Private	Bat Dec. 2, 1782	Bexar
Villafranca, Manuel	Private	Bat Nov. 2, 1778	Bexar
Villarreal, Manuel	Private	Bat Dec. 2, 1777	Bexar
X			
Ximenes, Jose Timoteo	Private	Bat Dec. 1, 1780	La Bahia
Y			
Yguera, Ambrocio	Private	Bat Census Jan. 3-5, 1780	La Bahia
Z			
Zeballos or Ceballos, Pedro	Private	Bat Jan. 1, 1778	La Bahia
Zepeda, Jose Cayetano	Armorer	Bat Sept 1, 1778	La Bahia
Zepeda or Sepeda, Xavier	Private	Bat Aug. 1, 1782	Bexar
Zerda, Francisco Sales de la	Private	Bat Nov. 2, 1778	Bexar
Zerda, Juan Maria de la	Private	Bat Nov. 2, 1778	Bexar
Zevallos, Nepomuseno	Private	Bat Feb. 3, 1774	Bexar

Presidio of San Antonio de Bexar (Texas) July 4, 1776

Cavalry Company of the Royal Presidio of San Antonio de Bexar Military roster of the above-mentioned Company in which the names of officers and enlisted men are included according to Article 1, Title 9, of the Real Reglamento issued by His Majesty for the settlement of new presidios.

Baron de Ripperda, Governor and Commandant of this Province of Texas
P (resent)   as Captain of this company...Lieutenant (Lt.) Don Joseph Menchaca...in Fort Cibolo
P...   Idem (same), Don Bernardo Fernandez
P...   2nd Lt. Don Joseph Hidalgo
               Sergeants
               Pedro Granados.....................................in the cav (b) allada (protecting the horses)
               Manuel Urrutia...Pursuing Indians
               Corporals

205

	Antonio Gallardo...............................	in Fort Cobolo
	Domingo Perez..................................	in the caballada
	Manuel Galvan.................................	in idem
P...	Julian Arocha	
	Andres de Sosa................................	pursuing Indians
P...	Prudencio Rodriguez	
Soldiers		
	Joseph de la Garza...in Fort Cibolo	
	Jose Miguel Gomez............................	in Fort Cibolo
P...	Andres Flores	
	Joseph Maria Rodriguez......................	in Fort Cibolo
P...	Manuel Villafranca	
	Gil Morin..	in the Cavallada
P...	Domingo Diego Acosta	
	Ildefonso Gomez...............................	in Fort Cibolo
	Francisco Camacho............................	in fort Cibolo
P...	Juan Remigio de Torres	
	Martin de Castro...............................	pursuing Indians
P...	Joseph Francisco Carabajal	
	Lorenzo Flores.................................	in the caballada
	Antonio Gonzalez..............................	pursuing Indians
	Mariano Rodriguez............................	in Fort Cibolo
	Joseph Antonio Flores........................	in Fort Cibolo
	Francisco Salas Gomez.......................	pursuing Indians
	Pedro Gonzalez.................................	in fort Cibolo
	Andres del Valle...............................	in Fort Cibolo
	Alejandro Hidalgo.............................	in the caballada
	Pedro Perez.....................................	in the cavallada
	Joseph Sosa de Rosas.........................	in fort Cibolo
	Juan Maria de la Zerda.......................	in the cavallada
	Facundo Mansolo..............................	in Fort Cibolo
	Eusebio Guzman...............................	in Fort Cibolo
	Juan Perez......................................	in San Luis Potosi
	Francisco Theodoro de Avila................	in Fort Cibolo
	Francisco Javier de Sosa.....................	pursuing Indians
P...	Joseph del Valle	
	Juan Joseph Sanchez..........................	in the cavallada
	Joseph Vicente Solis..........................	in San Luis Potosi
P...	Joseph Maria Hernandez	

	Juan Francisco Bueno	in Fort Cibolo
	Antonio Rodriguez Baca	pursuing Indians
	Francisco de los Santos Coy	in Idem
	Joseph Antonio Gutierrez	in the caballada
P...	Juan Urrutia	
	Javier Zepeda	pursuing Indians
	Pedro Javier Salinas	in Fort Cibolo
	Nicolas Carabajal	pursuing Indians
	Juan Casanova	in the cavallada
	Juan Joseph de Sosa	in San Luis Potosi
	Fernando Arocha	in the caballada
P...	Felix Ramon	
P...	Manuel Villarreal	
P...	Miguel Guerra	in the caballada
	Francisco Sanchez	in the caballada
	Carlos Hernandez	in Idem
	Juan Rodriguez	in Fort Cibolo
	Joseph Antonio Barron	in San Luis Potosi
	Juan Chirinos	in the caballada
P...	Toribio Jimenez	
	Thomas Antonio Oliva	in Fort Cibolo
	Miguel Martinez	in cavallada
	Joseph Guadalupe Rangel	in the caballada
P...	Juan Francisco Arocha	
	Francisco Antonio Urrutia	pursuing Indians
P...	Francisco Orandain	
	Pedro Mansolo	in Fort Cibolo
	Miguel Gutierrez	in Fort Cibolo
	Joseph Antonio Sausedo	in the caballada
	Vicente Leal	in the caballada
	Juan Antonio Urrutia	pursuing Indians
	Joseph Francsco de Castro	in the cavallada
	Joseph Farias	pursuing Indians
	Manuel Ramon	in idem
	Francisco Losoya	in the cavallada
	Francisco Sales de la Zerda	in the cavallada
	Patricio Rodriguez	in Idem

P...   Pedro Minon (invalid)

Company of San Antonio de Bexar, July 4, 1777

El Baron de Ripperda, Governor and Commander of Province of Texas.

Present As Captain of this company...

      Lieutenant Don Josef Menchaca...   detached

Present Idem, Don Bernardo Fernandeaz

Alferez Don Josef Hidalgo...	In Fort Cibolo
Sergeant Pedro Granados..	.in the caballada (Horse Herd)
Corporals	

Present   Manuel Vrrutia (Urrutia)

Antonio Gallardo.........	in idem
Domingo Perez............................	detached
Manuel Galvan............................	in the caballada
Julian Arocha..............................	in Fort Cibolo
Andres de Sosa..........................	.in the caballada

Present   Prudencio Rodriguez

      Soldiers

Josef de la Garza........................	in idem
Josef Miguel Gamez.................	detached
Andres Flores..............................	in Fort Cibolo
Josef Maria Rodriguez................	detached
Manuel Villafranca......................	in Fort Cibolo
Gil Morin....................................	in idem
Domingo Diego Acosta.................	in the caballada
Francisco Camacho......................	detached
Juan Remigio de Torres................	in the caballada
Martin de Castro.........................	detached
Jose Francisco Carabajal..............	in the caballada
Lorenzo Flores.............................	detached
Antonio Gonzalez.........................	in idem
(Illegible) Mariano Rodriguez...........in the caballada
Josef Antonio Flores.....................	detached
Francisco Sales Gamez..................	in the caballada

Present Pedro Gonzalez

Andres del Valle...........................	detached
Alexandro Hidalgo.........................	in the caballada

Present Pedro Perez

	Jose Sosa de Rosas..........................	in idem
Present	Juan Maria de la Zerda	
	Facundo Mansolo...........................	in idem
	Eusevio Guzman.............................	in Fort Cibolo
	Present Juan Perez	
	Francisco Theodoro de Avila...........	in the caballada
	Francisco Javier de Sosa...................	in idem
	Josef del Valle...............................	in La Bahia
Present	Juan Jose Sanchez...	
	Jose Bizente (Vicente) Solis.............	detached
	Jose Maria Hernandez.....................	in idem
	Juan Francisco Bueno.....................	in idem
	Antonio Rodriguez Baca.................	in idem
	Francisco de los Santos Coy.............	in Fort Cibolo
	Jose Antonio Gutierrez...................	in the caballada
	Juan Vrrutia (Urrutia).....................	in idem
	Javier Zepeda (Cepeda)...................	detached
	Pedro Javier Salinas.......................	in idem
Present	Nicolas Carabajal	
Present	Juan Casanova	
	Juan Jose de Sosa...........................	detached
	Fernando Arocha...........................	in idem
	Feliz (Felix) Ramon.........................	in the caballada
	Manuel Villarreal...........................	in idem
	Miguel Guerra...............................	detached
	Francisco Sanchez.........................	in idem
	Carlos Hernandez..........................	in La Bahia
	(Illegible) Jose Antonio Barron.........	in the caballada
	Juan Chirinos.................................	in idem
	Torivio Ximenez (Toribio Jimenez).	in Fort Cibolo
	Tomas Antonio Oliva.....................	detached
	Miguel Martinez...........................	in idem
Present	Jose Guadalupe Ranjel...	
	Juan Francisco Arocha....................	in idem
Present	Francisco Antonio Vrrutia (Urrutia).	in idem
Present	Francisco Orendain...	
	Pedro Mansolo...............................	in the Caballada
	Miguel Gutierrez............................	in idem
Present	Jose Antonio Saucedo...	

	Juan Antonio Vrrutia (Urrutia).........in La Bahia	
Present	Jose Francisco de Castro...	
	Jose Farias.......................................detached	
	Manuel Ramon.................................in idem	
Present	Francisco Sales de la Zerda (Cerda)...in the caballada	
	Patricio Rodriguez............................detached	
	Jose Romano Rodriguez....................in Fort Cibolo	
	Juan Antonio Casanova....................detached	
	Juan Jose Bueno...............................in idem	
Present	Pedro Minon (disable)	

San Antonio de Bexar
4 July 1777

El Baron de Ripperda

Royal Presidio of San Antonio de Bexar, January 2, 1782

Captain (Colonel Don Domingo Cabello, governor and commander
of arms of the said province, as captain of this company)   Present

1st lieutenant	Don Jose Menchaca	detached in the province of Coahuila
2nd lieutenant	Don Bernardo Fernandez	Present
1st alferes	Don Marcelo Valdes	Sick
2nd alferes	Don Francisco Amangual	Sick
Chaplain		Vacant

Persons de cuera (Leather Jacket soldier)

1st sergeant	Manuel de Vrrutia	detached duty at the fort of El Cibolo
2nd sergeant	Domingo Peres	Present
1st corporal	Pedro Peres	Present
1st corporal	Andres de Valle	detached in Coahuila for the estanco
2nd corporal	Jose Antonio Flores	detached at fort of El Cibolo
2nd corporal	Francisco Xauier de Sosa	detached with the horse herd
Privates		

Cadet	Don Nicolas Leme	Present
	Domingo Diego Acosta	detached with the horse herd
	Juan Remigio de Torres	detached with the horse herd
	Martin de Castro	detached at fort of El Cibolo
	Antonio Gonzales	detached at fort of El Cibolo
	Francisco de Sales Games	Sick
	Alexando Ydalgo	detached with the mail
	Juan Maria de la Cerda	detached at fort of El Cibolo
	Facundo Manzolo	Present
	Antonio Baca	detached in Coahuila for the estanc(i)o
	Xauier Zepeda	detached with the mail
	Juan Casanoba	detached in Coahuila for the estanco
	Fernando de Arocha	detached with the horse herd
	Carlos Hernandes	Sick
	Francisco Sanchez	detached at the fort of El Cibolo
	Juan Chirino	sick at Presidio San Juan Bautista Rio Grande
	Francisco Antonio Vrrutia	detached at fort of El Cibolo
	Pedro Manzolo	detached in Coahuila for the estanco
	Juan Antonio de Vrrutia	detached with the horse herd
	Francisco de Castro	detached with the horse herd
	Jose Farias	detached with the horse herd
	Manuel Ramon	detached with the horse herd
	Francisco Losoya	detached with the horse herd
	Francisco Sales de la Cerda	detached at the fort of El Cibolo
	Patricio Rodriguez	detached with the horse herd
	Juan Antonio Casanoba	detached with the horse herd
	Juan Jose Bueno	Present
	Jose Manuel Granados	detached with the mail
	Antonio Martinez	detached with the horse herd
	Cristobal Guerra	detached with the mail
	Manuel Salinas	detached with the horse herd
	Manuel de Castro	detached with the horse herd
	Manuel Leandro Martinez	detached at fort of El Cibolo
	Jazinto Ramon	detached with the mail
Armorer	Francisco Orendain	Present

Tropa Ligera

3rd sergeant	Mariano Rodriguez	detached with the horse herd
Drummer	Juan Jose Calderon	Present

211

1st corporal	Francisco Camacho	Present
1st corporal	Prudencio Rodriguez	Present
2nd corporal	Juan Jose Sanchez	detached with the mail
2nd corporal	Francisco de los Santos	detached with the horse herd

Privates

Lorenzo Flores	Sick
Pedro Flores	detached with the horse herd
Manuel Flores	Present
Pablo de la Garza	detached with the horse herd
Jose Agustin Hernandes	detached with the horse herd
Jose Gil de Leyba	detached with the horse herd
Pedro Hernandez	detached with the horse herd
Bizente Gonzales	detached at fort of El Cibolo
Mathias de la Garza	detached at fort of El Cibolo
Bonifacio Hernandes	detached with the hors herd
Eusebio de la Garza	detached at fort of El Cibolo
Lazaro de Torres	detached with the horse herd
Mariano de la Garza	Sick
Jose Maria Vraga	detached with the horse herd
Jose Joaquin Peres	Present
Juan Jose Cordoba	detached with the horse herd
Francisco Antonio Leal	detached with the horse herd
Jose Bruno Menchaca	detached at the fort of El Cibolo
Jose Antonio Baquera	Sick
Jose Miguel Sanchez	Sick
Jose Antonio Gomes	detached at the fort of El Cibolo
Jose Maria Olibarri	detached with the horse herd
Jose Francisco Padilla	Present
Jose Manzolo	detached with the horse herd
Juan Cadena	Sick
Pedro Antonio Ortiz	Sick
Ygnacio Flores	detached at the fort of El Cibolo
Ygnacio Peres	Present
Tomas de Luna	detached with the horse herd
Jose Flores	Present
Jose Antonio de la Garza	detached at the fort of El Cibolo
Pablo del Rio	detached at the fort of El Cibolo
Pedro Jose Enrique	detached at the fort of El Cibolo

	Juan Jose Cadena	detached at the fort of El Cibolo
	Jose de la Garza	detached with the horse herd
	Manuel Berban	Present
	Bentura Rico	detached with the horse herd
	Diego Carmona	Present
	Pedro Montalbo	detached with the horse herd
	Jose Alexandro de la Garza	detached with the horse herd
	Pedro Chirino	detached with the mail
	Jose de Sosa de Rosas	Present
	Francisco Xauier Peres	detached at the fort of El Cibolo
	Marcelo Borrego	detached at the fort of El Cibolo
	Jose Francisco de Villafranca	Present
	José de Arocha	Present
	Jose Ramon Flores de Abrego	detached at the fort of El Cibolo
	Andres Courbiere	Present

Ymbalidos (disabled)

Alferes	Don Juan Jose Ydalgo	Present
Sergeant	Pedro Granados	Present
Private	Pedro Minon	Present
Private	Bartholome Rosales	Present
Private	Manuel Villarreal	Present
Private	Jose Miguel Games	Present

Royal Presidio of San Antonio de Bexar, January 2, 1782
Signed: Domingo Cabello

Royal Presidio of San Antonio de Bexar, November 3, 1783

Captain (Colonel Don Domingo Cabello, governor and commander
of arms of the said province, as captain of this company)   Present

1st lieutenant	Don Jose Menchaca	detached in the province of Coahuila
2nd lieutenant	Don Bernardo Fernandez	in San Luis (Potosi) for the allowance
1st Alferes	Don Marcelo Valdes	Present
2nd Alferes	Don Francisco Amangual	Present

213

Chaplain		Vacant

Troops

Sergeant	Manuel de Vrrutia	P (resent)
Sergeant	Domingo Peres	D(etached) escorting the paymaster
Sergeant	Mariano Rodriguez	Detached with the horse herd
Drummer	Juan Jose Calderon	Present
Corporal	Pedro Peres	Present
Corporal	Andres del Valle	Detached in San Luis with the paymaster
Corporal	Prudencio Rodriguez	Present
Corporal	Francisco Xauier de Sosa	Detached with the horse herd
Corporal	Francisco de los Santos	E (nfermo) Sick
Corporal	Juan Casanoba	Detached with the horse herd
Carabineer	Domingo Diego Acosta	Detached with the horse herd
Carabineer	Juan Remigio de Torres	Present
Carabineer	Martin de Castro	Detached at San Luis with the paymaster
Carabineer	Antonio Gonzales	Present
Carabineer	Francisco de Sales Games	Detached with the horse herd
Carabineer	Alexandro Ydalgo	Detached with the horse herd
Cadet	Don Nicolas Leme	Present
Private	Juan Maria de la Cerda	Detached with the horse herd
Private	Facundo Manzolo	Detached in San Luis with the paymaster
Private	Antonio Baca	Detached with the horse herd
Private	Xabier Zepeda	Present
Private	Fernando Arocha	Detached escorting the paymaster
Private	Carlos Hernandes	Present
Private	Juan Chirino	Detached with the horse herd
Private	Pedro Manzolo	Present
Private	Juan Antonio Vrrutia	Detached with the horse herd
Private	Francisco de Castro	Detached with the horse herd
Private	Jose Farias	Detached at San Luis with the paymaster
Private	Manuel Ramon	Detached escorting the paymaster
Private	Francisco Losoya	Detached with the horse herd
Private	Francisco Sales de la Cerda	Enfermo Sick
Private	Patricio Rodriguez	Detached with the horse herd
Private	Juan Antonio Casanoba	Detached with the horse herd
Private	Juan Jose Bueno	Detached in San Luis with the paymaster
Private	Jose Manuel Granados	Detached in San Luis with the paymaster
Private	Antonio Martinez	Detached with the horse herd

Private	Manuel Salinas	Detached with the horse herd
Private	Manuel de Castro	Detached escorting the paymaster
Private	Jazinto Ramon	Enfermo	Sick
Private	Pedro Flores	Detached escorting the paymaster
Private	Manuel Flores	Enfermo	Sick
Private	Jose Gil de Leyba	Detached with the horse herd
Private	Pedro Hernandez	Detached escorting the paymaster
Private	Matias de la Garza	Detached with the horse herd
Private	Bonifacio Hernandez	Detached escorting the paymaster
Private	Eusebio de la Garza	Present
Private	Lazaro de Torres	Detached with the horse herd
Private	Mariano de la Garza	Detached with the horse herd
Private	Jose Joaquin Peres	Detached with the horse herd
Private	Juan Jose Cordoba	Detached escorting the paymaster
Private	Francisco Antonio Leal	Present
Private	Bruno Menchaca	Enfermo	Sick
Private	Jose Antonio Baquera	Detached with the horse herd
Private	Jose Miguel Sanchez	Detached with the horse herd
Private	Jose Maria Olibarri	Present
Private	Jose Manzolo	Detached with the horse herd
Private	Juan Cadena	Detached with the horse herd
Private	Ygnacio Flores	Present
Private	Ygnacio Perez	Detached escorting the paymaster
Private	Thomas de Luna	Present
Private	Jose Flores	Enfermo	Sick
Private	Jose Antonio de la Garza	Detached with the horse herd
Private	Pablo de el Rio	Detached with the horse herd
Private	Pedro Jose Enrique	Present
Private	Juan Jose Cadena	Enfermo	Sick
Private	Manuel Berban	Present
Private	Diego Carmona	Enfermo	Sick
Private	Pedro Montalbo	Detached with the horse herd
Private	Alexandro de la Garza	Detached with the horse herd
Private	Pedro Chirino	Present
Private	Jose de Sosa de Rosas	Detached with the horse herd
Private	Francisco Xabier Peres	Present
Private	Marcelo Borrego	Detached escorting the paymaster
Private	Jose de Arocha	Detached with the horse herd
Private	Ramon Flores	Detached with the horse herd

Private	Don Andres Courbiere	Present
Private	Nicolas Carabajal	Present
Private	Francisco Granados	Detached with the horse herd
Private	Francisco Menchaca	detached escorting the paymaster
Private	Francisco Berban	Enfermo Sick
Private	Jose Manuel Galban	Detached escorting the paymaster
Private	Juan Gabino Delgado	Present
Private	Jose Maria Hernandez	Detached escorting the paymaster
Private	Jose de Luna	Detached with the horse herd
Private	Jose Mariano Gamez	Present
Private	Jose Leandro de Sosa	Present
Private	Jose Losoya	Present
Armorer	Francisco Orendain	Present

Ymbalidos (Disabled or retired)

Captain	Don Luis Antonio Menchaca	Present
Alferes	Don Juan Jose Ydalgo	Present
Alferes	Don Balthazar Peres	Present
Sergeant	Pedro Granados	Present
Private	Pedro Minon	Present
Private	Bartholome Rosales	Present
Private	Jose Miguel Gamez	Present
Private	Lorenzo Flores	Present

San Antonio de Bexar, November 3, 1783

18th Century Spanish Musket

216

Criollo Cattle. Painting.
(Criollo means non-mixed descendants of early cattle from Spain)
Courtesy of Mimbres Ranch owners

Presidio La Bahia del Espiritu Santo - January 1, 1778

Captain	Don Luis Cazorla	Present
Lieutenant	Don Xavier Benites	Present
Alferez	Don Jose Santoja	Present
Sergeant	Jose Aguilar	Present
Corporal	Bernardo Gomes	Present
Corporal	Pedro Bezerra	Present

Soldiers

Jose Contreras	Present
Gerardo Flores	Present
Juan Guisar	Present: Detached to the horse herd
Jose Flores	Present: Detached to the horse herd
Anacieto Rios	Present
Ambrosio Higuera	Present
Hilario Maldonado	Present
Francisco Hernandez	Present
Eugenio de la Garza	Detached in the horse herd
Jose Carrion	Present
Antonio de la Garza	Present

217

Antonio Alvarado	Present: In the guard of the Mission
Juan Montalvo	Present
Juan Jose Martines	Present: Detached to the horse herd
Alexo de Leon	Present: In the guard of the Mission
Casimiro Cano	Present
Estevan Salas	Present
Juan Bautista Cano	Present
Andres del Rio	Present
Francisco Ramon	Present
Hermenegildo Gomes	Detached in the horse herd
Jose Gonzales	Detached in the horse herd
Ignacio Garcia	Present
Santiago Delgado	Present: in guard of the Mission
Francisco Vasques	Present
Tomas de la Garza	Present: Detached with the horse herd
Tomas Ortiz	Present
Francisco Bocanegra	Present
Pedro Zevallos	Present
Bernabe del Rio	Present
Juan Chirino	Present
Juan Cortes	Detached in the horse herd
Miguel Becerra	Present
Mariano Texeda	Present
Damacio Aldape	Present: Detached with the horse herd
Manuel Mendez	Present
Jose Bernardo de la Garza	Present: Detached with the horse herd
Fernando Galan	Detached in the horse herd
Jose Xavier Sais	Detached in the horse herd
Francisco Rios	Detached in the horse herd
Antonio Vazquez	Detached in the horse herd
Xavier Maldonado	Present
Antonio Trevino	Present

Chaplain (Bachiller) Don Jose Felix Ramos Present: (note Bachelor education level)

Presidio La Bahia del Espiritu Santo, January 1, 1778

Signed: Luis Cazorla

218

Cavalry Company of the Royal Presidio of La Bahia del Espiritu Santo, January 5, 1779

Captain	Don Luis Cazorla	Absent: Commissioned during the Inspection
Lieutenant	Don Jose Menchaca	Present: Provisional Commandant
Lieutenant	Don Xavier Benites	Present
Alferez	Don Jose santoja	Present
Sergeant	Jose Aguilar	Present
Corporal	Bernardo Gomes	Absent: In San Antonio de Bexar to be cured
Corporal	Francisco Basques	Present

Soldiers

Jose Contreras	Present
Gerardo Flores	Present
Juan Huisar	Present
Jose Flores	Present
Anacleto Rios	Present
Ambrosio Iguera	Conditionally present: Detached in the cavallada (horse herd)
Hilario Maldonado	Detached in the horse herd
Francisco Hernandez	Present
Eugenio de la Garza	Present
Francisco Zales	Detached in the horse herd
Antonio de la Garza	Absent: with the Captain (Inspection)
Cayetano de los Santos	Absent: In Rio Grande on furlough
Antonio Alvarado	Present
Juan Montalvo	Conditionally present: In the safeguard of the Mission
Juan Jose Martines	Present
Alexo de Leon	Present
Casimiro Cano	Detached in the horse herd
Estevan Salas	Present
Juan Bautista Cano	Present
Andres del Rio	Present
Francisco Ramon	Present
Hermenegildo Gomes	Detached in the horse herd
Jose Gonzales	Detached in the horse herd
Ignacio Garcia	In the safeguard of the Mission
Santiago Delgado	Detached in the horse herd
Tomas de la Garza	Present
Tomas Ortiz	Detached in the horse herd
Pedro Zevallos	Present

Bernave del Rio	Present
Juan Chirino	In the safeguard of the mission
Juan Cortes	Detached in the horse herd
Miguel Becerra	Absent: with the Captain
Mariano Texeda	Detached in the horse herd
Damacio Aldape	Present
Manuel Mendez	Present
Bernardo de la Garza	Present
Fernando Galan	Detached in the horse herd
Jose Xavier Sois (Solis)	Detached in the horse herd
Francisco Rios	Detached in the horse herd
Antonio Bazquez	Present
Xavier Maldonado	Detached in the horse herd
Antonio Trevino	Present
Jose Cayetano Zepeda	Present
Francisco Antonio Buentello	Present
Pedro de los Santos	Present

Chaplain (Fraile) Don Jose Felix Ramos	Present

Royal Presidio of La Bahia del Espiritu Santo, 5 January 1779

Signed: Josef Menchaca

Cavalry Company of the Royal Presidio of La Bahia, De Espiritu Santo December 1, 1779

Captain	Don Luis Cazorla	On inspection tour
Lieutenant	Son Josef Santoja	Present
1st Alferez	Don Josef Aguilar	Present
2nd Alferez Tropa Liguera	Don Policarpo Prada	Present
Chaplain	Don Josef Feliz Ramos	Present
1st Sergeant	Josef Francisco Basquez	Present
2nd Sergeant Tropa Liguera	Francisco Borra	Present
Drummer	Josef Andres de Ribas	Present
1st Corporal	Antonio Trebino	Present
2nd Corporal	Francisco Rios	Present
Private	Josef Contreras	Present: On detached duty

Private	Gerardo Flores	Present: with the horse herd
Private	Juan Guisar	Present
Private	Josef Flores	Present: with the horse herd
Private	Anacleto Rios	Present: with the horse herd
Private	Ambrosio Higuera	Present: with his captain (Cazorla)
Private	Ylario Maldonado	Present
Private	Francisco Hernandez	Present: with the horse herd
Private	Eugenio de la Garza	Present: Ill
Private	Francisco Salas	Present
Private	Antonio de la Garza	Present
Private	Cayetano de los Santos	Ill, in San Antonio
Private	Antonio Albarado	Present
Private	Juan Montalbo	Present
Private	Juan Josef Martinez	Present: on detached duty
Private	Alexo de Leon	Present
Private	Casimiro Cano	Present: on guard duty
Private	Esteban Salas	Present
Private	Juan Bautista Cano	Present: Ill
Private	Andres del Rio	Present: with the horse herd
Private	Francisco Ramon	Present: with the horse herd
Private	Hermenegildo Gomez	Present
Private	Josef Gonzalez	Present: Ill
Private	Ygnacio Garzia	Present
Private	Santiago Delgado	Present
Private	Tomas de la Garza	Present: with the horse herd
Private	Tomas Ortiz	Present
Private	Bernabe del Rio	Present with the horse herd
Private	Juan Chirino	Present: with the horse herd
Private	Miguel Bezerra	Present: with his captain
Private	Mariano Tegeda	Present
Private	Damasio Aldape	Present: ill
Private	Bernardo de la Garza	Present: ill
Private	Fernando Galan	Present: on guard duty
Private	Josef Jabier Sains	Present: Ill
Private	Antonio Bazquez I	Present: on guard duty
Private	Jabier Maldonado	Present: with the horse herd
Private	Josef Cayetano Zepeda	Present: Ill
Private	Francisco Antonio Buentello	Present: on detached duty
Private	Pedro Josef Grande	Present: on detached duty

Private	Juan Augustin de la Garza	Present
Private	Antonio Bazquez II	Present: with the horse herd
Private	Prudencio de San Miguel	Present: with the horse herd
Private	Josef Timoteo Ximenez	Present: with the horse herd

Ymalidos (disabled)

| Lieutenant | Don Jabier Benites | Present: absent with leave |
| Private | Pedro Ceballos | Present |

Signed: Eugenio Fernandez   Signed: Jose Santoja   Signed: Jose Aguilar
Signed Policarpo Prada

December 1, 1779

Presidio of La Bahia del Espiritu Santo (Texas) May 1, 1782

Cavalry Company of the Royal Presidio of La Bahia del Espiritu Santo
Report of the review passed on the officers, chaplain, sergeants, drummer, corporals, and privates of this company for the month of May. 1782, by Lt. Don Jose Santoja, interim commander of this presidio, in accordance with that which is prescribed by His Majesty in article 3 of title 9 of the Royal Regulations and instructions issued for the establishment of the presidios on the frontier line of the Interior Provinces of this kingdom of New Spain.

Captain	Don Luis Cazorla	CP commissioned in Coahuila
Lt.	Don Jose Santoja	P (resent)
1st Ensign	Don Policarpo Prada	D (ispached) in San Luis Potosi for the pay
2nd Ensign	Don Antonio de Mescieres	P

Chaplain	(B.A) Don Jose Felix Ramos	P
Leather Jacket Soldiers (tropa de Cuera)		
1st Sgt.	Francisco Vasquez	P
1st Corporal	Francisco Rios	P
1st Corporal	Bernave del Rio	P
2nd Corporal	Juan Chirino	P
2nd Corporal	Jose Ylario Maldonado	D protecting the horses
Soldiers		
	Jose Contreras	D protecting the horses

222

	Jose Flores	P
	Eugenio de la Garza	D protecting the horses
	Francisco Salas	D in San Luis Potosi for pay
	Antonio Alvarado	P
	Alexo de Leon	P
	Andres del Rio	D protecting the horses
	Hermenegildo Gomes	D protecting the horses
	Thomas Ortis	P
	Miguel Vezerra	P
	Mariano Texeda	D protecting the horses
	Fernando Galan	D protecting the horses
	Antonio Vasquez	P
	Xavier Maldonado	P
	Pedro de los Santos	D protecting the horses
	Pedro Jose Grande	P
	Agustin de la Garza	P
	Prudencio de San Miguel	P
	Jose Dionicio Liendro	P
	Jose Antonio Conejo	D protecting the horses
	Juan Jose Games	P
	Juan Jose de Leon	P
	Vicente Zerna	p
Armorer	Jose Cactano de Zepeda	P
Light Cavalry (Ligera Tropa)		
2nd Sgt.	Antonio Trevino	D protecting the horses
Drummer	Jose Andres Ribas	P
1st Corporal	Francico Buentello	D in San Luis with the paymaster
1st. Corporal	Francisco Ramon	P
2nd Corporal	Bernardo de la Garza	E (sick)
2nd Corporal	Anacleto Rios	D protecting the horses
Soldiers	Jose Maria Ramon	P
	Francisco de la Garza	D protecting the horses
	Justo Lopez	D in San Luis with the paymaster
	Diego de los Santos Cadenas	P
	Francisco Xavier Vasquez	D protecting the horses
	Marciano Trevino	P
	Francisco Venites	D protecting the horses
	Jacinto Martines	P
	Jose Manuel de la Garza	P

	Pedro Trevino	P
	Jose Gil	P
	Jose Polinario Peres	P
	Juan Nepomuccno Aldape	P
	Manuel Narciso	D protecting the horses
	Antonio Margil Ventes	P
	Antonio Ramon	P
	Sevastian Maldonado	P
	Joachin Galan	D protecting the horses
	Antonio de Rio	P
	Juan Andres Contreras	P
	Thomas Macias	P
	Jose Leonardo Ramon	P
	Juan Flores	P
	Pedro Jose Texeda	P
	Carlos Delgado	D protecting the horses
	Pedro Antonio de Luna	D protecting the horses

Retired (Ymvalidos)

Lt.	Don Xavier Benites	P
Private	Pedro Cevallos	P

Total 69

Summary

Total Active	Total 67
Total Inactive	Total 2
Total General	69

This I Certify as interim commander of this company, (as does) Don Antonio de Mecieres, 2nd Ensign of the same; at this Royal Presidio of La Bahia del Espiritu Santo, Today, the 1st of May, 1782.

Jose Santoja   Antonio de Mesieres

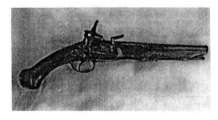

Spanish Musket Pistol
224

Calvary Company of the Royal Presidio of De Espiritu Santo
November 1, 1782

Captain	Don Luis Cazorla	On inspection
Lieutenant	Don Josef Sanxoja	Present
1st Ensign	Don Policarpo Prada	detached to San Luis for the allowance
Ensign	Don Antonio de Messierez	Present
Chaplain	Don Jose Feliz Ramos	Present
1st Sergeant	Francisco Vasques	Present
1st Corporal	Francisco Rios	Present
Corporal	Bernave del Rio	Present: the horse herd
2nd Corporal	Jose Ylario Maldonado	Present
Private	Josef Contreras	Present
Private	Jose Flores	Present
Private	Eugenio de la Garza	Present
Private	Francisco Salas	Present
Private	Antonio Alvarado	Present
Private	Alexo de Leon	Present
Private	Esteban Salas	Present
Private	Andres del Rio	Present
Private	Hermenegildo Gomes	Present
Private	Tomas Ortis	Present: with the horse herd
Private	Miguel Vezerra	Present
Private	Mariano Texeda	Present: with horse herd
Private	Fernando Galan	Present
Private	Xauier Maldonado	Present: meeting the paymaster in Laredo
Private	Pedro de los Santos	Present: with horse herd
Private	Pedro Jose Grande	Present: with the horse herd
Private	Juan Augustin de la Garza	Present: with horse herd
Private	Prudencio de San Miguel	Present: with the horse herd
Private	Jose Dionicio Liendro	at San Luis with the paymaster
Private	Jose Antonio Conexo	Present
Private	Juan Jose Games	Present
Private	Juan Jose de Leon	Present: meeting the paymaster in Laredo
Private	Vicente Zerna	Present: Sick
Armorer	Jose Cayetano de Zepeda	Present
Ligera Troops		
2nd Sergeant	Antonio Treuino	Present: with the horse herd

Drummer	Jose Andres Ribas	Present
1st Corporal	Francisco Buentello	Present
1st Corporal	Francisco Ramon	at San Luis with the paymaster
2nd Corporal	Bernardo de la Garza	to meet the paymaster at Laredo
2nd Corporal	Anacleto Rios	Present: with the horse herd
Private	Jose Maria Ramon	Present: with the horse herd
Private	Francisco de la Garza	Present: with the horse herd
Private	Diego Chirino	Present
Private	Justo Lopes	at San Luis with the paymaster
Private	Diego de los Santos Cadena	to meet the paymaster near Laredo
Private	Francisco Xauier Vasques	Present: with the horse herd
Private	Marciano Treuino	at San Luis with the paymaster
Private	Francisco Benites	Present
Private	Jacinto Martines	Present: with the horse herd
Private	Jose Manuel de la Garza	Present
Private	Pedro Treuino	Present
Private	Jose Gil	Present
Private	Jose Polinario Peres	Present
Private	Juan Nepomuceno Aldape	Present
Private	Manuel Narciso Venites	Present
Private	Antonio Ramon	Present
Private	Sevastian Maldonado	Present
Private	Joachin Galan	Present: with horse herd
Private	Antonio del Rio	to meet the paymaster near Laredo
Private	Juan Andres Contreras	Present
Private	Thomas Macias	Present
Private	Jose Leonardo Ramon	Present
Private	Juan Flores	to meet the paymaster near Laredo
Private	Pedro Jose Texeda	Present
Private	Carlos Delgado	Present
Private	Pedro Antonio de Luna	Present
Private	Antonio Gomes	Present
Private	Francisco Lara	Present

Ymalidos (disabled)

Lieutenant	Don Xavier Venites	Present
Private	Pedro Zevallos	Present

Signed: Jose Santoja   Signed: Antonio de Mezieres

November 1, 1782

Sources:

Library at the University of Texas, Austin, Texas, 78712, Archives Collection. Dolfph Briscoe Center for American History.

Online: http://www.cah.utexas.edu/projects/bexar/index.php

Thornhoff, Robert H., The Texas Connection, With the American Revolution, Eakin Press,

Burnet, Texas, 1981.

Villarreal, Jesse O. Villarreal, Sr., Tejano Patriots of the Amerrican Revolution, 1776-1783, privately published, 2011

Salamanca Archive: LEG,7279,EXP,1,148 San Antonio de Bexar; LEG,7278,EXP,6,151 San Antonio de Bexar;

Musket Gun Powder Pouch

Chapter XII

Colors of the Basic Spanish Regiment Uniforms

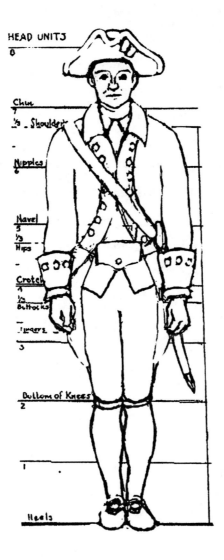

Unit	Coat	Cuffs	Collar	Lining	Waistcoat	Breeches	Buttons	Jacket
Rey	blue	red	red	red	red	blue	yellow	
Soria	white	red	red	white	red	red	white	
Navarre	white	red	red	white	red	red	yellow	
Hibernia	red	green	none	red	red	red	yellow	
Aragon	white	red	white	white	red	red	yellow	
Espana	white	green	green	white	white	white	yellow	
Flanders	white	blue	blue	white	blue	blue	yellow	
Principe	white	red	red	white	white	white	yellow	
Guadalajara	white	red	none	white	red	white	white	

Colors of the Basic Spanish Colonial Regiments

Unit	Coat	Cuffs	Collar	Lining	Waistcoat	Breeches	Buttons	Jacket
Habana	blue	yellow	yellow	blue	yellow	blue	yellow	
Louisiana	white	blue	blue	blue	blue	blue	white	
Voluntarios de Cataluna	blue	yellow	yellow	blue	yellow	blue	white	
Soldado de Cuera brim hat	blue	yellow	red	red	red	blue	yellow	leather-jacket flat

Source:
Smith, Digby, Kiley, Kevin F., An Illustrated encyclopedia of Uniforms from 1775-1783, The American Revolutionary War, Published by Joana Lorenz Books, 2008

XIII
Enlistment Papers of My Ancestors

1781 Santa Fe Presidio Military Muster

Tropa de Cuera (Leather Jacket Soldier)
2nd Sergeant Pablo Sandoval, later promoted to Lieutenant
Partial page with name of my ancestor Pablo Sandoval

"Don Pablo Sandoval, has ceased his functions as 1st Alferez of this company, retiring, taking his place is Don Juan Abrego, currently at Pueblo del Paso. 4 February 1795."

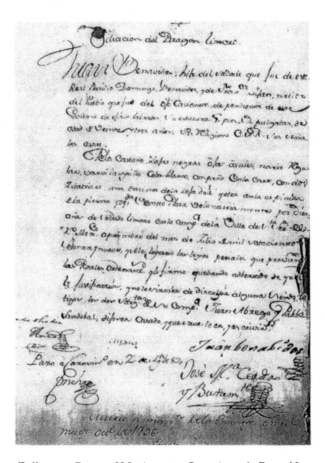

Enlistment Paper of My Ancestor Juan Antonio Benevides

Juan Benavides, son of soldier Domingo Benavides and Francisca Lujan, of Ojo Caliente.
Record: "Farmer, 5' 3", 22. Chestnut hair, black eyebrows, blue eyes, straight nose, thin beard,
fair skin, dark spot on face, scars above ritht eyebrow and on calf of left leg. 1 July 1779." Also
recorded was "Married. Literate. Signed. Died in combat 6 October 1796."

234

Index

239

241

243

244

245

249

250

251

252

259

267

269

Leroy Martinez, JD

Leroy Martinez was born on February 10, 1945, and raised in Los Angeles, California. His parents provided an excellent education in private schools which gave him the foundation to earn a Bachelor's degree and Law degree.

He served in the Army from February 1966 to February 1968 and worked for the Los Angeles County for thirty-one years.

He began his family research and learned that his father and mother came from earlier influential Spanish families. As a result, he collected a large amount of genealogy and history research which included his direct ancestor Sgt. Hernan Martin Serrano, who was part of the 1598 expedition to settle New Mexico. Since, he has authored articles, has given historical presentations, and has participated in ceremonial re-enactments as a 1780 Spanish soldier.

He is a member of the Sons of the American Revolution and the Order of the Founders of North America 1492-1692. These societies align themselves with ancestors relating to Spanish soldier Patriots contributing to the American Revolution and prior to the settlement of North America.

Leroy Martinez has collected as many Spanish archive records from Arizona, California, Louisiana, New Mexico, and Texas to connect military soldiers in what is America today from the period of 1776-1783. This writing presents the English version of the Spanish copy records in my possession.

CPSIA information can be obtained
at www.ICGtesting.com
Printed in the USA
FSOW02n0712310717
37054FS